Issues in Community Policing

Peter C. Kratcoski
Kent State University

Duane Dukes
John Carroll University

ACJS Series Editor, Dean J. Champion

Academy of Criminal Justice Sciences
Northern Kentucky University
402 Nunn Hall
Highland Heights, KY 41076

Anderson Publishing Co.
Criminal Justice Division
P.O. Box 1576
Cincinnati, OH 45201-1576

Issues in
Community Policing

Copyright © 1995 by Anderson Publishing Co. and
Academy of Criminal Justice Sciences

ISBN 0-87084-506-3

Library of Congress Catalog Number 94-73244

Gail Eccleston *Editor*   *Managing Editor* Kelly Humble

Cover photograph courtesy of the
Cincinnati Police Division

This work is dedicated to the memory of Robert C. Trojanowicz (1942-1994), the intellectual "father" of the modern community policing movement.

Acknowledgments

The presentation of the tremendous amount of information given in this book would not have been possible without the cooperation of the many contributing authors. In addition, the assistance and encouragement of Dean J. Champion, ACJS/Anderson Monograph Series Editor and Gail Eccleston, Editor, Anderson Publishing Co. are very much appreciated.

Many others assisted with the production, editing and indexing of the material, including Diane Harris, Janet Hamilton, Scott Meyer, Karen Swearingen, Marcy Valenzuela, Mike Luterzo, and Andrea Clapsaddle. Lucille Dunn Kratcoski also gave tremendous assistance with this project.

Peter Kratcoski
Department of Criminal Justice
Kent State University

I must thank Nancy for her tremendous support during the preparation of this book; the process has tried her patience as a wife, a colleague and a friend, but it could not have been completed without her love, advice and words of encouragement. Mrs. Carolyn Clifford, our department secretary, deserves special thanks for her instrumental and expressive abilities; she has organized voluminous materials and kept communication lines open among the multitude of authors and editors involved in this enterprise. My thanks also extend to Jennifer Wheeler and Elizabeth Osborne, who have been especially helpful in the final stages, working diligently in the final weeks on galley proofs. Last and certainly not lease I would like to thank the officers and supervisors of the Cleveland Police Mini-Station Program; they introduced me to community policing and have shown me how a good idea can become a great program when it is applied creatively and with care.

Duane Dukes
Sociology Department
John Carroll University

Foreword

Peter Kratcoski and Duane Dukes have assembled a timely and interesting collection of essays and research about community policing. Community policing is not new. It was the mode of policing in the early 1900s. Each neighborhood had one or more "beat" cops who acquired a familiarity with all community residents. Police officers dined at local restaurants in neighborhoods they patrolled. They took a personal interest in the lives of citizens. Their work involved the problems of small children, intervening in family disputes, delivering babies in emergencies, and a host of other activities unrelated to crime. They also protected the community. When crimes occurred, these officers did their best to apprehend the perpetrators.

Over time, advancements in communication and mechanization led to the widespread use of patrol cars or units with two-way radios. More modern police departments were increasingly typified as having a larger portion of their police forces relegated to patrol vehicles. Mobilizing police officers in this fashion enabled police departments to bring police services and security to wider community areas. Response time was greatly improved, so that officers could appear at crime scenes within minutes or seconds following these incidents. In general, the effectiveness of police patrols was substantially enhanced.

While police departments were able to expand their services to larger segments of communities, a subtle detachment occurred relative to "beat" patrols. Greater mobilization of officers through motorized patrols meant fewer "beat" cops on foot patrols, walking through neighborhoods on a regular basis. Foot patrol units became antiquated. Gradually, the police became distanced from the community as anonymous officers in cruisers replaced the personable "beat" officers on foot patrols. The large-scale reorganization of police departments made it more bureaucratically expedient to assign area patrols according to objective criteria rather than traditional subjective criteria. Departments became obsessed with increasing organizational efficiency and effectiveness. Cruiser patrols made it possible to be in more places throughout the community in shorter time periods compared with officers on foot patrols. Most police departments assumed that since sheer police presence would be enhanced through such modern and streamlined patrolling methods, citizens would regard this greater police presence favorably. Few persons anticipated the adverse consequences of such major organizational changes.

Bureaucratization of police organizations and policing generally had numerous proponents. Many critics of traditional police patrols cited widespread corruption and police misconduct that seemed an integral part of foot patrol. Becoming closer to the public through foot patrol meant greater susceptibility to various forms of corruption. Some of this corruption involved minor infractions, while other forms of corruption involved considerable felonious activity. For instance, police officers on foot patrols might receive free meals at local restaurants in exchange for not citing delivery trucks for parking in "no parking" areas in front of these same restaurants. Traffic tickets might be fixed in exchange for other gratuities (e.g., free dry cleaning, discounts on furniture, household appliances). The well-known story of Frank Serpico, a former New York City police officer, involved all forms of police corruption, including the use of police officers as drug couriers and sources of drug money laundering and exchange.

By establishing more objective patrolling criteria and other bureaucratic features, police departments have made it more difficult for certain types of police corruption to occur. But *no* patrolling method has ever eliminated such corruption completely. In the aftermath of large-scale organizational changes, police departments have had to reassess what gains and losses they have produced. One consequence of bureaucratization has been to further alienate citizens from officers who are sworn to protect them. Police work is difficult enough to perform with citizen cooperation. It is even more difficult without it.

Since the 1970s, police departments have begun to reassess their patrol styles. In an effort to restore public confidence in the police as interested and caring enforcers of the law, many police departments have undertaken experiments involving community policing. Some critics say that this is nothing more than a rediscovery of "beat" patrol. But those who study police organization and policing know that community policing is something more than simply placing officers back into neighborhood "beats." Community policing is a dynamic synthesis of citizen interests and police resources dedicated to aggressive crime prevention. Citizen involvement in law enforcement is of paramount concern. It is increasingly important for citizens to understand why police officers perform their tasks in certain ways. It is also important for citizens to become actively involved in diverse ways in helping the police to solve certain kinds of community problems.

This work describes the general nature of community policing and provides several explanations for its emergence and current importance. For some persons, at least, community policing is controversial, since it departs from accepted standards of police conduct and operations. The nature of the controversy about community policing is presented. Various community policing programs are described. These programs are found in cities ranging from Delray Beach, Florida to Kalamazoo, Michigan. The internal dynamics of police organizations are explored in an attempt to portray certain organizational obstacles that may hinder the establishment of community policing programs in various communities. Some essays also describe community reactions to community policing in different contexts.

Finally, Kratcoski and Dukes identify several key issues involving community policing as a viable concept for law enforcement and crime prevention.

I am indebted to Ralph Weisheit, the former ACJS/Anderson Monograph Series Editor, for his initial contact with Professors Kratcoski and Dukes. It is a pleasure to include their work under my aegis and tenure as the current Series Editor.

Dean J. Champion
ACJS/Anderson Monograph Series Editor
Minot, ND

Preface

Policing is a prevalent feature of society today. It has become a part of popular culture as well as an integral part of the law enforcement and justice systems. Policing has become a highly organized and expensive division of all major cities, requiring billions of dollars in local, state, and federal funds. In the media images of popular culture, policing is made up of crime-busting cops who, through force, stealth, and superior intellect, interdict and apprehend the myriad street criminals plaguing society today.

In all of the media images and organizational emphases, we sometimes lose the sense that police work is performed by police officers who are real people. The community police officer is clearly unlike the image established for police officers in either the media or the predominant professional literature. Today, this literature is providing a fuller and clearer characterization than just five years ago (Wilson, 1989; Green, 1989). But the real success is in what the community police officer is doing for the community and the department as a whole.

The limited amount of time spent by neighborhood police officers on actual crimes is consistent with the charge for their unit. They are intended to be "proactive" and not "reactive." They conduct Crime Watch training sessions, organize community block organizations and youth groups, meet the people of the neighborhood and work with the elected officials in the ward. The police officer with the skills and temperament suited for this may be rare.

As one example of Neighborhood Police activity, we witnessed a 34-year-old community police officer in a one-hour time span: (1) counsel a mentally ill woman in the office, then follow her home to check on her safety; (2) when flagged down by a neighborhood resident while on patrol, keep a domestic disturbance scene reasonably quiet until district officers could arrive; (3) issue a carefully phrased bilingual warning to a Hispanic resident to move illegally parked vehicles; and (4) passively back up a district officer on a suspicious moving violation.

This effective, flexible, responsive policing was typical of community police officers and was found throughout our research. These officers are accessible, informative, and helpful. Their work, as we have reported elsewhere, has resulted in improved citizen relations, greater feelings of safety in the neighborhood, and higher rates of crime reporting (Dukes, 1987; Dukes & Waycaster, 1991).

The place of the community police officer in the department is also important. Although not intended to answer radio calls, every officer we interviewed had backed up a district officer and/or answered a call as the first car within the last 12 months. In short, while Neighborhood Police officers tend to be older and more prevention oriented, they still exercise their general charge to enforce the law. And, they support their fellow officers in high-risk situations.

To fulfill their charge to prevent crime through the development of community relations, perhaps the single greatest contribution that Neighborhood Police officers make is in their availability. This produces an atmosphere of closeness to the police that has not been felt in many neighborhoods for literally decades. One officer is so respected for this that people come from other neighborhoods to his ministation to report crimes.

Finally, the patrol would seem to be indispensable as a part of neighborhood policing. We joined officers in walking and riding "beats" where they were greeted on a first-name basis by residents and retailers alike. The greatest personal contact is made on foot patrol, of course, but this is possible in only some neighborhoods. In today's police department, the areas covered are so extensive that they require a car. It is our conclusion that the time spent by neighborhood officers communicating with citizens and patrolling the neighborhood serves the community and the department very well.

Peter C. Kratcoski
Duane Dukes

Contents

Section I

WHAT IS COMMUNITY POLICING?

In 1987 we "discovered" community policing in Cleveland, Ohio while conducting a program evaluation of Cleveland neighborhood organizations and their application of local funds to implement the Crime Watch Program. We refer to our experience as a "discovery," since this creative application of police personnel and citizens was not highly publicized outside the participating neighborhoods. We were unaware of it but, of course, the police and safety departments were well aware that they were employing community policing; they had received separate funding for the concept and had developed a community policing division within the police department. Hard working and dedicated staff within the police and safety departments had spent many long hours putting together the "package" that would allow a major U.S. city recovering from serious financial problems to continue both to put safety forces on the streets and to encourage residents to participate in their own protection. This effort, begun in the early 1980s, was fueled by the desperate need to do more with less.

The talent, energy, and foresight of both the police and the staff of the safety director, who were turning concepts into reality, impressed us, but our commitment to the Crime Watch research made it impossible to begin a completely new research project regarding community policing at that time. The city of Cleveland was interested when we were able to return in 1992 to look more closely at the community policing features of Cleveland's crime prevention efforts. In 1992, we conducted extensive research with neighborhood residents, police officers in the community policing unit, their supervisors, and police officers in the community policing unit, their supervisors, and police officers not in the unit. We gathered quantitative date on crime incidence and computerized samples of the community police duty logs.

Showing the success of community policing quantitatively is a difficult enterprise at best, but we have experienced the qualitative difference that has come from the implementation of this one program. We have concluded that crime prevention through community policing and neighborhood Crime Watch in Cleveland is working. Exactly how it works, why it is successful, and how successful it is are

1

complex questions that we have been addressing through a series of papers at professional meetings. Some of the findings reported by us in professional papers over the past two years appear here in print for the first time, along with the strong contributions of a wide variety of other thinkers and researchers in the field.

A number of works in the area of community policing have begun to appear in the literature. Most of these have been either general treatments of paradigms associated with community policing or case study descriptions of programs in various cities across the country. This volume is prepared with a somewhat different orientation. It is intentionally not an attempt to do either of the above. Rather, it is an attempt to begin to address important aspects of community policing that have yet to be collected under one title. Our guidelines in doing so are based on whether the information would have utility in the development and understanding of community policing as an operating entity. While the paradigmatic discussions and the case studies to date have shed some important light on the growing practice of community policing, we have felt that issues important both to criminal justice practitioners and to academicians in related disciplines have remained relatively undeveloped. They have rarely appeared in the literature and have never been subsumed within a single treatment of the topic.

We will present some case studies and identify topics that need further examination. The reasons for this are simple: in the first instance, we feel that the actual cases provide important illustrations of the principles discussed in this volume; in the second instance we have forged ahead with some research in areas that are yet to be fully developed.

Community policing, as perceived and understood by criminal justice professionals, involves both identifying and dealing with community problems and responding to the expressed and experienced concerns of community members. Whether such policing is termed COP (Community-Oriented Policing) or POP (Problem-Oriented Policing), its primary focus is on close involvement of police administrators, police officers, and community members in decisions and activity that will make the community a safer and better place to live.

Through our research project on community policing in Ohio, which surveyed several thousand police officers and administrators, we discovered that community policing was sometimes equated with public relations programs, drug prevention programs for school children, or a return to foot patrols by officers, instituted to attempt to recapture the relationships that formerly existed between community members and the officers who served the neighborhoods.

Both police administrators and those examining community policing as researchers sometimes fail to distinguish between the underlying philosophies or attitudes that are considered vital for community policing and the various techniques that are employed to accomplish the goals established for community policing. Cardarelli and McDevitt (1992:4-5) reported that police administrators equated community policing with foot patrols and periodic meeting width citizens, while Taylor and Greene (1993:7) found that many police departments they surveyed had developed bicycle and foot patrols, neighborhood crime watches, and citizen advisory boards, but did not identify these activities as community policing.

In Chapter 1, by Kratcoski and Dukes, "Perspectives on Community Policing" defines community policing, distinguishes community policing from public relations, crime prevention and problem-oriented policing, discusses its essential elements, traces its evolution, and describes how its goals can be accomplished under various organizational structures. The second selection, by J.S. Albritton, "The Technique of Community-Oriented Policing: An Alternative Explanation," attempts to delineate the essence of community policing and show that it must be intricately interwoven with community problem solving if it is to go beyond a public relation image.

Chapter 3, "Community Policing: The Implementation Gap" by Eli B. Silverman, examines organizational obstacles that are likely to affect collective efforts to implement community policing. Drawing from the experiences of a number of police departments who have tried to implement community policing, the author suggests that confusion of the goals of community policing, a lack of commitment from both the administration and patrol officers, and a lack of sufficient resources are organizational factors inhibiting community policing implementation.

1

Perspectives on Community Policing

Peter C. Kratcoski
Kent State University

Duane Dukes
John Carroll University

INTRODUCTION

Lee P. Brown, the current Director of the U.S. Office of National Drug Control Policy (commonly referred to as the Drug Czar), formerly served as Police Chief of Houston, Texas, and as Police Commissioner of New York City. He was responsible for instituting community policing in both cities. When Brown was Police Commissioner of New York City, he gave the following as a definition of community policing:

> We define community policing here in New York as a partnership between the police and the law-abiding citizens to prevent crime; to arrest those who choose to violate the law, to solve recurring problems where we tend to go back to the same places over and over again, and to evaluate the results of our efforts. The whole objective is to improve the quality of life in the neighborhoods throughout our city. (Rosen, 1992)

Trojanowicz (1990) observed that, "Community policing requires a department-wide philosophical commitment to involve average citizens as partners in the process of reducing and controlling the contemporary problems of crime, drugs, fear of crime and neighborhood decay; and in efforts to improve the overall quality of life in the community" (1990:125). He also noted:

> Community policing requires everyone in the department, sworn and civilian personnel at all levels, to explore how they can carry out the mission through their actions on the job. Equally essential is that the department must permanently deploy a portion of its patrol force as community officers in specific beats so they can maintain direct, daily contact with average citizens. Yet the ultimate success or failure of community policing rests primarily with the new community officers, the generalists who operate as mini-chiefs within their own beat areas (1990:175).

When community policing is defined and explained to officers working with police agencies in small communities, some officers often respond with a comment that "this is what we have always been doing." Policing in a small community is conducive to developing the types of interpersonal and cooperative interaction between the citizens and the police that serve as the cornerstone of a community policing orientation. In fact, Greene (1993:7) found that the police in many small communities surveyed in Florida apparently were employing some form of community policing, such as team policing or foot patrol, even though it was not specifically defined as community policing. On the other hand, one cannot conclude that if the police and citizens communicate that this interaction constitutes community policing. Much of it may be time-passing chatter that is not structured toward solving community problems or enlisting the citizens' help in preventing potential problems.

With community policing, much of the interaction is purposeful and goal oriented. The police share the information and strategies they have available with community members. Community policing rests on the philosophy that law-abiding people deserve input into the policing process, and that solutions to problems require freeing both residents and police to explore creative options.

Trojanowicz (1990) noted that the theoretical framework of community policing is grounded in organizational theory, open systems theory, critical theory, normative sponsorship theory, and public policy analysis (1990:174). Wilson and Kelling (1982) described community policing theory in practical terms, by emphasizing that it involves protection of all individuals in the community where they reside. Police are responsible for order maintenance, crime reduction, and allowing citizens to maintain a quality of life which gives them an opportunity to interact freely in their community.

The *ICMA Workbook on Community-Oriented Policing* suggests that this form of policing is built on five assumptions:

1. The effectiveness of any strategy to reduce neighborhood-based crime will vary in proportion to the degree and breadth of support given that strategy by neighborhood residents.

2. Neighborhood support of a crime reduction strategy will vary in proportion to the degree of trust and respect neighborhood residents and local government officials give to each other.

3. The effectiveness of a neighborhood-based crime reduction strategy will vary in proportion to the combined effectiveness of incident-driven and problem-oriented responses.

4. The effectiveness of COPS [community-oriented policing] will vary in proportion to the degree that COPS is understood and accepted by neighborhood residents, elected officials, administrative managers, and implementing employees.

5. The effectiveness of COPS will vary in direct proportion to the degree of decentralization [that] occurs. (1982:14)

HISTORICAL DEVELOPMENT OF COMMUNITY POLICING

Bowman (1992) identifies the historical roots of the modern community policing movement in nineteenth-century British and American law enforcement. In the British system, the primary emphasis was on crime prevention through the maintenance of order. The role of all police officials included securing the cooperation and respect of community residents. They viewed themselves as members of the community.

Braiden (1992) traces the reemergence of community policing to the philosophy of policing promulgated by Sir Robert Peel. He refers to item seven of Peel's original principles, "the police are the public, and the public are the police," to emphasize that the police and the public have common concerns, interests, and goals. Braiden states:

> It was Peel's contention that a community must literally police itself, with certain members paid to do it full time in uniform while the rest did it part-time as they went about their daily work. (1992:18)

Early American policing was even more democratic, with responsibility for order shared between government officials and private citizens. However, rapid urbanization and industrialization in the nineteenth century produced greater reliance upon full-time law enforcement professionals (Bowman, 1992:59).

Kelling and Moore (1988) have shown that the police establishment, like all other institutions, is subject to change, with the changes often resulting from the reaction of the citizenry to occurrences in the community that they find to be intolerable. In the early 1900s, police organizations were closely linked to such entities as political parties, city councils, and mayors. In this "political era," policing had many of the characteristics of modern community policing including a decentralized neighborhood based structure and close personal relationship with members of the community. At that time, officers employed techniques grounded in the practice of beat patrol, but also conducted investigations, maintained public order, and performed service-type activities.

There is a tendency to romanticize our past, but not all was rosy in this early application of community policing. Although policing included the virtues of direct communication and problem-oriented police activity, being close to sources of political power was often corruptive. In short, the law as it was commonly practiced in some cities in the late nineteenth and early twentieth centuries involved principles and transactions that did not appear in any of the legal codes. In response to this, a reform era emerged in the 1930s, but for the next two decades police involvement in politics was not an uncommon practice (Kelling & Moore, 1988).

By the 1960s, American policing had evolved into another distinct phase. Major police departments had begun to base police work on the professional model. This approach required a highly centralized organizational design, with specialization of labor and a bureaucratic structure. It also developed a practice of detached, formalized communications between the police and citizenry for reasons not unrelated to the advent of modern technology and as a means to process an increased amount of crime. Outcome was measured in terms of crime control, with increases and decreases in the crime rates used as measurements of success or failure. The technologies of the 1960s included increased emphasis on auto patrol since the squad, patrol, or zone car could cover much more ground than an officer on foot and could be dispatched readily to a crime scene via radio. With more hours in the car, it only made sense to make officers more comfortable via air conditioning; so, eventually, the officer became disconnected from the very community being served, talking with residents only to take crime reports and being sent to the scenes of these crimes by the central radio dispatch. Later, sophisticated communications systems included installing computers in the patrol cars.

The current community policing movement gained some support in the 1970s, and received much more attention during the late 1980s. It is the result of many factors, including the knowledge that the professional, centralized police organizational model did not lead to the expected reduction in crime.

Dissatisfaction with police performance also stimulated the growth of community policing. Those most often directly in touch with the police, including minority group members, the socially and economically disadvantaged, and young people, increasingly let it be known that they felt the police were unresponsive to their needs. Urban unrest and the growth of youth gangs underlined the point that the traditional approaches to crime control, and particularly to street crime problems, were not working.

DIFFERENTIATING COMMUNITY POLICING FROM POLICE-COMMUNITY RELATIONS

Trojanowicz (1990) noted that considerable confusion still exists between definitions of community policing and police-community relations. The following diagram illustrates the differences between the two concepts:

Community Policing	Police-Community Relations
Goal: Solve problems—improved relations with citizens is a welcome by-product.	**Goal:** Change attitudes and project positive image—improved relations with citizens is main focus.
Line Function: Regular contact of officer with citizens.	**Staff Function:** Irregular contact of officer with citizens.
Citizens nominate problems and cooperate in setting police agenda.	"Blue ribbon" committees identify the problems and "preach" to police.
Police accountability is insured by the citizens receiving the service.	Police accountability is insured by civilian review boards and formal police supervision.
Meaningful organizational change and departmental restructuring ranging from officer selection to training, evaluation, and promotion.	Traditional organization stays intact with "new" programs periodically added, no fundamental organizational change.
A department-wide philosophy and acceptance.	Isolated acceptance often localized to PCR Unit.
Influence is from "the bottom up." Citizens receiving service help set priorities and influence police policy.	Influence is from "the top down"—those who "know best" have input and make decisions.
Officer is continually accessible. In person or by telephone recorder in a decentralized office.	Intermittent contact with the public because of city-wide responsibility, contact is made through central headquarters.
Officer encourages citizens to solve many of their own problems and volunteer to assist neighbors.	Citizens are encouraged to volunteer but are told to request and expect more government (including law enforcement) services.
Success is determined by the reduction in citizen fear, neighborhood disorder, and crime.	Success is determined by traditional measures, i.e., crime rates and citizen satisfaction with the police.

Source: Robert C. Trojanowicz "Community Policing is Not Police-Community Relations." *FBI Law Enforcement Bulletin*, vol. 1 (October 1990), p. 10.

DIFFERENTIATING PROBLEM-ORIENTED POLICING (POP) AND COMMUNITY POLICING

Problem-oriented policing (POP) has been viewed by some as clearly distinguishable from community policing (COP) (Eck & Spelman, 1987; Goldstein, 1990) and by others as a component of COP (Cordner, 1988; Rosen, 1992; Trojanowicz & Bucqueroux, 1990). Moore (1992) views POP and COP as overlapping concepts, with each having a distinctive thrust. He describes POP as an approach developed to respond to specific situations whereas COP fosters a more permanent working partnership between the police and the community that will continue to exist even if the community is not facing immediate serious problems.

According to Goldstein (1990:32), problem-oriented policing is a comprehensive plan for improving policing in which the high priority attached to addressing substantive problems shapes the police agency, influencing all changes in personnel, organization, and procedures. Trojanowicz and Bucqueroux (1994) differentiate between problem-oriented policing and community policing in the following way:

> All community policing involves problem solving, but not all problem-oriented policing is community policing. Problem-oriented policing does not always include permanent assignment of the officers, the officers working from a decentralized station, and the officers soliciting input from citizens regarding their ideas about the problems and how to solve them . . . Problem-oriented policing does not necessarily involve long-term evaluation to ensure that the solutions to the problems are long lasting. (1994:17)

Hoover (1992) differentiates between problem-oriented policing and community policing in the following manner:

> Problem-oriented interventions may involve modifying a community's infrastructure, but there is an end point to the intervention. Changes are made and the police "withdraw." It is an intermediate level of order maintenance responsibility. This is not so with community-oriented policing. The police come to a neighborhood, and are there to stay as generalist government agents responsible for the quality of life in the microcommunity (1992:10).

A problem-oriented policing approach grounded in the directives of the National Institute of Justice requires that the problem-solving system follow five basic principles:

1. Officers of all ranks and from all units should be able to use the system as part of their daily routine.

2. The system must encourage the use of a broad range of information, including but not limited to conventional police data.

3. The system should encourage a broad range of solutions, including but not limited to the criminal justice process.

4. The system should require no additional resources and no special units.

5. Finally, any large police agency must be able to apply it.

The problem-solving process adopted in Newport News, Virginia included four stages:

1. Scanning—identifying an issue and determining if it is a problem.

2. Analysis—collecting information on the problem from all available sources.

3. Response—using the information to develop and implement solutions to the problem.

4. Assessment—determining if the response to the problem was effective.

(Eck & Spelman, 1987a:xix-xx)

Thus, *community-oriented policing* may be considered as a general management strategy toward policing, that is, as an approach to *delivering services* to the public, whereas *problem oriented policing* is only one component of *community policing*.

THE STRUCTURE OF COMMUNITY POLICING

Almost everyone is in agreement that the community policing philosophy must permeate throughout the entire police organization if community policing is to be effective. For example, Trojanowicz and Bucqueroux (1994) state, "Community policing organizational strategy first demands that everyone in the police department, including both civilian and sworn personnel, must investigate ways to translate the philosophy of power-sharing into practice" (1994:4).

However, in the majority of the cities employing community policing, some type of specialized community policing unit or program is developed and this unit is specifically designated a community policing program. The term is applied to a wide range of specialized units, such as mini-stations, team policing, or foot patrols.

Trojanowicz emerged as the chief spokesperson for community policing, with many departments and professional police associations relying on his advice and expertise to assist with the development their programs. He emphasized the necessity for the entire police department to embrace the community policing philosophy, and the need to have some officers designated as community policing officers, but did not outline a specific administrative structure under which these officers would work. Trojanowicz and Bucqueroux (1994) emphasized that, "Community policing is not a tactic, technique, or program" (1994:6). Instead, he saw community policing as a new approach to policing by the entire department.

Varying structures for the implementation of community policing have emerged. In the following section, approaches to community policing in four cities are described in detail.

COMMUNITY POLICING IN CLEVELAND

In 1954, the city of Cleveland reached its largest population, about 750,000 residents. For the next 35 years, Cleveland's population declined, standing at 500,000 residents as of the 1990 census. The decline was more than numeric. In this same time, the traditionally educated, politically active, middle class residents of Cleveland were leaving, moving predominately to the surrounding suburbs. The heavy industrial base that built Cleveland was also declining; some old factories went out of business altogether, while others left the state in pursuit of economic advantages.

By the 1970s, the Cleveland Safety Department faced a crisis situation of declining city budgets and increasing crime rates. The lower budgets necessitated reductions in safety personnel even though the city needed them more than ever. As the city found it increasingly difficult to meet the challenge of rising crime, yet another problem emerged: growing citizen alienation and distrust.

The Cleveland Safety Department began to look for creative solutions to the problems mentioned above. Some of the solutions would bring revenues into the department, while others would look toward creative ways of addressing safety issues. Fortunately, various state and federal funding appeared in the 1980s that helped in both regards. First, there was Crime Watch funding, and finally there was direct funding for community policing.

Designing a Program

Designing a community policing program to meet the needs of Cleveland meant also meeting some of the internal needs of the department. At first, the idea of community policing was not well received. There was considerable concern that officers would be diverted from important tasks of traditional law enforcement and crime solution. So, in 1984, the department pursued the development of a special unit.

Community policing in Cleveland was organized through the Neighborhood Police Unit. This unit was deployed into neighborhoods following the "Detroit Model" of neighborhood based police mini-stations. In 1983, the city was divided into 32 districts and each was assigned a mini-station. The 64 officers who staffed the mini-stations were independent of the existing police districts. They did not answer radio calls, but reported directly to their supervisor stationed at police headquarters. Their duties during the day were to be dictated by the needs of the community, and included answering questions, resolving problems and disputes, assisting in reporting crimes, and following up on crimes that had been reported. Part of the day would be spent in the mini-station, taking calls and walk-ins; the rest of the day would be spent on patrol in the neighborhood, usually in a car, but sometimes on foot, when the area was small enough to allow it.

The officers were also given responsibility for providing crime watch training in the community. This became a large part of the job, and officers spent many evenings with neighborhood organizations, working to establish crime watch programs.

In this first phase of the Cleveland Mini-Station Program, two officers were deployed to each mini-station in overlapping shifts. These shifts overlapped by four hours. This allowed the station to be staffed and operational for 12-hour days. The two key components of the program, a storefront office and a patrol car, could be utilized fully in this scheme. The officer on the first shift would spend the first four hours in the mini-station and, when the officer on the second shift arrived, would then patrol on auto or foot for the remainder of his/her shift. The officer on the second shift would man the office until the first shift was over and then would take over patrol duties.

This procedure allowed the mini-station to be covered for an eight-hour day and allowed a mini-station officer to patrol or complete other duties in the neighborhood for an eight-hour day. Since the mini-station was left uncovered for 16 hours of the day, two adaptations emerged: (1) the installation of telephone answering machines, and (2) the support services of the Auxiliary Police of Cleveland. The former adaptation was retained in all mini-stations. The latter proved to be effective in only a few stations. Even where the auxiliary police shared quarters with the neighborhood police, in some cases their services were not extensively used. This fact may be the result of some neighborhood police officers expressing a lack of confidence with auxiliary police working in their units. While the community relations potential of the auxiliary police was great, the mini-station officers were generally not confident regarding their abilities in real emergencies and were distinctly negative about having them in the same room when potentially confidential telephone conversations could be overheard.

By 1989, the politics and economics of the city had taken a toll even on the mini-station program. The principal threat to the program appears to have been the continued financial drain on the city and its Safety Department. The number of officers assigned to the program was reduced to 34.

During this time of reduction in force, the mini-station officers were often assigned policing tasks that took them out of the neighborhood. The mini-station officers began to receive "special assignments." These included policing major league sporting events, protecting the mayor, and policing all public and privately sponsored events occurring in the city.

Recently, the program has been restructured. Council members who initially argued against the implementation of the program now felt that the program was a good idea and recommended that it be expanded. The program had shown successes on many fronts by this time. Although it received virtually no media attention, the "word" about the program had spread from resident to resident and neighborhood to neighborhood. People in neighborhoods with the program accepted the opportunity to play a part in the movement to improve their living situations. This translated into greater satisfaction with city governance and safety services. The successes were recognized by the local politicians who did not have mini-stations in their wards, and they began to demand the same kinds of services (with, of course, the same kinds of results) in each of their neighborhoods. The Safety Department and the Police Division were unable to provide such services under the existing structure, and the entire community policing program was renovated. The program was expanded geographically to cover the entire city for the first time and the number of officers was expanded to 42.

Two additional changes actually had the most impact in changing the character of the program. First, the actual number of mini-stations was reduced to 21. The model that was originally initiated and had worked so well was now being reimplemented. In addition, two officers were assigned to each mini-station in overlapping shifts. The number of mini-stations was now smaller, while the geographic area to be covered was larger.

By the end of 1993, political fortunes had shifted yet again. Federal funding became available for policing initiatives. Local politics had become favorable to community policing and internal police issues had shifted so that a restructuring of the program was possible. With a supportive mayor at the helm, the most recent structural change elevated the program to an equal status with each of the six District Headquarters. This was accomplished by making the head of the Community Policing Division a Commander.

COMMUNITY POLICING IN EDMONTON, CANADA

In 1987, the police department of Edmonton, Canada established the goal of incorporating community-based policing into the philosophy of the department.

(Hornick et al., 1989) The Neighborhood Foot Patrol Program (NFPP) was implemented in 21 "neighborhood areas" of the city. Edmonton had 1,092 police constables and 279 support staff employed by the department at the time NFPP was started. The city had a population in excess of one-half million. The economy of the city, heavily dependent on raw resources industries, was experiencing an economic recession. As is common in such economic circumstances, health and social programs were losing funding, while unemployment and crime rates were increasing (1989:5).

The goals of NFPP were very similar to those of most community policing programs; that is, to prevent crime and help to improve the quality of life in the neighborhood. This required that the constables consider how poverty, racism, unemployment, homelessness, and other social ills were associated with crime. The constables were given the charge to become proactive and assist with finding solutions to community problems by relying on community leaders to help in identifying and solving community problems.

NFPP was structured in the following manner:

1. A constable patrolled a small geographic area on foot.

2. Each patrol area had a store-front office that was used to promote community involvement in police work and provide a place for volunteers to work.

3. Community liaison committees were established. These committees include leaders in the neighborhoods and focused on community problem solving.

4. Volunteers were recruited and actually assisted the constable.

5. Problem-solving strategies for both short-range and long-range solutions were employed by the constables.

The constables selected for NFPP were volunteers. Of 46 who were initially interviewed, 21 were chosen. They worked eight-hour shifts, but could be flexible in terms of the specific hours worked during any given shift. The overall project was supervised by a project manager who provided general direction. The day-to-day supervision of the foot patrol constables was the responsibility of the four division commanders.

The program was evaluated externally, and it was concluded that the program was successful to some degree in accomplishing its program objectives. It was stated that structurally there were some problematic matters that would need adjustment, but the flexibility of the program, the officers' semiautonomous work patterns that enabled them to tailor their schedules to best fit the needs of the neighborhood, the use of foot patrol and "storefront" stations, and utilizing problem-solving techniques were all conducive to the movement toward goal accomplishment (Hornick et al., 1989:129).

COMMUNITY POLICING IN DAYTON, OHIO

The Dayton Community Policing Program was established in 1991. Prior to this time, Robert Trojanowicz provided some community policing training for the command staff, city officials, and interested people in the neighborhoods in which community police officers would eventually be assigned. In 1993, 19 officers (three white females, three black females, eight white males, and five black males) were assigned to 16 neighborhoods located in various areas of the city. These neighborhoods were selected for the community policing program on the basis of an analysis of the characteristics of the neighborhoods and the belief that community policing would work in these areas.

The community police officers had flexible hours but typically worked during the day time. From time to time, they attended special events in the community or participated in crime prevention activities, such as helping to organize "block watch" programs. The community police officers were under the direct control of the Operations Division. However, a lieutenant was assigned to serve as coordinator of the Community Policing Program. This person oversaw the activities of the officers, served as a liaison with central administration and the district commanders, and provided training for the community police officers who volunteered for this assignment.

Currently, the community police officers have considerable discretion regarding their specific activities during their shift. They normally walked a beat, but also had an office in the neighborhood. This office was donated by the people of the neighborhood. The Dayton Police Department only covers telephone costs. The community police officer focuses on improving the "quality of life," in the neighborhoods, addressing persistent problems such as repeat offenders, assisting the district officers who provide auto patrol services to the area, and occasionally answering 911 calls when the district officers are backed up.

The response to the program by the citizenry has been quite positive. Periodically, the citizenry is contacted through a door-to-door interview. The residents in every fifth household are interviewed. They are questioned on their perceptions of neighborhood problems and asked if they have been involved in any way in trying to improve the neighborhood. If not, they are asked if they would they like to become involved. Various members of the city council who do not have community police officers in their wards requested that the program be expanded to include them. A dramatic decrease in calls for service has occurred in some neighborhoods. A Juvenile Diversion Program was started in 1992 for first-time misdemeanor offenders, and several community educational programs were started with the help of the community police officers. The community police program appears to be accepted by the rank-and-file patrol officers and administration. However, there is still some lack of understanding of the community policing philosophy and apparently some administrators have difficulty separating community policing from police-community relations.

COMMUNITY-ORIENTED PROBLEM SOLVING POLICE—ST. LOUIS

The St. Louis City Police Department developed its Community-Oriented Problem Solving Unit (COP) in 1991. At an earlier date, representatives of the Police Executive Research Forum came to St. Louis and held a three-day training session with a group of police commanders, middle managers, sergeants, and beat officers on the problem-solving technique. After the training was completed, three small areas of the city were selected to introduce COP. Two officers were assigned to each area, and these officers were to handle all calls in that area along with trying to eliminate or reduce some of the persistent community problems.

The COP officers were receptive to the additional responsibilities placed on them. According to Sgt. Robert Heimberger, a coordinator of COP:

> The officers themselves seemed more receptive to this style of policing because they felt it gave them a little more say in how they policed their beat. They were no longer tied to "just the facts," they were allowed to experiment, try and solve problems, and arrest was no longer their number one tool in dealing with community problems. They were allowed to contact other agencies and get them involved and more importantly get the community involved in helping take care of some of their own problems.
>
> (Taped interview with Sgt. Robert Heimberger, 1994)

Realizing that the community policing philosophy and problem-solving approach must be accepted and applied throughout the department, a department-wide training program was developed. It was hoped that all officers would internalize the community policing philosophy and incorporate the problem-solving techniques into their daily work habits. Through department-wide training, the notion that community-oriented policing should be integrated into all units will be fostered.

Typical of many cities initiating a community policing program, the residents of the community and the politicians were more receptive to COP than were the police administrative staff and field officers. Rather than outright resistance, their attitudes might be characterized as guarded, qualified acceptance. Sgt. Heimberger noted that community policing was an easy sell in the St. Louis neighborhoods in which it was employed:

> The people are not satisfied with the old style of policing. They feel that the police are not receptive to their needs. We had a private company conduct a telephone survey of citizens, to answer some of our questions about how the community feels about police services. The results, I think, were typical of most communities, in that all of the community showed that they like the police, they felt the police have a very difficult job to do, and they also felt that the police were not as sensitive to their needs as they could be, so they were willing to buy into COP.
> (author interview with Sgt. Robert Heimberger)

He also emphasized that a large part of the success of this program is due to "City Hall's commitment to this. "It gave the officers more tools and resources to work with, and it also let them know that they were not alone in their fight to try and improve the well being of our community and citizens." Community policing appears to be accepted by more officers and administrators now that the program has been in effect for several years. Perhaps this is the result of the training that is being provided to the officers or perhaps it is the result of community policing receiving mass media coverage.

> I think this style of policing is pretty much getting a grip in St. Louis, and I think that they believe that it is here to stay. We are seeing more officers buying into the philosophy, more officers taking part in it, and as more get involved it has a snowball effect. When we go out and talk to the officers on the street, it seems to be happening on its own without anyone else pushing or prodding it along (Taped interview with Sgt. Robert Heimberger, 1994).

To date, the effectiveness of the COP in St. Louis has not been formally evaluated. However, the gut feeling of one officer is that the program is working. He states:

> Taking a cursory look at it from just going to the district meetings and talking with the neighborhood officers, I would have to say that relationships with the community have improved. The people are getting to know the beat officers by name. The officers are now being issued pagers. The citizen can contact the officer that he knows to help him deal with problems. In that term, yes, there has been a marked increase in support from the community.

The four community policing programs described above illustrate the fact that the specific structure of the community policing unit and the extent to which community policing is employed depend on the needs and structure of the community as well as the needs and structure of the police organization. Albritton (1991:3) noted that "Police organizations have often transformed reform proposals and experiments to fit their own agenda and priorities; rarely have they adapted these proposals in all their theoretical "purity" (1991:14).

EXTENT OF COMMUNITY POLICING

Trojanowicz and Bucqueroux (1992) estimate that two-thirds of all police departments serving communities with populations greater than 50,000 are either now employing community policing or are planning to do so in the near future. Although we cannot discuss the programs in all cities, it is important to note that, for each city, important variations on the basic models have been made to adapt community policing to the unique needs and characteristics of that city. The proliferation of programs is itself testimony to the attention being given to community policing.

In a survey of large city police departments conducted by Cardarelli (1993), it was found that, in 25 large city departments that indicated they had a community policing program, 24 were started in the past three to five years and the newness of these programs was reflected in the confusion of law enforcement administrators on the meaning of community policing. Some equated community policing with foot patrols and periodic meetings with community residents, others with community relations. Only a small number stated that community policing must involve the residents in the decision-making process related to policing policies (Cardarelli & McDevitt, 1992:4-5).

Skolnick and Bayley (1986) have identified a number of obstacles to the introduction of community policing into the police department. These include resistance from police administrators, police unions, and patrol officers, and the prevailing culture of policing. The resistance of the administration may stem in part from the fact that with community policing, officers have autonomy and have the authority to make decisions. As a result of extensive media coverage, the rank-and-file patrol officers in some cities have reacted against community policing by downplaying the importance of COP programs. Not fully understanding the essence of community policing, police administrators and patrol officers in some cases have characterized COP as a police-community relations and have not regarded it as within the realm of "real" police work.

SUMMARY

Regardless of the specific definition of community policing given, there appears to be a general consensus that it encompasses a specific philosophy and involves an organizational strategy that facilitates a working arrangement between the police and the community in solving problems and working toward improving the overall quality of life.

Perhaps it is best to think of the police and the community as one unit. That is, the police officer assigned to a specific neighborhood is as much a part of that neighborhood as any other citizen residing there. Community policing is working when the officer begins to think of his/her assigned area in terms of "my neighborhood," rather than "my beat." The committed community policing officer responds to problems emerging in the neighborhood in a manner similar to the way a resident would respond by developing strategies to eliminate the problem and trying to find means to prevent it from recurring.

Community policing should not be equated with specific units or techniques. Its goals can be achieved through a number of different means. Foot or bicycle patrol units, storefront or mini-station programs, or combinations of these have been employed to facilitate the community policing process.

2

The Technique of Community-Oriented Policing: An Alternative Explanation*

James S. Albritton
Marquette University

INTRODUCTION

In recent years, community-oriented policing (COP) and its corollary, problem-oriented policing (POP), have been widely touted as the most promising "strategic innovations" in policing in decades (e.g., Goldstein, 1979,1987,1990; Wilson & Kelling, 1982; Skolnick & Bayley, 1986; Sparrow, 1988; Trojanowicz & Bucqueroux, 1990). While declaring "traditional-reactive" modes of policing resounding failures in achieving their crime-fighting, peace-keeping and public service objectives, some COP/POP enthusiasts announce, with unmitigated confidence, that a "quiet revolution" in police operations and philosophy is presently under way (e.g., Kelling, 1988). Indeed, in a recent volume on these matters, Trojanowicz and Bucqueroux (1990) set forth a virtual catechism of essential principles, beliefs, values, and exhortations to animate this new ideological orientation and its implementation in contemporary policing. Guided, henceforth, by the "lessons of police history," and the "search for more effective strategies of policing," the "community era" of policing is ostensibly upon us (Kelling & Moore, 1988).

The purpose of the present discussion is not to review in detail either the internal consistency of the principles and programs of COP/POP or the prescribed means and methods of implementation. There has already been ample and substantive criticism of the COP/POP ideology in previous works (e.g., Manning,

---

* Revised version of paper previously presented at the annual meeting of the Academy of Criminal Justice Sciences, March 14, 1992, Pittsburgh, PA.

1984; Walker, 1984; Weatheritt, 1986; Greene & Mastrofski, 1988; Riechers & Roberg, 1990). Thus, very little would be accomplished by yet another critical appraisal of COP/POP principles, assumptions, and prescriptions. Rather, this discussion raises a much broader issue suggested by the COP/POP controversy: i.e., the tendency of many police specialists to focus on police "reforms" or "innovations" like COP/POP as if they occurred in a self-contained, undifferentiated social vacuum—without reference to, or recognition of, the larger social forces and determinants in modern policing.

To illustrate the contours of this broader issue, it is instructive, nonetheless, to examine further one of the more categorical assertions in the Trojanowicz and Bucqueroux catechism that has much deeper and salient implications for policing than these authors apparently realize: namely, their contention that community policing is not a "technique" (1990:20-21). However insignificant or routine such an assertion may seem on the surface, it reveals, upon closer scrutiny, much more than semantic difficulties in understanding both the COP/POP agenda and modern developments in policing. More importantly, it points to the need to place our understanding of police development, strategies, reforms, and innovations in a much larger context of socio-historical reflection and analysis—a context that incorporates an inclusive, holistic grasp of the influence of *technique* on modern social institutions.

One of the most provocative and convincing macro-level analyses of the impact, influence, and implications of *technique* on modern society exists, for example, in the works of Jacques Ellul (esp. 1964,1980). Ellul's rigorous conception of the *Technological Society* (1964) is one of numerous studies that attribute to *"technique"*—most often understood, incompletely, as an aspect of "technology"—either powerful correlation or causal determination in the development of modern social institutions.[1] Consequently, Trojanowicz and Bucqueroux's seemingly innocuous assertion that community policing is not a "technique" must be measured against Ellul's broader analysis of the role and meaning of *technique* in a *Technological Society*.[2]

Addressing the broader implications of *technique* for modern policing requires three additional but interrelated steps in this discussion: first, defining more precisely the concept and meaning of technique; second, relating the concept to the general development of modern policing techniques; and finally, demonstrating the specific consequences of policing-as-technique for the community policing movement today.

DEFINING TECHNIQUE

Although the precise connotations that Trojanowicz and Bucqueroux attribute to the term "technique" are not entirely clear, they obviously use it both restrictively and pejoratively to imply that "community policing is not a technique that departments can apply to a specific problem until it is solved. . ." (1990:20). In the same context, they state that "community policing is not something to be used periodically, but it is a permanent commitment to a new kind of policing that provides decentralized and personalized community problem-solving" (1990:21). In effect, Trojanowicz and Bucqueroux's narrow use of the term reveals a common misconception about the nature of *technique*—i.e., that technique is nothing more than a limited, neutral device, a simple means or stratagem, that can be willfully chosen, applied, and controlled for any given purpose or end.

The Technical Imperative

In Ellul's analysis of the *Technological Society*, we immediately encounter a unique interpretation of *technique* that is far more encompassing and profound in its implications than in previous studies. Although term "technology" is often used interchangeably with *technique* in general discourse on these matters, Ellul demonstrates that technology, as we commonly define and comprehend it, is only one manifestation of the technical phenomenon in society (1964:5-22; 1980:23-33). *Technique* actually encompasses a wide array of processes, means, and methods, of which technology is only a part (See Ellul, 1980:23-33).

According to Ellul, *technique* generally incorporates "the *totality* of methods rationally arrived at and having absolute efficiency (for a given stage of development) in every field of human activity" (1964:xxv). *Technique* is neither an abstract theoretical construct, nor an isolated methodological device that one can employ at will; it is a holistic sociological phenomenon that affects all human institutions through an identifiable, tangible process of growth and development in every area of modern society. Technical growth is governed by certain "laws" of development: in particular, a technical imperative to search for the "*one best means*," at a given stage of development, that will produce the most efficient, rational, and effective result for the objective pursued (1964:79-147).

Western machine technology provided the fundamental impetus for the growth of modern techniques historically; but techniques have since spread to every major social institution. For example, the economy, the state, commercial and industrial corporations, the military, policing, the sciences, education, propaganda, and even human relations are inseparable from the technicized infrastructure that surrounds them (See, e.g., Mumford, 1963; Ellul, 1965; Galbraith, 1967; Toffler, 1970). *Technique* has become so pervasive today that it can now be described as an autonomous *system*—our new, and historically unique, social environment (Ellul, 1980).

Symptomatically, the *language* of technique saturates every major contemporary human activity and institution. Every significant task is measured, analyzed, and evaluated in terms of technical efficiency. Common discourse in every major field is infused with such technocentric watchwords as "efficiency," "effectiveness," "rationality," "standardization," "organization," "planning," "administration," "centralization," "decentralization," "change," "innovation," "new," "revolutionary," "problem-solving," "means," and "methods." The crucial point is not that these watchwords are pure rhetorical devices, but that they betray a universe of discourse that breeds a predictable mentality, approach, and method in *any* given activity or advocate (Postman, 1992). This is quite obviously the case with the theoreticians of the COP/POP orientation in policing (as well as many of their critics), where the language of *technique* permeates virtually every discussion about community— and problem-oriented policing.

Herman Goldstein, for example, exudes the idiom of technique in pointing to the many perceived benefits of community policing: "e.g., decreased tensions between the police and the community, more effective use of police resources, an increased quality of police service, increased effectiveness in dealing with community problems, increased job satisfaction for the police participating in the programs, and increased accountability to the community" (1987:8). Indeed, all of the perceived benefits of COP/POP are couched in the vocabulary of "effectiveness," and "new," "progressive," "innovative" modes of thinking about policing.

As Cordner and Hale conclude in a recent summation of what works in policing, the combination of COP/POP offers "one of our brightest prospects for improved police effectiveness" (1992:14). In fact, even the most staunch critics of the COP/POP ideology are often reduced to a mere demand that COP/POP rhetoric become tangible reality, and that community policing *prove* its effectiveness by technical-empirical standards of scientific research (e.g., Manning, 1984; Greene & Mastrofski, 1988; Riechers & Roberg, 1990).

The Technical Phenomenon

Expanding on the implications of his definition of *technique,* Ellul shows clearly how technical growth and development are transformed into the *technical phenomenon* (1964:79-147). The cumulative effect of the proliferation of techniques historically leads to the inexorable imposition of technical means and methods on all aspects of social life. For example, the demonstrably efficient modes of industrial and commercial organization and production (as exemplified by the time and motion studies of F.W. Taylor, for instance) eventually affect the bureaucratic, administrative, and managerial structures of the modern state. Although there are obvious variations in individual technical operations and applications between the industrial and governmental spheres of activity, both spheres have tended to grow exponentially during the nineteenth and twentieth centuries.

Ellul attributes the growth of both the modern state and the capitalist economy to technical advances common to each. Standardization of technical procedures, rationalization of organizational means and methods, increasingly precise measures of efficiency, and a conscious and deliberate commitment of human thought and energy to the pursuit of the "one best way" to achieve a given result— all combine to engender the *technical phenomenon* (1964:19-22).

Among the many consequences of this phenomenon is the growth of the modern state in all of its complexity, powers, and responsibilities. In particular, *technique* galvanized the extension of the state's police powers into the increasingly formal, bureaucratic, and centralized agencies of policing that have characterized the Western world specifically since the nineteenth century (Cf. Miller, 1977; Walker, 1977,1980; Critchley, 1972).

POLICE POWER AND POLICING TECHNIQUES

The growth of the modern state and the pressures of technical and industrial development made necessary the creation of formal agencies of public policing over the last two centuries (Ellul, 1967:100-103). There is no question that other types of policing precede historically (See e.g., Albritton, 1992; Carrot, 1992; Critchley, 1972). But it is primarily in the nineteenth century, and thereafter, that policing techniques converge with wider technical developments to create the truly modern forms of centralized policing. This historical convergence required initially that the police powers of the state be rationally translated and structured into police organizations, and subsequently into increasingly technicized police practices and procedures (Ellul, 1964:100-103; Carte, 1976; Marx, 1988).

The Police Organization

The concentration of police powers in formal organizations of public policing followed a highly differentiated pattern of development initially. Much of this variability was determined by the relative stages in technological development achieved by each society. Nevertheless, the highly centralized, bureaucratic, paramilitary, and professionally oriented model of police organization—encouraged, for example, in England under Sir Robert Peel—remained a relatively stable example of technical efficiency well into the twentieth century. The major reason for the durability of this organizational model was that it conformed to the "laws" and imperatives of all technically structured organizations during this specific stage of technical development. Moreover, this type of "scientific" organizational structure was consistently promoted and implemented by "innovators" like F.W. Taylor and Henry Ford in industry, and eventually, August Vollmer, O.W. Wilson, Bruce Smith, and William Parker in specific areas of American policing (Cf. Carte, 1976; Wilson, 1950). The historically "fragmented" and "decentralized" nature of American policing has always presented a special problem to organizational reformers, who have persistently called for greater centralized control over American policing (Walker, 1977,1992; Munro, 1974). Yet American policing, especially in its twentieth century evolution at the urban, state, and federal levels, tends to mirror precisely the general process of centralization encountered elsewhere.

Thus, the principles of centralized, scientific management and organization have remained the dominant credo of organizational experts until recently (Cf., e.g., Walsh & Donovan, 1990; Goldstein, 1990; Roberg & Kuykendall, 1990). With the proliferation of new technical means, however, comes the possibility of *deconcentrating* the highly centralized, bureaucratic, and hierarchical nature of traditional organizations. This new threshold in technical development does not imply, in any manner, a radical *reversal* of the trends identified earlier. On the contrary, despite enthusiastic exhortations to "decentralize" or "democratize" many complex organizations, including the police (Cf., e.g., Naisbitt, 1984), we are simply witnessing a necessary re-adaptation and re-adjustment of the technical system to cumulative modifications in the technical environment that favor the process of *deconcentration* (Ellul, 1980:76-121).

For example, one of the more serious fallacies in the COP/POP "philosophy" is the idea that police organizations can be effectively "decentralized," both organizationally and managerially, by adopting community policing strategies alone (e.g., Moore & Trojanowicz, 1988). The implementation of foot patrols, mini-stations, greater autonomy for line officers or CPOs, more direct and cooperative communication between police and citizens, and police involvement in creating "communities of interest" with citizens, are all examples of what Ellul (1980:55-75) refers to as measures of *deconcentration*. These kinds of necessary adaptations or "innovations" in policing strategy should not be confused with authentic processes of "decentralization." Deconcentration measures in policing allow for a degree of "democratization" in decision-making out of technical necessity, but actually retain greater factual *centralization* of the police organizational apparatus in the long run. This aspect has been demonstrated clearly in the historical development of centralized police agencies, and most recently in experiments with team policing (e.g., Walker, 1992).

The inadequacy of decentralization experiments lies not in the choice of strategy, planning, or personnel, but in the failure to understand the *technical imperative* of centralization of police organizational powers and authority, as Ellul's analysis consistently demonstrates for other complex organizations. This kind of paradox is not, however, the consequence of some Machiavellian scheme or ill will on the part of police administrators or planners. Instead, it is the result of *technical necessity* and the evolving nature of the relationship between the police, the state, and society as a whole. This complex relationship makes it imperative for the police to maintain autonomous control over their operations, both to meet increasing social demands for police services, and to secure their domain of technical expertise. Again, Ellul illustrates how this is part of an impersonal, inexorable progression of *technique* through all domains of the Technological Society (See esp. 1980:55-75; 1964:247-318).

The Progression of Police Techniques

In order to reinforce their ideological position as reformers of contemporary policing, the advocates of the COP/POP orientation offer a generally simplistic and artificial dichotomy between "traditional" or "efficiency-oriented" policing on the one hand, and "community" or "effectiveness-oriented" policing on the other (e.g., Goldstein, 1979,1987,1990; Skolnick & Bayley, 1986; Moore & Trojanowicz, 1988). However, not only are efficiency and effectiveness *synonymous* as technical terms and methods, they are *inseparable* aspects of the same technical progression and phenomenon noted earlier.

Understandably, frustration with the highly centralized, bureaucratic, "traditional" model of policing has led many police analysts and administrators to seek viable alternatives. There is, nonetheless, a remarkable *permanence* in the overall centralized-bureaucratic model of American policing—despite numerous small agencies and the many efforts at reform during the twentieth century (Cf. Walker, 1992). The permanence of processes of centralization can only be understood adequately in terms of Ellul's description of the *Technological Society,* and the pervasiveness of centralized, techno-bureaucratic organizational forms in all areas of institutionalized society.

Moreover, the *technique* of policing a Technological Society has undergone a number of transformations during the last two centuries, most of which have tended to accomplish any combination of the following: (1) reinforce the general centralization process, (2) concentrate police powers in formal public policing agencies, (3) perfect the various technical practices and procedures of policing itself, and (4) render the police increasingly autonomous in relation to external controls. In the meantime, police agencies have acquired a progressively sophisticated and efficient technical apparatus for all kinds of police operations (e.g., Marx, 1988), as well as a legally sanctioned monopoly over the legitimate use of coercive force (Bittner, 1970; Klockars, 1985).

It is highly significant, for example, that Klockars (1985) devotes a generous portion of his analysis of the "idea of police" to demonstrating that only "means-based" (as opposed to "norm-derivative") definitions of police are adequate to the task of understanding the police role in society. This is precisely Ellul's contention, for different reasons, about *The Technological Society.* Technique is *always* "means-based," and most often represents the triumph of means over ends, or ultimate values, in any area of application. Since the police derive their powers from the order of social *necessity,* this reality places an indelible mark on the nature of police powers, as well as any effort to transform them in any substantial manner.

Furthermore, in spite of national scandals and official investigations, along with the so-called "police crisis" of the 1960s, the "due process revolution" of the Supreme Court, the academic "research revolution" of the 1970s, and now the COP/POP challenge to traditional forms of policing, the police have remained remarkably autonomous in their *essential* objectives and operations. Indeed, as

Cordner and Hale (1992:12) note in regard to COP/POP's impact: "In most departments, community policing is not intended to completely substitute for motor patrol, but rather to supplement and complement motor patrol's reactive efforts." Although their observation is perceptive and undeniably correct, it unavoidably weakens what every COP/POP enthusiast promotes as "authentic" community policing (esp. Trojanowicz & Bucqueroux, 1990).

Nevertheless, Cordner and Hale's observation unwittingly identifies the probable fate of the COP/POP agenda, especially in the United States. Police organizations have often transformed reform proposals and experiments to fit their own agenda and priorities; but rarely have they adopted these proposals in all their theoretical "purity," as the Team Policing era apparently demonstrates (Walker, 1992:363-368). It would seem, moreover, that the burgeoning problems of crime, violence, and drugs nationwide would make it impossible, as well as technically impractical, for police agencies to convert globally to the model of policing proposed by the COP/POP advocates.

Again, none of this is due, in the final analysis, to the evil intent of police officials, the epiphenomenal "police subculture," or deliberate managerial inertia in police departments. The decisive and determining factor is *technical necessity* itself—i.e., the search for the most efficient means to achieve both the organizational objectives of contemporary police agencies and the demands for ever more effective crime-fighting technologies from both the police and public. Pursuing the "traditional," crime-fighting mandate remains, therefore, the single most efficient way for urban police to justify their operations *and* maintain a relative degree of public credibility and support from the citizenry. Consequently, the traditional form of policing *must* continue to function in priority and predominance over reform measures, while perhaps incorporating the most technically useful aspects of COP/POP innovations and applications into traditional practices and procedures.

CONSEQUENCES OF THE COP/POP TECHNIQUE

To the extent that COP/POP principles have seemingly passed from the stage of theoretical elaboration to that of experimental application, they certainly qualify as an *emerging techniques* under Ellul's definition. However, the extent to which these principles offer efficient and useful methods for future policing will be determined by a number of social and technical factors that have little to do with the original intent of their theoreticians.

Contrary to the assumptions of its architects, COP/POP strategies are not simply a matter of making appropriate policy choices between traditional modes of policing and reform. The success of COP/POP will be based solely on the technical criteria of potentially efficient results. These results will most likely occur, if at all, in the areas of efficient neighborhood restructuring and more effective means of information-gathering at the local level. A preliminary assessment of the probable outcome of the COP/POP experiments can only be based, therefore, on an evaluation of the present strengths and weaknesses of its potential enhancement of the traditional technical means of policing, as well as its future utility for urban police operations.

Major Strengths

One of the major preoccupations of a *Technological Society* is the establishment of *social order* (Ellul, 1964:esp. 295-299). By reinforcing the emphasis of policing on order-maintenance and "peacekeeping" functions, COP/POP theoreticians such as Wilson and Kelling (1982), Goldstein (1990), and Skogan (1990) may have an appreciable impact on refocusing police thinking and operations on "community problems" and "disorder." The deconcentration of police resources to deal with specific, manageable problems of urban decay and disorder has already been partially achieved in some areas (e.g., Eck & Spelman, 1987); and it is not difficult to foresee the useful application of some of the "problem-oriented" techniques advocated by Goldstein (1990). In particular, the "new and more effective strategies" proposed by Goldstein, Eck and Spelman—i.e., scanning, analysis, response, and assessment—could become useful tools for police strategists in systematizing and rationalizing procedures that may have been spontaneous or haphazard to this point. The passage from such "pure" theoretical procedures to the stage of routine practical application simply illustrates a fundamental characteristic of all techniques in any field. Since order-maintenance responsibilities are both a general and pervasive function of contemporary policing, the police can only strengthen their legal and paralegal powers by adopting the problem-solving strategies inherent in the COP/POP orientation (See, e.g., Skogan, 1990:Ch. 7).

A second major strength of the COP/POP movement is the continued impetus it has brought to the so-called "research revolution" (Alpert & Dunham, 1992:30-31; Walker, 1992:24-25) in contemporary policing. Although this "revolution" extends over the last three decades, it has brought an ever-increasing number of advisors, researchers, theorists, practitioners, and experts into the field of police research. At the same time, this concentration of experts constitutes an emerging "technical intelligentsia" in policing operations, management, and analysis. In fact, the elaboration of the COP/POP agenda is primarily the work of academic researchers, in combination with major public and private sources of support and funding—such as NIJ, the Police Foundation, PERF, the VERA Institute, the Ford Foundation, and others. In other words, law enforcement is beginning to constitute its own *technostructure,* with the same impact and implications that Galbraith (1967) attributed to private industry and government decades ago. The consequences of this development for the future of policing are considerable, since the general "search for more effective strategies of policing" today revolves principally around the COP/POP ideological orientation (Kelling & Moore, 1988).

It is also quite revealing that Moore and Trojanowicz (1988), in one of the most interesting articles to emerge from the *Perspectives on Policing* collection at the National Institute of Justice, discuss policing strategies as "corporate strategies," analogous to those of private industry. When they state that "a strategy is defined when the executive discovers *the best way* to use his organization to meet the challenges or exploit the opportunities in the environment," (1988:2) they point, once again, to the technical imperative that unifies the quest for the most efficient means in *every* area, whether public or private, commercial or political. This imperative propels the *Technological Society*, as we have seen, and makes it impossible and impractical to isolate policing from other institutions and activities that characterize and define it.

Regardless of the outcome of experiments with COP/POP strategies, the COP/POP movement has erected an intricate bridge between law enforcement and academia. And this bridge has been forged by an emerging theoretical and technical elite in the areas of police analysis, planning, and research whose future is inextricably linked to the outcome of COP/POP experimentation.

Major Weaknesses

As is the case in general technical development, the success of a new set of technical means is not necessarily determined by the inherent intellectual weaknesses in the proposed innovations (Ellul, 1980:Ch. 4). The effect of *technique* is both *cumulative* and *causal;* it can never be understood in isolation, or as a result of what Ellul calls "abstract empiricism" (1980:89-91). The attempts by enthusiasts of the COP/POP movement to create a new *paradigm* for policing often defy theoretical and historical logic, as well as careful empirical research techniques (See Greene & Taylor, in Greene & Mastrofski, 1988:Ch. 11). Yet the hyper-empiricism promoted, for example, by Greene and Taylor will hardly retard, or significantly modify, technical innovation and application for two principal reasons: (1) few scientific research projects today are truly "disinterested," and (2) "good technique" presently requires immediate, utilitarian application, regardless of evidence of contrary effects. This fact is cogently illustrated by Skolnick and Bayley as they symptomatically shift the "burden of proof" to others:

> Our recommendations about the usefulness of community-oriented policing are based . . . on arguments that such innovations "make sense" or on conclusions developed from field observations. But if some of the new we have praised is unproven, so too is the old. Rarely have traditional police practices been subjected to rigorous evaluation . . . Because doubts about traditional strategies are so widespread, the burden of proof should be on those who seek to maintain them. (1986:226)

Thus, for the "innovators," the onus is on the disbeliever to disprove the validity of the new paradigm. The innovators are committed *only* to the technical imperative of change itself—i.e., the old or traditional that must be discarded in the face of the new and commonsensical that must be immediately embraced. This mentality represents, nonetheless, a primary weakness in the general COP/POP orientation. The reluctance of proponents to subject their most cherished assumptions to honest scrutiny and critical evaluation actually defies the logic upon which their original demands for change in policing were purportedly based. It also makes doubtful the ultimate durability of community policing as a viable *technique,* as Ellul defines it in the context of the *Technological Society.*

A second major weakness lies in the conceptual infrastructure of the COP/POP "philosophy" itself. While the conceptual defects are many, this discussion focuses on two that are central: i.e., the concept of "community" on the one hand, and that of "policing" on the other. The concept of "community" that underpins COP/POP discourse is as naive, sociologically imprecise, and equivocal as it is unsatisfactory to the careful observer. Yet it is precisely this conceptual ambiguity that lends power and persuasion to the COP/POP orientation as an ideological technique, in that it simplifies, rearranges, reduces, makes operational and instrumental, *any* social reality it encounters (Ellul, 1980:45-46).

Insofar as the idea of "community" has posed a persistent *dilemma* to traditional philosophers and social theorists for centuries (See, e.g., Nisbet, 1969), there is little evidence to indicate that COP/POP architects have somehow resolved it today. On the contrary, these theorists persist in addressing "community" as if it were a "problem" to be resolved by COP/POP initiatives and interventions, along with CPOs in the "neighborhood" (yet another ambiguously defined term). In this environment of ambiguity, "community" is taken as a *given,* whereas the actual *disappearance* of natural, organic human communities and extended families has been a major theme in nineteenth and twentieth century sociological literature and research, as well as a pervasive by-product of the *Technological Society* itself (Ellul, 1964:esp. 126-127).

The *illusion* of community is, of course, constructed upon the progressive disappearance of authentic communities from urban social reality today. This explains, in turn, the cogent and inevitable appeal of the COP/POP philosophy to a wider audience. On the foundation of this illusion, the police play a dual role as the governmental agency of choice and change. First, they must regain the "goodwill" of the neighborhood citizen by giving him/her a greater sense of participation in the police decision-making process; and second, the police must become the agency of change through which "community" is reinstated, or re-created, as social reality (e.g., Skolnick & Bayley, 1986). No other agency of local government is expressly empowered to intervene in this process of "community-building," except through the auspices of the police. Only the problem-solving interventions and mediations of the police are called upon to effect such a daunting transformation.

After a perceptive review of previous "circumlocutions" in policing, Klockars (in Greene & Mastrofski, 1988:Ch. 13) correctly points out that "police can no more create communities or solve the problems of urban anomie than they can be legalized into agents of the courts or depoliticized into pure professionals." In practice, the police have not constructively assumed this new, creative role of community-building in any of the COP/POP experiments to date. And it is doubtful they ever will, voluntarily. In any case, none of the present circumlocutions and mystifications about "community" emanate from police officials. They emerge, most often and unfortunately, from the idealistic and somewhat romantic ruminations of academic observers.

A second conceptual defect relates to the very idea of "policing" that is proposed in the COP/POP strategy. A prime assumption of this strategy is the perceived *need* to re-integrate the police into "the community" by making the former more responsive to the latter. Ideally, the line-officer and the citizen should eventually become *unified*, as the police provide more services and the citizen more information. However harmonious and democratic these projections may appear, they obscure many stark realities of police power and certain delusions in the COP/POP philosophy about "honest citizens." For example, in playing the "devil's advocate" to this philosophy, Bayley (in Greene & Mastrofski, 1988:Ch. 12) provides an unusually honest account of several of these delusions. Specifically, he concedes that community policing materially legitimates the penetration of communities by powerful agents of government, while transforming the citizens into potential interest groups favorable to the police. Furthermore, he notes that the new strategy will most likely increase the relative power of the police among government agencies, and eventually weaken the "democratic rule of law." What Bayley fails to underline, however, is the fact that all of these scenarios are perfectly consistent with the growth and direction of police techniques in a *Technological Society*.

Indeed, the technical utility of COP/POP experiments may inadvertently supply the breeding ground, or conduit, for the extension of policing techniques to the most intimate, grass-roots level of society—something "traditional" modes of policing were rarely able to accomplish, either operationally or systematically. Because the COP/POP strategists cannot accept a natural *tension* and *ambivalence* in the relationship between police and society, they are perhaps sowing the seeds of a greater and more subtle tyranny than they ever imagined "philosophically." In the final analysis, as Ellul consistently points out, every progression in *technique* exacts a corresponding cost, and that cost is most often paid in strictly human currency.

CONCLUSION

Throughout this discussion, an attempt has been made to demonstrate the value of incorporating the much narrower focus on the internal characteristics of police reforms like COP/POP into a macro-level understanding of policing in a

Technological Society. Ellul's definition and analysis of *technique* provides such a holistic context, as well as a powerful explanatory matrix in which to understand the nature and determinants of policing as a sociological and technical phenomenon. In this broader context, COP/POP can be understood not as a new or revolutionary strategy for policing, but as part of a *progression* of technical innovations that has led to policing techniques that are now on the verge of penetrating the most intimate level of social existence. None of this is happening by deliberate design, but the process is facilitated materially by the uncritical and naive encouragement of COP/POP doctrines.

Furthermore, the analysis of *technique* exposes a process of growth and development that is both impersonal and implacable. The police mandate in the *Technological Society* has been forged out of necessity and involves an incessant search for the most efficient and effective means to exercise police powers toward a given objective. This is not the product of Machiavellian scheming by police administrators, but a *technical imperative* that has led the police to pursue the widest autonomy in their functions and operations throughout modern history. It is therefore naive and unrealistic for COP/POP strategists to assume they can transform the technical imperatives of traditional policing through enthusiasm and exhortation alone. Moreover, their failure to perceive the broader implications of *policing-as-technique* may end by encouraging a more oppressive extension of police powers into grass-roots society than they ever imagined in their rhetorical excesses. Such are some of the lessons to be learned from a broader understanding of policing in a *Technological Society*. Yet we may also discover, to a degree, that rhetoric can *become* reality in the world of *technique* . . .

NOTES

1   The theme of technology's pervasive and multifaceted influence on modern society has been pursued by many prominent social thinkers in recent history. A recommended sampling would include such works as Mumford, 1963,1970; Galbraith, 1967; Ellul, 1967,1980; Bell, 1968; Mesthene, 1970; Toffler, 1970; Kuhns, 1971; Burke, 1972; Gendron, 1977; and Teich, 1990. The literature on this topic is remarkably vast, and it is somewhat surprising that police analysts have tended to ignore the magnitude of its impact on policing (Cf. Walker, 1983, 1992).

2   The composite term, *Technological Society,* is employed here as Ellul (1964) defines it. It implies a type of society in which *technique* has become the organizing force and efficient cause for all subsequent societal developments. Since a full and fair treatment of this complex thesis is beyond the scope of the present discussion, the reader is urged to consult Ellul's recent clarification of definitional matters in *The Technological System* (1980:esp. Ch.1).

3

Community Policing:
The Implementation Gap

Eli B. Silverman
John Jay College of Criminal Justice—City University of New York

INTRODUCTION

The amount of ink spilled debating community policing's meanings, contents, advantages and disadvantages has far exceeded extensive analyses or even satisfactory explanations of how this supposedly new mode of policing has been or can be operationalized. With the exception of chapters in this volume and a few others (Kelling & Bratton, July, 1993, Sparrow, 1988), the literature on community policing implementation is quite scanty, primarily anecdotal and superficial. Therefore we know very little about the obstacles which face the implementation of community policing.

It is the intention of this paper to explain how and why: (1) explorations of community policing's implementation record are scanty and frequently contradictory and; (2) the obstacles confronting community policing implementation lack systematic examination and learning transferability among various police departments.

CONCEPTUAL AMBIGUITY AND IMPLEMENTATION

Assessment of community policing implementation is severely hampered by conceptual issues that pertain to policing in general and community policing in particular. The multiple and sometimes conflicting goals and purposes of policing have been extensively explored by others (Wilson, 1968; Bittner, 1970; Hoover, 1992).

It is not necessary to take a position on the relative merits of the respective positions regarding, for example, law enforcement, order maintenance, or conflict resolution. It is important to note, however, that confusion and ambiguity among these missions not only makes it difficult to assess what police are supposed to achieve, but also how to achieve these goals. It is difficult to know how to introduce appropriate police strategies and changes if we do not know what the these changes are supposed to yield. These complexities are further compounded by community policing's changes and/or additions to the police mission. For community policing often talks about fear reduction, crime prevention, quality of life crimes, and problem solving (Goldstein, 1990; Kelling & Moore, 1988).

As a problem solver, the community police officer must be willing to and capable of entertaining a wide range of alternatives in terms of identifying, defining, and addressing problems. This range of cognitive and behavioral actions entails an outlook and value system profoundly different than the law enforcement role. Police departments, which publicly proclaim community policing, acknowledge these outward behavioral changes.

In a February 1992 department publication, former New York City Police Commissioner Brown raises and responds to several questions. Two of the questions are: *What is Community Policing?* and *Aren't We Doing All Those Things Now?* The answers are instructive:

> Community Policing is a partnership with the public aimed at reducing crime, arresting offenders, reducing the fear of crime, and improving the quality of life in every neighborhood in the City of New York. You have been doing an excellent job of pursuing and arresting offenders and answering calls for services as rapidly and efficiently as possible. As a department, however, we have not had a strategy for resolving the problems that cause many 911 calls to come from the same locations. We were able to react to crimes once they were committed, but we were not organized to reduce and eliminate the conditions that cause crime and fear of crime (Brown, 1992:1).

An even more fundamental change in policing values and behaviors is captured in community policing's emphasis on joint police–public cooperation in the determination and resolution of community problems and issues. "Partnership" and "coproduction" are typical of the words used to describe this enterprise (Skolnick & Bayley, 1986; Trojanowicz & Bucqueroux, 1990). Police and community interaction often takes place in the neighborhoods where officer and residents may share different perspectives, outlooks, lifestyles, racial, religious, and ethnic backgrounds and consequently view similar behavior from very different perspectives. In addition, the police officer, as the previously labeled "professionally trained expert," is no longer the sole repository of the explanation and determination of the types of crimes that should receive priority attention and the greatest claim on police and other community resources. It can easily be argued that the expectation that field police officers should act as general government agents responsible for virtually all neighborhood conditions—in effect neighborhood managers—will at times require that they take adversarial positions with the municipality that employs them. "Instead of police merely intervening in threats to community peace or safety as emergency workers, they would become long-term treatment specialists" (Guido, 1993).

If police officers are now to engage in a far wider and more extensive range of policing functions, how are these newer and more complex range of police functions, roles, responsibilities, and their attendant risk-taking activities to be introduced into existing police organizations and structures? Should these changes replace or be grafted on to existing police functions? Or are existing responsibilities to be entirely restructured and recast? Are the desired changes to be introduced at the outset in a single, separate pilot unit, several units, or the entire department at once?

ORGANIZATIONAL AMBIGUITY AND IMPLEMENTATION

Community policing's implementation is not only beset by the ambiguities and complexities that surround the police mission, but these difficulties are further compounded by the ambiguities that are inherent in complex organizations, including large police organizations (Bolman & Deal, 1991; McCaskey, 1982). It is appropriate to briefly note these sources of organizational ambiguity and relate them to the incomplete and contradictory findings regarding community policing's implementation.

1. *We are not sure what the problem is.* Definitions of the problem
   are vague or competing, and any given problem is intertwined
   with other messy problems (Bolman & Deal, 1991:27).

With polls showing rising attention to crime, the fear of crime has given rise to facile political solutions which rests on simplistic explanations of the causes of crime (Walker, 1993). Given the complexities inherent in the crime issue and the criminal justice system, it is easy to understand why some urge caution in the rush to adopt community policing's departure from the so-called professional policing model.

"Community policing is being oversold. It is widely perceived as some kind of miracle municipal antibiotic, promising to cure or alleviate the intractable problems of contemporary society" (Guido, 1993:1). Judged against anything approximating such lofty goals, no policing strategy can succeed. If we are to make intelligent and informed choices, we must come to a better understanding of what community policing entails and promises, as well as the problems which must be overcome in implementing it.

2. *We are not sure what is really happening.* Information is incomplete, ambiguous, and unreliable, and people disagree on how to interpret the information that is available (Bolman & Deal, 1991:27).

The record of community policing is a vivid testimony to this observation. A 1992 survey of the 25 largest police departments in the country reveals that 78 percent reported practicing community policing, 13 percent were planning for the near future and only 9 percent reported not having a community policing program. This is despite the fact that the actual components of their community policing practices varied significantly (Cardarelli & McDevitt, 1992). A more recent survey by the National Center for Community Policing and the FBI reported 50 percent of the police departments in cities with more than 50,000 population following community policing. An additional 20 percent planned to adopt it within a year (*U.S. News & World Report,* August 2, 1993:28). It seems apparent that it is considered acceptable for a police department to proclaim its allegiance to community policing.

Houston's police department presents a vivid example of the varying interpretations which are applied to incomplete and ambiguous information in community policing. There have been numerous laudatory reviews of Lee P. Brown's introduction of "rapid change. . . wide range of innovations, reflecting extraordinary sensitivity to all of the insights and research findings in police" (Goldstein, 1990:59) during his tenure as Chief of Houston's Police Department from 1982 until 1990 (Skolnick & Bayley, 1986; Brown & Wycoff, 1987). The praise has been effusive. Chiefs like . . . Lee Brown . . . essay the greatest departures from the path laid out by reform policing. They have deliberately sought to open their organization to effective collaboration with citizens at every level; from the chief's office through the precinct captains to the patrol officer. They have reorganized to put the full resources of their forces at the disposal of low levels of the organization. They have sought help from citizens in controlling crime and disorder. They have rallied support from other government agencies to deal with the problems that the community and the police together view as most important" (Sparrow, 1990:113).

"The most ambitious are, with Sir Kenneth Newman and Lee Brown, testing their department's capacity to handle change itself, to manage rapid and wholesale movement into many new areas at once (Sparrow, 1990:198). Brown had a different approach to making those changes than did many of his fellow chiefs, however. He was convinced, probably more than any of them, that community policing is not simply a matter of good ideas and programs built on them but requires—if it is to work and to last—a complete transformation of policing and police departments. . . . His job, he thought, was to change the Houston department's style: how it thought, how it worked, what it believed, what it valued" (Sparrow, 1990:92).

Given the immense obstacles confronting community policing and the necessity of fundamental organizational change, Brown proposed a two-pronged strategy. The first phase consisted of implementing specific, separate department programs which do "not require a complete change in the organization's operation style (Brown, 1989:4). Phase II, on the other hand, does require such changes in all aspects of the entire department. Houston's two-phase timetable was initiated with Phase I from 1982 to 1987 when Phase II began as the "the department made an organizational commitment to adopt community policing as its dominant operating style" (Brown, 1989:4). Many accomplishments were listed for Phase I. They primarily focused on growing acceptance, adoption, and reassurance within the department:

1. Break down barriers to change.

2. Educate its leaders and rank-and-file members for community policing.

3. Reassure the rank-and-file members that the community policing concepts being adopted had not been imported from outside the department but instead were an outgrowth of programs already in place.

4. Reduce the likelihood that members for the department would reject the concepts of community policing as 'foreign' or not appropriate for the department and the community (Brown, 1989:5).

Two years later, in 1991, an evaluation of Houston's police department was released. This consultant evaluation [assuming the research was completed no earlier than 1990] meant that it included Phase I and 3 years of Phase II when a new way of thinking and behaving was incorporated into the entire department. The report finds many difficulties with the results and implementation of Houston's community policing called Neighborhood Oriented Policing (NOP).

In terms of achievements, the report finds a lack of any "comprehensive improvement in performance. . . . Results appear quite limited in their tangible effects on citizen security and quality of life" (CRESAP, 1991:Executive Summary). While the report noted individual examples of problem solving, "this evidence is anecdotal only, and no comprehensive change in behavior has been observed or documented"(CRESAP, 1991:OM–6). In addition, officer and supervisor resistance was observed. Many officers seem entrenched in their opposition to the program, perceived as a public relations gimmick. Reportedly, there is a tendency among patrol sergeants and lieutenants to be 'negative leaders' not inclined to support officers' initiative. (CRESAP, 1991:NOP 3).

These liabilities are partially attributed to organizational issues and difficulties that impinge on implementation. This includes a "great diversity of interpretation among officers as to the meaning and emphasis of NOP. . . The report goes farther and wonders whether "It may be unreasonable to expect all or even most officers to fundamentally alter their approach to their job, particularly to 'manage all the problems in their beat'" (CRESAP, 1991:NOP 2).

Others have joined in the critical assessment of Houston's community policing efforts. Writing, ".. . ten years after initiating neighborhood-oriented patrol efforts in Houston . . ." Hoover observes that. . . "at least 80 percent of the patrol officers involved remain strong skeptics. Most are outright cynics. Command staff indicate that at best 20 percent of the officers who have been involved in the neighborhood-oriented patrol effort are supporters. Indeed, skeptical managers point out that the 20 percent of the officers who have been involved in the neighborhood oriented patrol effort are supporters. Indeed, skeptical managers point out that the 20 percent support may well represent individuals who have decided that the politically correct way to get ahead in the organization is to support the initiatives of central administration. Keep in mind that these are not patrol officers who have merely received a one-hour orientation to community policing. They have had a great deal of training, have been in numerous discussion sessions on neighborhood oriented patrol, and have been assigned to neighborhood-oriented patrol areas for a number of years" (Hoover, 1992:23, 24).

3. *We are not sure what we want.* We have multiple goals that are either unclear or conflicting or both. Different people want different things, leading to political and emotional conflict (Bolman & Deal, 1991:27).

As discussed above, the situation could not more aptly characterize the diverse missions and goals of community policing. In addition, these divisions among policing goals and strategies are not restricted to the upper echelons of police organizations. Numerous studies, for example, have noted divergent goals and other conflicts among the different levels of police departments (Reuss-Ianni, 1983).

4. *We do not have the resources we need.* Shortages of time, attention, or money make a difficult situation even more chaotic (Bolman & Deal, 1991:27).

The scarcity of resources has repeatedly plagued community policing implementation efforts. For example, the widely heralded and often-cited 1977 Flint Michigan Foot Patrol project originally consisted of 22 police officers in 14 neighborhood which were selected partially on the basis of their support for the program. Within a year after it began, the program extended to two-thirds of the city; at one time it included 44 officers in 44 beats and then was reduced to 36 officers in 36 beats. This accordion-like implementation had, according to its primary evaluator, an undesirable impact on the program.

The rapid expansion caused headaches for the program and for the researchers. The original plan allocated 22 officers to the 14 beats, so that two-person teams with overlapping morning and afternoon shifts, could cover high-density, high-crime areas. The luxury of doubling up officers quickly disappeared and further expansion caused many officers to complain that they were being stretched too thin. Many beats expanded, so that it was increasingly difficult for one officer to cover so much more territory or so many more people. (Trojanowicz & Bucqueroux, 1990:208).

An in-house New York City Police Department review as well as an independent study found similar issues of inadequate management and diffusion of community policing resources during the period when community policing was extended from a few precincts to all of the city's 75 precincts (*New York Daily News,* January 24, January 25, 1994; *New York Times,* January 25, 1994).

The degree to which community policing requires additional funding in excess of the level of the professional-reform model has been debated and partially hinges on the nature and extent of an agency's community policing. Nevertheless, adequate funding for community policing seems to be a perennial issue, especially as it pertains to the expensive "labor intensive" foot patrol (Rosen, 1992:17). A review of community policing in New York State, for example, underscores community policing's vulnerability to the fluctuations of local economies and the revenues they generate. One city's police chief, for example, notes: "I'm facing budgetary cutbacks, and if I lose two officers, I have to put neighborhoods officers back onto a line position just to handle the number of calls we get."(Rosen, 1992:17).

Due to the critical issue of revenue support, some jurisdictions have attempted to safeguard their community policing efforts through what they considered to be separate, and perhaps sacred, revenue sources. The Flint Foot Patrol project was financed in 1979 with a three-year $2.6 million grant to augment existing motor patrol, crime prevention, and undercover operations. The Flint experiences provide graphic evidence of the tenuousness of police organizational reform in the fact of a declining economy and dwindling tax base.

By the time the Flint project was launched, the number of sworn officers had declined substantially despite the fact that grant money was supposed to be used exclusively to pay for new foot patrol officers above and beyond existing staffing, the number of officers in the department as a whole never really grew. Quite obviously money saved by not using the new funds to increase total numbers helped cover shortfalls elsewhere in the system.

While the motivation was understandable, and the economic pressures intense, the fact remained that the police department had launched an ambitious, ever expanding, and widely popular effort with no ultimate increase in staffing. It also meant the chief had to 'rob Peter,' who in this case was motor patrol, to 'pay Paul'—the new foot patrol initiatives, further fueling internal dissent and straining both kinds of patrol to the breaking point (Trojanowicz & Bucqueroux, 1990:209).

The negative impact of declining resources in the midst of increased police activity, public expectations, and support (as evidenced by public referendum support for special tax levies for foot patrol) has led one participant to conclude that ". . . Flint serves as a lesson that Community Policing must never be funded separately, by a special pot of money" (Trojanowicz & Bucqueroux, 1990:213). One participant in the experiment observed, "In many communities, people have demonstrated that they are willing to tax themselves more to pay for improved and expanded police service, but there is obvious danger in putting those funds in a special account where it can become a temptation" (Trojanowicz & Bucqueroux, 1990:213).

New York City's 1991 community policing introduction was supported by State passage of $1.8 billion to fund the City's "Safe Streets, Safe City" community policing program. The revenue sources were personal income tax surcharge extensions beyond 1992, property tax hikes earmarked for public safety and an instant lottery game which has fallen far short of prediction. The ability of the specific dedicated funding mechanism to ensure long run support enabling New York to escape the fate of the Flint experience is questionable. It is noteworthy to observe that the State legislature's funding package stipulated that the city's failure to achieve stated goals of patrol police levels within a 24 percent margin will trigger proportionate reductions in surcharge revenue support. In addition, a recent 1994 Mayoral task force questioned the adequacy of current patrol staffing levels. (*New York Times,* March 12, 1994).

Finally, even if special dedicated funding does ensure the security of a police agency's funding, it is relevant to examine the impact that guaranteed police funding may have on other city agencies when there are revenue shortfalls. If community policing requires police and other city agencies to cooperatively join in solving problems, what will happen if these other agencies have decreasing support? New York Police Deputy Commissioner of Training, says her prime concerns are the budget cuts that city agencies face. In light of the direct or indirect role that such agencies play in realizing the full potential of community policing, such cutbacks could undermine the effectiveness of the concept. Given the nature of community policing, the public could be disappointed, and they could direct their disappointment at the police if their expectations are not met (Rosen, 1992:18).

5. *We are not sure who is supposed to do what.* Roles are unclear, there is disagreement about who is responsible for what, and things keep shifting as players come and go (Bolman & Deal, 1991:27).

Confusion and ambiguity surrounding role responsibility has been repeatedly noted in reference to the implementation of community policing. This is particularly applicable in regard to the internal clientele not directly involved in the community policing program. A review of the Flint Michigan program includes the original evaluation of a major police researcher:

> They did a great job of educating the community and the officers involved in the program, but they forgot to include motor patrol in the educational process.' Traditional officers not only felt neglected but insulted, laying the groundwork for hostility between the two units (Trojanowicz & Bucqueroux, 1990:207).

Regardless of the merits of these perceptions of mistreatment, organizational implementation must come to grips with the appropriate way to introduce changes. The highly influential E. Edward Deming raised 14 points in the famous Deming Management Method. The fourteenth point is "Take Action to Accomplish Transformation." In order to take action, top management needs to " . . .explain . . . to a critical mass of people in the company why change is necessary and that the change will involve everybody. Enough people in the company must understand the Fourteen Points, the Deadly Diseases, the obstacles. Top Management is helpless otherwise." Dr. Deming regards a critical mass as vital. Just as workers cannot act alone, neither can top management. Enough people must understand the Fourteenth point to know what to do and how to do it (Walton, 1986:88).

The vast bulk of the community policing implementation efforts have not involved the entire internal constituency. The results have been remarkably similar to Flint. In Baltimore County's widely heralded COPE program, its select officers are "sometimes referred to by other officers as 'cops on pensions early'"(Goldstein, 1990:173). Goldstein noted in 1990 that New York's CPOP (Community Patrol Officers Program). ". . . who are insulated from the pressures of daily calls made to the police, are sometimes referred to by other officers as the 'untouchables" (Goldstein, 1990:173).

Today, in 1994, this author's interviews in three precincts finds the vast majority of these same officers, officially known as Community Police officers, but more commonly still called CPOP, frequently criticized by other police for not doing "real" police work, a reflection of the disdain and perhaps misunderstanding of this role. So tensions and resentments often are projected upon what is perceived as a special, elitist, favored group engaged in a different kind of policing. Thus, internal clientele becomes divided into hostile camps.

The problem-solving initiative in Newport News, Virginia, with its emphasis on "agency wide strategy" which focuses on all department members has received considerable attention (Eck & Spelman, 1989; Spelman & Eck, Feb. 1987). At this point, however, no one is prepared to declare widespread acceptance and clear understanding of respective roles. "Obviously, making problem-solving an integral part of the daily operations of the Newport News department will require a sustained effort over a much longer period of time than has elapsed since the project was initiated" (Goldstein, 1990:56). Lack of clarity of roles and turnover among high level police official only contributes to uncertainly plaguing community policing implementation in many jurisdictions. It is one thing to argue that police should be accomplishing different things under community policing; it is another to actually provide resources and explain how this should be done.

6. *We are not sure how to get what we want.* Even if we agree on what we want, we are not sure about what causes what (Bolman & Deal, 1991:27).

In addition to the confusion and ambiguities about the appropriate division and assignment of community policing responsibilities, there are also uncertainties as to the actual nature of the "partnership with the community." Numerous commentators have addressed these related issues such as: who speaks for the community; to what extent the community is a partner; what if the community is at odds with the police; how do police work with agencies; what role do they have in setting agency priorities; how involved do the police get in addressing an underlying problem that breeds crime (Manning, 1988, 1992; Klockars, 1988; Reichers & Roberg, 1990). A call for problem solving in not sufficient, especially with inadequate, poorly supported training. For many, community policing is longer on intentions than it is on strategies and tactics.

7. *We are not sure how to determine if we have succeeded.* We are not sure what criteria to use to evaluate success. If we do know the criteria, we are not sure how to measure them (Bolman & Deal, 1991:27,28).

Since police goals and missions are often multiple, contradictory, and confusing, measurement of degrees of community policing, success can be very difficult indeed. Furthermore, since community policing makes such claims as fear reduction, reduction in actual crime, improvement in quality of life conditions and increased public satisfaction with the police, it remains unclear as to which of these should receive what degree of weight and in what combination. In this regard, a 1993 interview with Lee Brown, former head of the New York City and Houston police departments, is quite instructive. Brown, a leading advocate of community policing makes many claims but cites "customer satisfaction" as the central indicator for community policing.

"Are the people happy with their police? Are they willing to work with them? That is important, because if you look at what we traditionally do—that is, evaluate police based on the crime rate—well the police don't control the factors that produce crime. It's inappropriate to use that as a criterion for evaluating police effectiveness" (*Congressional Quarterly Research,* 1993:101). Brown says that "the two community policing programs he was associated with, Houston's and New York's, both passed the customer satisfaction test" (*Congressional Quarterly Research,* 1993:101). This remarkable statement is not substantiated by any evidence of supportive or positive public surveys nor is it supported in the literature. Police, of course, are not unique in their reluctance to establish benchmarks in advance and\or declare victory after the introduction of organizational change. New York City, for example, only submitted a proposal to the National Institute of Justice in June 1992 for funding of an evaluation of their community policing efforts which began two years earlier. Ultimately that evaluation was awarded to a respected research organization, which, nonetheless had a leading role in the very development of the city's community policing.

IMPLEMENTATION LESSONS

This chapter has focused on several central issues surrounding community policing implementation. The first notes the very formidable odds that challenge the conversion of community policing plans to community policing practice. These challenges reside in the conceptual issues which are inherent in: (1) policing in general; (2) community policing in particular and; (3) large complex organization, such as police departments in large cities.

There seems to be little prospect of arriving at consensus as to the most appropriate weights that should be awarded to the various police missions and community police goals. It is therefore appropriate that we now center the discussion on those organizational factors that have most repeatedly presented formidable obstacles to community policing implementation. It is our contention that if more attention is devoted to these frequently found obstacles, the road to implementation would be less rocky.

Organizational Obstacles

Although there are many organizational factors that impact on organizational change, we will center our discussion on a few salient features. Firstly, we have discussed inadequate resources devoted to community policing efforts. This, however, includes more than financial resources. It also includes human and informational sources. If policing is to change or evolve into community policing, then other divisions in the department must be included and encouraged to support these efforts. Otherwise noncommunity police officers and/or specialized units, such as detectives, will go their own way. As Kanter notes "Other structures and patterns also need to change to support the new practice: the flow of information, the division of responsibilities . . ." (Kanter, 1983:300). In another context, Kanter notes that ". . . institutionalization requires other changes to support the central innovation and thus it must be integrated with other aspects of the organization. If innovations are isolated, in segmentalist fashion, and not allowed to touch other parts of the organizational structure and culture, then it is likely that the innovation will never take hold, fade into disuse, or produce a lower level of benefits than it potentially could" (Kanter, 1983:299).

We also note the key role of hierarchical arrangements. Many large police organizations have advanced the intention of reducing the levels of their bureaucratic hierarchy and increasing the autonomy of precinct commanders and the local community policing officer. This objective, however, has often proved elusive. In New York City, for example the rhetoric of the Police Commissioner of 1991 is now still echoed by an advisor to the Police Commissioner of 1994 (Brown, 1991; Kelling, 1994).

The crucial role of middle management has been repeatedly noted in all studies of organizational change. In policing, with the 1960s advent of foot patrol for example (Kelling & Bratton, 1993), the key role of the sergeant level was noted even before community policing. What is missing, however, is not only early involvement of middle management but examination of the basis of their resistance if that is the case. Resistance, for example, may be based on the belief of middle managers that strategic changes will not work or they may feel that they are "incapable of executing that strategy" (Guth & MacMillan, 1986:325).

Segmentalist vs. Integrative Police Organizations

The organizational obstacles we have described may be subsumed under what Kanter calls a segmentalist organization (Kanter, 1983). In segmentalist organizations, the individual is trusted less than the system which "is often designed to protect against individual actions" (Kanter, 1983:34). In segmentalist organizations, "Participation is something the top orders the middle to do for the bottom" (Kanter, 1983:244). Without trust, authority will not flow to the bottom, problems will not be shared, and natural bureaucratic resistance will prevail. Middle management resistance will be well justified and specialist units will continue to remain the favored route for reward and recognition.

In integrative organizations, on the other hand, new changes will be supported because there is a previous history of support for changes (Rogers & Shoemaker, 1971). Similarly, the involvement and participation of all levels will be encouraged because of stability that rests on an integrative arrangement of shared responsibilities, security in expressing views and inquiries, and the absence of constant top-level turnovers. The integrative organization supports cooperation and has a history of rewarding change over tradition, collaboration over isolated specialists (Kanter, 1981: 154, 212, 237, 297). It is from this history that change agents are supported with the appropriate financial, informational, and human resources required for their tasks.

Community policing's implementation can only forge ahead with future consideration to change in organizational arrangements, procedures, and cultures. Devolution of authority, enhanced roles for precinct commanders, middle managers, and the community police officers may best be facilitated by the cultivation of an integrative organization. By pursuing this path, the gap between the possibility and the reality of implementation may be narrowed.

Section II

VARIATIONS IN COMMUNITY POLICING ORGANIZATIONAL MODELS

Part II describes different organizational models used to guide community policing programs and operations. In Chapter 4, "Operation Cul-De Sac: LAPD's Experiment in Total Community Policing," James R. Lasley, Robert L. Vernon, and George M. Dery, III report on the results of a survey of community attitudes toward the Los Angeles Police Department's implementation of what it termed "Total Community Policing." Using a random sample of citizens affected by community policing efforts, the researchers explored opinions of their attitudes toward the police and their fear of crime. Forms of police-citizen contact and the locations of the contract were explored, to determine the types that created the most effective changes in attitudes. Official crime rates in the areas where community policing had been instituted were also examined.

The researchers reached a number of interesting conclusions. In addition to reporting reductions in actual crimes and fear of crime, and improvement in police-community relations and citizen satisfaction with police performance, the study also explored the reactions of the officers involved in the community policing efforts. They identified female and veteran male officers as those who tended to perform best in community policing, and found that assignment to a particular area for a year or more was needed to establish trust and rapport with the residents.

Chapter 5 is a contribution from Michael Wiatrowski, titled "Community Policing in Delroy Beach." This chapter presents an interesting study of the employment of community policing in a "resort" area. The characteristics of the residents of this community include the upper class rich as well as the lower working class and the poor. He explains how a multi-faceted foot patrol, bicycle patrol, and decentralized mini-station is employed by the police with positive results.

In Chapter 6, "Dynamics of Community Policing in Small Communities," Peter C. Kratcoski and Robert Blair discuss the results of their survey of community policing programs in three small Ohio cities. They explored the various ways the communities had implemented community policing, the police administrators' and officers' perceptions of what community policing should involve, and the community's response.

Reactions of administrators, officers, and citizens varied widely. Anecdotal data presented in this chapter provide interesting insights into the problems involved in gaining officers' and community members' acceptance of the concept, as well as the ways these three cities adapted the community policing idea to fit their own citizens' specific needs. Officer training was identified as a key element in the levels of success attained.

4

Operation Cul-De-Sac: LAPD's "Total Community" Policing Program*

James R. Lasley
California State University—Fullerton

Robert L. Vernon
Los Angeles Police Department (retired)

George M. Dery III
California State University—Fullerton

INTRODUCTION

Although the importance of the community to police work was first identified by Peel nearly 200 years ago (see Trojanowicz & Bucqueroux, 1990) it was not until the last decade that police administrators began to truly recognize the community's potential for controlling inner-city crime. Much of this renewed interest in the community on the part of police has been prompted by favorable results from policy evaluations of contemporary "community-based" policing programs (Greene & Taylor, 1988). In essence, findings from these studies suggest that police who foster informal social control through increased community sensitivity are more effective at controlling crime than police who maintain com-

* This project was supported by a grant awarded to California State University, Fullerton by The John Randolph Haynes and Dora Haynes Foundation. Points of view or opinions stated in this document are those of the authors' and do not necessarily represent the position(s) of the Haynes Foundation or the Los Angeles Police Department.

munity distance and rely exclusive on formal "reactive" enforcement strategies (for a comprehensive review, see Trojanowicz & Bucqueroux, 1990; Skolnick & Bayley, 1988).

Unfortunately, many police administrators (especially those serving large metropolitan areas) who attempt to transform their agencies into so-called community-based models may encounter significant difficulties. First, and foremost, among these is the identification of a specific "community" wherein particular needs of citizens can be identified and met by police.

According to Herbert J. Gans, an eminent authority on social organization, a community is defined as "an aggregate of people who occupy a common and bounded territory in which they establish and participate in shared institutions." However, few, if any, of today's urban centers conform to the latter definition of a "community." Instead, most moderate to large metropolitan areas are comprised of nebulous territorial, demographic and institutional boundaries. Thus, police administrators who seek the benefits of community-based policing within crime-ridden inner-city neighborhoods are likely to conduct an endless search for a necessary starting point: the identification of a "true" community.

The above situation, and the various problems it poses to police attempting to implement community-policing, is no more evident than in the City of Los Angeles. Specifically, rapid population growth and demographic shifts that have occurred in Los Angeles over the past two decades have thrown many L.A. inner-city neighborhoods into a "community identity-crisis." That is, many communities that once shared similar demographic and institutional identities have now become "transitional" neighborhoods comprised of residents who share no common social bonds. For occupants of these once stable inner-city neighborhoods, drive-by shootings, narcotics trafficking, homicide, prostitution and a series of other felony and misdemeanor crimes have become the norm. For the police, attempts to implement crime-control in the form of community-based policing have been formidable.

In the following sections, a recent attempt by the Los Angeles Police Department devised to restore community presence and to enable effective community-based policing within transitional inner-city neighborhoods is described and evaluated. This program, nicknamed "Operation Cul-de-Sac," represents the an experiment in what we call "Total Community Policing."

TOTAL COMMUNITY POLICING: THE THEORY

The construction of the Total Community Policing (hereafter referred to as TCP) concept is based on four related propositions:

1. Crime control is best achieved through informal (i.e., citizen-based) rather than formal (i.e., police-based) control networks;

2. Police and citizens cannot realize the benefits of informal crime control in the absence of clearly defined communities;

3. Informal crime control networks can be created or recreated within any grouping of citizens or neighborhoods by creating either implicit or explicit community boundaries; and

4. The creation of community boundaries will result in the development or redevelopment of permanent informal social control networks that produce long-term reductions in neighborhood disorder and criminal activity.

As Proposition One illustrates, the basic foundation of TCP rests on the general principle of community-based policing; that is, the belief that crime is ultimately controlled by the public and not the police. The logic here suggests that crime is mainly the product of factors such as inadequate family life, poor schools, improper guidance—not inadequate policing (Trojanowicz & Moss, 1975; Trojanowicz & Dixon, 1975). Therefore, TCP theory predicts that increased enforcement measures taken by police in neighborhoods lacking a sense of "community" will have only a marginal impact on crime.

The second proposition of TCP is based on James Q. Wilson's and George Kelling's (Wilson & Kelling, 1982) concept of "broken window" community disorder. In other words, residents of neighborhoods that are characterized by both physical and institutional decay (i.e., have lost their sense of community) become anonymous to each other, fearful of crime, and targets for increasing criminal activity. In addition, police may label such neighborhoods as "a lost cause" or "a place where crimes are expected to happen," which may result in providing citizens with only the most basic services and/or treating all citizens as if they were offenders (for a thorough discussion of these issues, see Goldstein 1977a, 1977b, 1979, 1991).

Wilson and Kelling (1992) metaphorically suggest that by fixing "broken windows" (i.e., repairing the physical and social decay) community presence and social control will be restored, and crime will go down. However, TCP theory assumes that some inner-city neighborhoods are so overcome by physical and social blight that there are no "windows" left to fix. In other words, some communities lack even the most basic physical or institutional structure and can only be revitalized by starting from scratch; in effect, they must be "totally" rebuilt.

Proposition Three represents the community building aspect of TCP. Regardless of the social or physical state of a particular neighborhood or group of neighborhoods, TCP theory holds that the definition of community boundaries will begin a process whereby community cohesion and informal crime is regenerated. By using their crime control function, the police may initiate the latter process by constructing either implicit or explicit boundaries around neighborhoods lacking a common identity. This process will create both an outward and inward symbol to both police and citizens that a "community" now exists. However, care should be taken to create symbolic community boundaries that are strong enough to be observed and respected by all.

For citizens, the value of defining community boundaries is two-fold: First, citizens living within newly defined community boundaries experience a greater sense of physical unity that is conducive to social interaction—the basic building block of informal crime control; second, citizens entering these defined areas from the outside will readily sense order, cohesion, and unity and be more apt to treat the "new community" and its residents with greater respect. The latter aspect of TCP is especially important for deterring crimes of opportunity. More often than not, offenders who seek easy prey within disorderly neighborhoods will think twice about entering and committing a crime within a "community" setting— where they run a greater risk of their criminal activities being observed and reported to police.

The construction of symbolic community boundaries is beneficial for police as well. Knowing where a community begins and ends enables police not only to tailor their style to the specific citizens they serve but also to detect people, places, and things that are usual and unusual. Most important, the goals of community-based policing (for example, positive interpersonal contact, citizen respect for police, police respect for citizens) can be more effectively carried out when police and citizens share common community boundaries. Thus, according to TCP, the establishment of a "community" is a necessary first step in establishing a police-community partnership.

The last proposition of TCP is that the formation of communities will enable citizens, with the assistance of police, to form lasting informal controls over criminal behavior. It is here reasoned that the formation of a strong community presence will serve to foster new institutions of social control as well as to revitalize those that have been weakened by urban decay (Reiss & Bordua, 1967; Reiss, 1971). Furthermore, at the community-level, police need to become involved in assisting citizens during this institutional rebuilding process.

In fact, the ultimate success of TCP lies in the formation of police-citizen partnerships that help form a "total community." Borrowing from the concept of Problem-Oriented Policing advanced by Herman Goldstein (1991), TCP assumes that combined efforts on the part of police and citizens to restore physical community order will eventually restore citizen-based informal crime control. Such police-citizen community building activities include the removal of gang graffiti, the cleaning of trash, the permanent closure of abandoned dwellings, and so forth.

This "problem-oriented" phase of TCP is essential for long-term crime control. With the creation of both real and perceived community order, the roots of informal social control begin to form: neighbors are no long afraid to communicate; children are no longer afraid to walk to school; and, in general, citizens are no longer afraid to spend their leisure time in their "community" as opposed to some other area which they perceive as "safer." In turn, the enhancement of community interaction enables the establishment and strengthening of basic socializing institutions (i.e., schools, churches, families, that provide lasting community order and informal control crime). Thus, strong police-citizen partnerships are of critical importance for communities established under TCP programs to maintain their crime resistent qualities over time. In the following section, a description and analysis of a model TCP program carried out by the Los Angeles Police Department, "Operation Cul-de-Sac," is presented.

OPERATION CUL-DE-SAC: PUTTING THEORY INTO PRACTICE

For the most part, Operation Cul-de-Sac (OCDS) represents the first specialized community-based policing effort by LAPD since the inception of "Team Policing" in the 1970s (e.g., see Sherman, 1973; Vernon, 1992). The primary goal of OCDS was to conduct an "experiment" that, if successful, could serve as a model for future community-based policing programs targeted toward inner-city neighborhoods characterized by violent crime and a lack of community presence. The following sequence of events outlines the street-level implementation of OCDS:

1. *Site Selection.* Because OCDS was designed to test community-based policing under the most difficult of circumstances, prerequisites for an appropriate test site included (a) consistent patterns of heavy Part I crime activity and (b) the absence of an observable community identity. Based on these criteria, the neighborhoods within one patrol sector or "reporting district" (corresponding to one census tract) within LAPD's Newton Division were selected as the OCDS testing ground.

The OCDS program site, known as RD 1345, was comprised of inner-city neighborhoods occupying a 10-square-block area within South Central Los Angeles. Although this location was largely residential, it also included various businesses and a major high school. However, obstacles to community presence in RD 1345 were numerous.

First, the population was very dense, consisting of some 5,000 residents occupying less than 700 dwellings; and second, most residents lived in extreme poverty, with over one-half of all household incomes falling below the poverty level. Added to this was the fact that these neighborhoods had undergone rapid ethnic transition. In 1988, approximately 95 percent of residents in RD 1345 were African-American. Now only 40 percent are African-American, with the remainder being of first- and second-generation Hispanic descent.

As far as criminal activity, the neighborhoods of RD 1345 ranked among the top five most dangerous in the entire city of Los Angeles. During 1989, for example, more than 150 assaults and street robberies were recorded within the area's less than one-square mile perimeter. In addition, the City's most violent gangs had staked their claim in the streets of RD 1345. The 1989 total for drive-by shootings in this area was 34—the highest of all neighborhoods served by LAPD.

2. *Community Acceptance.* To ensure that OCDS was indeed a police-community partnership, it was essential to gain citizen approval for the program. Footbeat officers, many of whom were spanish-speaking, canvassed all 700 households within the OCDS program area asking residents how they felt about the prospect of police imposing community boundaries—even if it mean the closure of certain streets—within their neighborhood. Similar discussions were also held at the local high school. Only 10 of all 700 households surveyed objected to the OCDS plan.

3. *Community Identity.* Shortly after citizen approval was obtained, the "community identity" phase of OCDS began. On February 1, 1990, police and various public works entities installed a series of temporary concrete barriers and signs reading "Narcotics Enforcement Area" at street locations along the outer boundaries of the "new community." Resembling freeway dividers, the concrete barriers were strategically placed so that they did not unnecessarily obstruct business, school, and residential traffic, or emergency fire access. In particular, streets with a history of high drive-by shooting activity were targeted for barricade placement.

4. *Community Rebuilding.* After establishing strong external community boundaries recognizable by both police and citizens, the building of an internal community structure was undertaken. Examples of activities used in this process included:·

   • The assignment of 15 regular and other cash overtime OCDS officers working footbeat, bicycle and mounted patrols who had a primary mission of "getting to know residents and the neighborhood" rather than "making arrests."

   • The development of various task forces composed of public agencies and community groups to assist in the clean up of garbage, graffiti and other signs of physical decay. The creation of a police-sponsored tutorial program in the local high school involving overtime pay for teachers who instructed afterschool classes on life skills for teenagers.

   • The creation of "block clubs" composed of residents within each neighborhood whereby police and citizens could communicate their specific needs to each other during periodic informal meetings.

- The initiation of public picnics and other social gatherings in local parks to facilitate police-community relations as well as to allow the "new community" to establish their presence in neighborhood leisure areas.

PROGRAM RESULTS

Community-Level Program Assessment

The following program assessment sections (detailing both community—and officer-level factors) present results from an independent program analysis of OCDS conducted by researchers at California State University, Fullerton (for a thorough discussion of sampling and design methods used in collecting these data, see Lasley, 1993). This analysis was initiated just over one year after OCDS had begun at the street level; hence, findings presented here represent the effects of the OCDS program following one year of full operation. Study findings were based on a variety of official and unofficial data sources: LAPD agency crime statistics (i.e., Part I crime data), CRASH Unit (Community Resources Against Street Hoodlums) gang intelligence information, community surveys and police officer interviews.

- *Sense of Community was Strengthened:* Approximately 82 percent of residents surveyed felt that placement of barricades around their neighborhoods created a stronger sense of community. In further support of an improved community presence, nearly all residents (93%) claimed that had become personally acquainted with more of their neighbors since the beginning OCDS than during any other time since moving to their present home. In fact, one El Salvadorian resident claimed that she was "always afraid of her American neighbors," but after making personal contact with them "they were now giving her English lessons" so that they could better communicate.

- *Part I Crimes were Reduced:* For the year following OCDS, Part I crimes were 15 percent lower than the previous year. Furthermore, displacement of crime to adjoining patrol sectors was not discovered. Part I crimes in these areas were also down, on average, approximately nine percent. Thus, it appeared as though the barricades had caused a "bleed off" of community presence and not criminal activity.

- *Drive-by Shootings and Gang Activity were Reduced:* There were 70 percent fewer drive-by shootings during the first year of OCDS than during the year preceding the program. This was a significant finding considering the fact that crimes of a predatory nature are rarely impacted by traditional "community-based" policing efforts. Interviews with local gang members indicated that many gangs were unwilling to continue long-time rivalries on neighborhood streets with "cul-de-sacs", such as those within the OCDS project area. Many stated that the new community presence gave them an uncomfortable feeling of being "trapped-in."

In addition to the above information, numerous personal interviews conducted with about 75 members of local street gangs revealed that about one out of every two gang members felt that the OCDS program was beneficial for curbing gang warfare. Gang members offered two explanations for their feelings. First, they felt that the more personal attitude of the Cul-de-Sac officers served to reduce already high frustrations that the average gang member experiences daily while living in the ghetto or barrio. Second, gang members felt that the barricades were an effective deterrent to drive-by shootings. About one-half of the gang members interviewed stated that they felt safer because of the barricades. When asked "Why?", many respondents felt that the increased security of the barricades offered gang members a good excuse not to continue a feud or fight without loosing honor or looking like a "chicken." Several gang members who lived out of the Cul-de-Sac area expressed a strong desire to have barricades placed in their neighborhood in order to protect themselves and their families.

• *Fear of Crime among Citizens was Reduced:* Surveys taken before and after the implementation of OCDS revealed that a majority of the project area residents were significantly less concerned about becoming the victim of a crime in the street or in their homes. Approximately 65 percent more residents were willing to walk in their neighborhoods at night after OCDS than before (Lasley, 1991). And 82 percent were more willing to go into their neighborhoods during the day. Furthermore, visual inspection of citizen residences further suggested a significant lifestyle change as the result of OCDS.

For example, visits to households during the pre-OCDS period revealed the extent of these citizens' fear of becoming crime victims: windows and doors nailed shut, boards over windows, beds on floors to avoid random gunshots. However, during the post-OCDS period, many of these drastic security measure has been removed or lessened to enable a more normal, less crime-concerned, style of life.

• *Positive Changes in Socialization Patterns were Observed:* Perhaps the most surprising positive effect of OCDS was evidenced at the local high school. Just a few weeks after OCDS began, high school attendance increased approximately 10 percent. Most students who were interviewed stated that they were "no longer afraid to walk to school." In response to this trend, high school officials began scheduling dances and other afterschool activities that had been previously discontinued due to the perception of unsafe neighborhood conditions.

- *Police-Community Relations were Improved:* Survey results indicated that citizen attitudes toward police steadily increased during the first year of OCDS. Prior to the program's state date, 49 percent of area residents gave the police a highest possible rating of "very helpful," six months into the program 63 percent considered police "very helpful," and after one year this rating increased to 78 percent. Interestingly, the last rating was taken following the highly publicized "Rodney King" incident—which, according to *Los Angeles Times* surveys, served to significantly lessen general public opinion toward LAPD. When OCDS residents were asked why they still held the police in high regard despite the "King" incident, the response heard most often was "the police we have gotten to know are different, they would never do anything like that."

- *Informal Crime Control was Improved:* After OCDS, citizen calls for service had increased four-fold. In addition, 58 percent of residents surveyed claimed that they were better able to identify a "stranger or strange situation" in their neighborhood after OCDS than before. Furthermore, approximately 70 percent said that they were more likely to report a crime after OCDS because they felt the police were "able to do something about it." When asked whether they would be willing to testify in court about criminal activity they observed, 39 percent of residents shifted their answer from "no" to "yes" after living under OCDS for one year. In explaining the latter change in attitude, many stated, as did one resident, that "if the police were willing to help fix their neighborhoods, they weren't just going to stand by and watch."

- *Citizen Acceptance of "Barricades" Increased Over Time:* Baseline figures established at the beginning of OCDS suggested that approximately 63 percent of residents survey indicated that they thought the use of barricades in their neighborhood was either a "good" or "very good" idea. Data obtained from the one year follow-up revealed that citizen approval toward the use of OCDS barricades had increased approximately 29 percent. Within response categories, approximately 81 percent of the follow-up sample felt that the barricades in their neighborhood were either a "good" or "very good" idea. Although some residents expressed concern over their neighborhoods resembling "housing projects" as a result of the barricades; however, they also stated that they would not like their neighborhoods to go back to the way they were before OCDS if the barricades were removed.

POLICE-CITIZEN CONTACTS: WHICH ARE MOST IMPORTANT?

In order to determine how existing negative attitudes toward police are best "unfrozen," and positive attitudes are likewise made stronger, the OCDS partnership process was systematically studied (Lasley & Vernon, 1992). The purpose of this investigation was to find out which aspects of police-citizen contact have the greatest potential for improving working relationships between police and citizens. Four types of contact were examined:

1. Type of Contact
   - visual only
   - physical

2. Frequency of Contact
   - the number of visual police-citizen contacts
   - the number of physical police-citizen contacts

3. Location of Contact
   - home only
   - street only
   - both home and street

4. Quality of Contact
   - officer demeanor/politeness
   - officer helpfulness
   - officer understanding
   - officer caring

The effects of the above contact varieties on community attitudes toward police-citizen partnerships were assessed by asking OCDS residents to respond to the statement "I will do anything possible to work with the police to make my neighborhood a better place to live." Responses were rated on a scale of 1 (Agree Strongly) to 5 (Disagree Strongly). By measuring change in responses to this item over the first year of OCDS, it was revealed that certain modes of contact proved more effective than others in building police-citizen partnerships within inner-city neighborhoods. These findings were as follows:

Type of Contact

Visual Only: Residents who claimed that their only contact with OCDS officers was of a visual nature improved their outlook toward police-community partnerships by approximately 12 percent over the one-year study period.

Physical: Residents who claimed to have made at least one physical contact with OCDS officers evidenced a 38 percent improvement in attitudes toward police-community partnerships.

Frequency of Contact

Visual: For those residents who only "saw" officers in their neighborhood, frequency of contact did nonetheless condition their attitudes toward partnerships with police. Those claiming to see an officer once daily improved their opinion by 33 percent, compared to 14 percent and 9 percent for those seeing an officer once per week or once per month (respectively).

Physical: The frequency impact of physical contact between citizen and police was nearly two times higher than that observed for contact that was visual only. Specifically, residents who made a daily personal contact with officers improved their relationship with police by a margin of 69 percent. By comparison, a weekly contact resulted in a 32 percent improvement, and a 19 percent improvement was the result of making contact only once per month.

Location of Contact

Home and Street: Among those making personal contact with police, contact in the home improved partnership attitudes to a much larger extent (29%) than did contact made in the streets (17%). However, those citizens who made contact with police in both their homes and in the streets improved their attitudes by 34 percent.

Quality of Contact

Demeanor/Politeness: Residents responding "yes" to the statement "officers who patrol my neighborhood are generally polite to me" improved their partnership outlook by 37 percent.

Helpfulness: When asked whether officers were "helpful in matters requiring their assistance," respondents who agree with this question evidenced a 35 percent improvement in partnership opinion.

Understanding: Answering "yes" to the question "officers generally take time to understand my particular problem" resulted in the second strongest opinion change discovered among OCDS residents (72%).

Caring: The greatest improvement in partnership opinion (80%) was discovered for those residents who felt that "officers cared about them as a person."

SUMMARY

Several lessons in community-based policing can be drawn from the above analysis of Operation Cul-de-Sac. First, and foremost, community-based policing can be used as an effective tool to "unfreeze" perceptual gaps between police and citizens. As discovered here, this appears to be the case even in inner-city neighborhoods where crime, lack of community presence, and deep-rooted anxieties toward police are typically found.

Even more important, the art of favorable community interaction can and should be converted into a science. That is, all types of police-citizen interaction do not appear to provide the same pay-offs where change in community perception toward police activities is concerned. Simply put, some modes of community-based policing interaction seem to build citizen confidence more than others.

With respect to evidence presented here for inner-city neighborhoods, police agencies engaging in community-based policing efforts would be well advised to focus their efforts on the quality rather than quantity of police-citizen interactions. In other words, expressions of helpfulness and understanding on the part of officers toward citizens appear to be many times more important to the overall effectiveness of community policing programs than are factors such as visual presence, frequency of contact, or even officer politeness and helpfulness.

In sum, it is here generally recommended that job designs of officers assigned to building community partnerships be structured to maximize the potential for quality police-citizen contacts. On a supervisory level, quality of police contact should be emphasized in performance evaluation criteria. With regard to field operations, stability of assignment should be practiced for individual officers so that they will be afforded enough time to develop quality interpersonal relations with the citizens they serve. These and other measures taken to ensure quality contacts between police and citizens, may provide one of the many keys to "fine tuning" the newfound science of community-based policing (Lasley & Vernon, 1992).

OFFICER-LEVEL PROGRAM ASSESSMENT

In this section, interview data gathered from police officers who have been assigned to OCDS details are presented. The contents of these interviews are here used to highlight some of the successes and failures of community-policing in urban Los Angeles neighborhoods, as seen through the eyes of the OCDS police officers. Although the following discussion represents experiences and opinion specific to the OCDS program, it can be argued that many of these accounts may prove useful for structuring future community-policing efforts in the inner-city areas of Los Angeles as well as other urban centers. Because OCDS is thus far the nation's most comprehensive effort to implement community-policing in a high-crime urban setting, the findings presented below provide state-of-the-art insights for discovering what works and what does not work with regard to the formation of police-community partnerships.

Female and Veteran Male Officers Tend to be Most Adaptable to Community-Based Policing Assignments. Most of the OCDS officers interviewed, including supervisors, indicated that female and older, more experienced male officers were by far the most effective at carrying out the mission of community-based policing. According to one OCDS officer, who attempted to explain this discovery,

> Younger male officers tend to be caught up in the hook and
> book syndrome and they sometimes don't equate community-
> based policing with 'real' police work . . . when they are
> young, they are anxious to get out there and make arrests not
> friends.

It was the consensus among those interviewed that female officers, regardless of age and experience, tended to adapt more easily to an enforcement role of "community liaison" (Lasley, 1992; Lasley & Felkenes, 1993). Greater patience and more flexible police officer role identities are some of the more frequent explanations for the observed success of female officers in community-policing assignments. The key explanation for the success of veteran male officers was that these officers, more than their younger counterparts, tended to find positive community contact refreshing and enjoyable after enduring many years of negative encounters with the public during a typical career as a "reactive" patrol officer.

Officers Selected to Work Community-Policing Assignment Must Possess a High Degree of Self-Motivation. Interviews and personal observations revealed that officers who lacked self-motivation and personal initiative were also the least successful at carrying out community-policing assignments. In brief, officers who adhered to the "reactive" police management style of "merely following orders" given to them by their supervisors tended to be the least productive when given unstructured time during community-policing assignments.

Stability of Assignment is Necessary to Build Strong Police-Community Partnerships. Most citizens and officers interviewed indicated that for a community-policing officer to be effective, he or she must spend a large amount of time working the same patrol area—getting to know people, places, and activities. Consensus of opinion revealed that it usually took officers and citizens no less than one year to "warm up" to each other. Many residents of the OCDS program neighborhood felt that trust could be built between themselves and officers in as short as a six-month period; however, most of the residents expressing this opinion were those who were either block club leaders or retired, affording them the greatest amount of free time to engage in casual contact with OCDS officers. Among those citizens interviewed who had significant daytime responsibilities, most felt that the six-month time period was simply too short to develop a bond of trust between themselves and the officers.

Community-Policing Assignments Can Lead to Boredom and Burnout Among Officers. Officers interviewed expressed two concerns about how they were affected by long-term (i.e., over one year) community-policing assignments. First, some officers complained that the restricted geographic area of OCDS patrol sectors often caused boredom. Many claimed that the repetition of seeing the same faces and places day-in and day-out—regardless of how much work there was to be done—simply "gets boring after a while." Other officers expressed concerns over the possibility that prolonged assignments to community-policing activities may impede their professional development and opportunities for varied policing experiences that are necessary for obtaining promotions.

On the other hand, it was apparent that the most dedicated, most highly self-motivated officers were at risk of professional "burnout" due to the unlimited work potential of community-policing assignments. For the most part, community-policing assignments are what an officer makes of them. For those officers who take their assignments most seriously, there is always the risk of taking on so many responsibilities that a normal shift provides nowhere near enough time to get everything accomplished. It was observed that OCDS officers falling into the latter situation became so personally dedicated to maintaining community partnerships that they regularly continued to work in the OCDS program area when their shift had ended and even on days off.

Difference in Uniforms Appears to Assist Community-Policing Efforts. An unlikely finding was the effect that the "lighter shade of blue" uniform worn by OCDS officers appeared to have on both officers and citizens. Citizens interviewed claimed that they soon learned to associate the OCDS officer as "a different type of LAPD officer." Many citizens claimed that when they saw the OCDS uniform they felt at ease and knew that they could trust the officers who wore them. One citizen stated that she "feared retaliation from gangs if [she] told the police who was a neighborhood criminal." However, she also stated that she knew the officers in the OCDS uniforms were "special officers" would do everything they could to protect her and her identity; thus, she felt more comfortable informing police about untoward activities in her neighborhood.

Difference in uniforms also appeared to affect officers and their outlook toward citizens. Officers interviewed indicated that they "felt different" while wearing the OCDS uniform as opposed to wearing the traditional LAPD patrol uniform. As one officer commented, "At first, I didn't think it [the uniform change] would change me, but it really did make me, and I think the citizens, more open to others."

The Community Can Expect Too Much from Officers Who Work Community-Policing Assignments. A common complaint among many officers who were assigned to OCDS was that community members possessed unrealistic expectations for service. In particular, officers encountered many situations where citizens demanded service that was far beyond the nature and scope of police work. OCDS officers stated that it was not uncommon for some community members to intentionally abuse the promise of "special services" provided by community-policing. One citizen who was interviewed complained that community-policing was "not all it was cracked-up to be" because an OCDS officer refused, on several occasions, to help him mow and rake his lawn.

The Success of Community-Policing Requires Community Members to Share Equal Responsibility for Crime Control With Police. Although a great many community members affected by OCDS provided a great deal of assistance to police in efforts to control neighborhood crime, some did not. OCDS officers indicated that some community members failed to "carry their weight" in making efforts to control crime. In general, officers claimed that the promise of increase service provided by OCDS was perceived by some citizens as a signal that the police could handle all problems by themselves. One officer stated that "the reaction of some residents to community-policing was to get lazy and expect the police to do all the work." In some instances, it was observed that a few residents failed to clean up trash or cover up graffiti because they expected OCDS officers to have taken over the responsibility for such community maintenance activities.

Some Community-Building Activities May be Beyond the Scope of Community-Policing. Many community-building activities were "experimented" with during the course of OCDS. Some of these activities proved more successful than others. Among the more promising of these activities were community picnics, the showing of feature movies, community newsletters, graffiti clean-ups, and crime-prevention block clubs. However, some OCDS officers stated that various activities attempted were not met with a great deal of success. Among these were a high school tutorial program and an athletic program geared toward teenagers.

Officers interviewed claimed that the tutorial program was valuable in theory, but did not capture the attention of the teenagers for whom the program was established. OCDS officers who coordinated the tutorial program with various high school instructors expressed that it was very difficult to attract teenagers to attend tutorial meetings that were held immediately following normal school hours. Some students felt that the program may have had a greater degree of success had it been scheduled less frequently or during hours that did not compete with their normal after-school activities.

In addition, OCDS officers felt that the athletic program was not successful because officers who were assigned to the administration of the program did not have the appropriate expertise to do so. However, officers did state that the program had a high degree of potential for community-building among teenagers. In particular, they felt that such a program was not beyond the scope of community-policing and could have been successful had OCDS officers had the knowledge and ability to organize the appropriate athletic activities.

Community Members Need Rewards for Their Efforts. Several OCDS officers commented that community members were highly responsive to recognition given to them by the LAPD for their positive participation in the OCDS program. One OCDS supervising officer commented that the greater use of commendations for active community members would have a strong impact on the strengthening of police-citizen partnerships.

Community-Policing Demands Increased Resources. A common complaint expressed by OCDS officers concerned a lack of appropriate resources needed to effectively carry out their mission. The program began with some 12 patrol officers and two supervising sergeants (one handling administrative duties, the other handling field supervision). At present the program has been reduced to approximately 9 patrol officers and one supervising sergeant (who must handle both administrative and field supervision responsibilities). Furthermore, the future of these resources depends upon the ability to obtain external funding through State and Federal Law Enforcement Grants. Many officers expressed the concern that if resources continue to decline, the future of OCDS and the quality of service that can be afforded to the public will be greatly jeopardized.

Fear of Injury is a Concern Among Officers Who are Assigned to Inner-City Community-Policing Assignments. It was discovered that several OCDS officers perceived themselves to be at greater risk of personal injury as the result of giving up their patrol cars for footbeats or bicycle patrols. As one officer stated, "When you work an area where patrol cars get a few bullet holes in them every month, you start to think about what it will be like without the patrol car." From these observations, it may be assumed that community-policing assignments within crime-ridden inner city areas evoke additional concerns for personal safety among officers. However, OCDS officers further claimed that they felt much safer walking or riding bicycles in the OCDS program area because of the strategic placement of street barricades. In short, officers felt that the barricades reduced the type of criminal activity that placed them most at risk, i.e., drive-by shootings. Several officers stated that they would have severe reservation about taking a community-policing assignment in the inner-city without the construction of barricades or something like them.

CONCLUSION

Amid the excitement, promise, and skepticism that currently surrounds the concept of community-policing, there are few solid answers to guide the abandonment of "reactive" policing models in favor of police-community partnerships. To the contrary, our current state of knowledge on the subject merely generates a plethora of critical policy questions.

From an historical standpoint, it is of little use to trace community-policing back to its roots in nineteenth century England to seek answers. Although Sir Robert Peel cast the conceptual mold of community-policing nearly two centuries ago for use by the London Metropolitan Police, this mold is today merely an anachronistic icon of professional policing. It is safe to say that the founding principles of community-policing are no longer valid to address the complex issues that face the social and political complexities of contemporary communities.

Furthermore, it can be argued with a high degree of confidence that an appropriate "method" of community-policing that best addresses the needs of today's society has not yet been discovered. Perhaps there is not one but several models of police-community partnerships that are both efficient and effective given a variety of community circumstances. Therefore, it is critical that many innovative programs like Operation Cul-de-Sac be introduced and tested under a variety of social settings so that the roots of modern community-policing programs can be established.

Undoubtedly, many of these innovative policing efforts, such as Operation Cul-de-Sac, will be controversial. In fact, most rapid changes in social control are met with a high degree of resistance. So long as these programs are implemented in a legal, moral, and ethical fashion, they will ultimately be of benefit in uncovering the true definition of "community-policing."

At present, OCDS continues and is approaching its second year of operation. As an applied test of the Total Community Policing concept, many lessons have been learned. The most important among these has been the discovery that imposed community boundaries can serve as a vital point of reference for effective police-community partnerships and the regeneration of lasting informal social control networks. Most important, the Total Community Policing model provides a community-based alternative to traditional "reactive" policing models that are currently the norm in inner-city neighborhoods characterized by community disorder.

In closing, one important point should be stressed regarding the comprehensive nature of Total Community Policing programs: Barricades or any other physical symbols of community boundaries by themselves are insufficient for creating a "community." Police and neighborhoods must work together to rebuild social cohesion once "new communities" are defined. In addition, any imposition of community boundaries should be perceived by residents as a "positive" rather than a "negative or invasive" change. Specifically, residents should never feel stigmatized by their "new communities." Without strong community acceptance and participation, efforts to implement Total Community Policing in any neighborhoods will undoubtedly fail.

5

Community Policing in Delray Beach

Michael D. Wiatrowski
Florida Atlantic University

INTRODUCTION

The decision to initiate a community policing program represents a recognition by both the police and the community that the previous patterns of interaction have not been effective in confronting the crime and disorder problem that the community faces. In the fall of 1990, a neighborhood task force was appointed by the city of Delray Beach, Florida. The citizens, community leaders and government of Delray Beach conducted an extensive survey of the neighborhoods of the city. The problems and conditions of the communities were examined to provide an objective assessment of the conditions and problems of the neighborhoods. The communities were divided into three groups:

1. Those that were stable and viable;

2. Those that were in a state of decline and that required additional services; and

3. Those that were deteriorated and that required considerable assistance.

This provided the basis for recommending which neighborhoods would receive the community police program. At a meeting of the neighborhood commission, the rationale for the selection of the neighborhood to receive the commu-

*   This research was made possible through the cooperation of the Delray Beach Police Department, Major Richard Lincoln, and City Manager David Harden.

nity policing program was explained. The neighborhood that was chosen was geographically bounded to the west by an interstate highway, to the north by an access road, to the east by railroad tracks, and to the south by a major commercial access road. The community, an older and historically racially segregated, predominantly residential area that was black with significant representation from Haitian, Nicaraguan, Guatemalan, and other Central American and Caribbean groups.

The officer selection process began with the orientation of the entire department to the goals and purposes of community policing as a philosophy. The officers were given information about community policing and what it would attempt to accomplish. The officers were also solicited to volunteer for the program. In the interviews the officers were questioned about their commitment to interacting with the community in direct contact with both citizens and community groups.

The group that was selected for the community police program was comprised of four officers and a sergeant who would serve as supervisor. The officers received 24 hours of training. This training included instruction about the philosophy and goals of community policing, and the development of communication skills needed to interact with the community. These skills were necessary to provide the officers with the confidence to interact with both individuals and community groups.

EVALUATION OF THE COMMUNITY POLICING PROGRAM

Community policing as a model of policing has under gone more than the professional model at a corresponding stage of its development. In part this is because evaluation research has emerged as a major goal in program development and implementation. The two major questions relate to program evaluation. First, Has the program been implemented as designed? Secondly, Has the program had the effect that it was designed to address? The conceptual framework and evaluation instruments used in the evaluation of the Delray Beach Community Policing Program were derived from previous interview schedules and surveys designed for evaluations of the Flint, Michigan; Houston, Texas; New York, New York; New Haven, Connecticut; and Edmonton, Canada.

It was determined that a before-and-after research design would be used. This would allow for changes in the attitudes of the residents towards the community policing program to be measured and their victimization experiences to be determined. Because of the pattern of historical segregation that existed until the early 1970s in Delray Beach, there was no control area against which the residents could be compared, thus a more sophisticated research design could not be developed. The individual respondent was the unit of analysis on which the data for this study was based.

A group of interviewers were selected and trained by the researchers. Additionally, a list of addresses in the area of the community policing program was developed for the sampling of residents of the community. The residents were given a token payment of $5 as compensation to complete the approximately one hour required for the interview schedule. This was done on philosophical as well as pragmatic considerations. The community is comprised largely of blacks who settled into the area because it was historically an area in which they were permitted to live. Recent immigrants from Haiti and a large contingent of migrant farm workers from Central and South America who perform seasonal work in the area have also moved into the area. It was felt that this was necessary to insure a representative response and was appropriate compensation in return for their time.

During the first wave of interviews, almost 400 interviews were obtained in March and April of 1991 and in the second wave, 290 interviews were completed in May of 1992. There was a slightly higher refusal rate for the second wave of interviews. The interview schedule was divided into discrete sections that addressed issues of community concern and the functioning and impact of the community police officers in the community.

CONCERN FOR NEIGHBORHOOD ISSUES

The first area to be assessed was the concerns of the residents about the major issues that confront their neighborhoods and communities.

Table 5.1 Neighborhood Concerns

	Amount of Change	Significance
Crime	+	.000
Drugs	+	.000
Schools	+	.000
Shopping	+	.000
Police Visibility	+	.000
Abandoned, Unrepaired Buildings, Houses	+	.000
Loitering	+	.000
Drunks, Loud Persons	+	.000
Neighbor Interaction	+	.000
Recreation	+	.000
Community Activities	+	.000
Police Community Interaction	+	.000

The following measurement scheme was used to assess the level of concern in the neighborhood.

1. Much worse
2. Worse
3. Same
4. Better

Ideally, this should provide the officer with information about what the community views as its major concerns. This is of concern because as the level of concern increases, it should also affect the level of informal social control in the community. As communities develop higher levels of concern after the completion of the community policing program, this should be reflected in an increased capacity to confront community problems. The perception of the residents of the communities in which the community policing program is located is that there was an improvement in major problem areas including crime, drugs and police community interactions and that the level of disorder in the community was reduced. The police-and crime-related factors represented areas of specific interest because it demonstrates that community policing can achieve demonstrable improvements in areas directly related to the crime problem in the community.

COMMUNITY SOCIAL COHESIVENESS

The relationship between crime and disorder in the community is well documented in the community policing literature. Wesley Skogan (1990) in *Crime and Disorder* demonstrates that as disorder increases in the community, citizens retreat from the streets and relinquish the control that they have over their physical and social environment. The result is that the informal social control that is strong in communities with low crime rates begins to erode and that disorder becomes more pervasive, manifesting itself in an increased crime rate. Where social control is high, nonresidents are monitored by the community, problems are addressed before they become significant, and the community functions better as a community.

In community policing, it is becoming recognized that it is possible for the police to affect some elements of community life, but cannot improve all of the diverse aspects of a community. Community policing has come to recognize that CPOs can help a community to become more organized, they can make appropriate referrals to appropriate departments in cities, they can also attempt to consolidate efforts in the community that are logically connected. For example, delinquency prevention and parenting classes in a community center might logically be brought together. Correspondingly, the CPO probably cannot immediately do too much about improving lighting or fire protection. In fact, there may be more perception of problems in the community as the community is becoming more aware of the problems that confront it.

In the area of neighborhood cohesiveness, the citizens report that while cohesiveness has not improved, that they are meeting to deal with community problems and that they believe that neighborhoods are safer places in which to live. There is also the perception that the drug and crime problems have been improved. Typically, community policing programs are placed in communities where the quality of life has deteriorated. While this part of Delray is not the most desirable area in which to live, it appears that the residents are *beginning* to interact with each other and to improve the level of social control in the community.

Neighborhood Intervention and Neighborhood Problems

One characteristic of low crime communities is the willingness of residents to intervene when confronted with a problem. This research indicates that the residents of the part of Delray Beach in which the community policing program was implemented were less likely to intervene if they heard a scream or glass breaking, or if they saw someone breaking into a house. In small communities, there may be an increased fear of retaliation that manifests itself in the increased unwillingness to intervene.

Despite the negative information with respect to the willingness to intervene, there are substantial indications that the residents believe that the quality of life in their community has improved. In community policing, the police role shifts from one that stresses the reaction to crime to one that emphasizes the relationship between the quality of life in the community and the crime problem. As a result, one outcome of the community policing program is the emphasis on the improvement of the ability of the residents to affect the factors that make life in the community desirable.

This research assessed 29 indicators of the quality of life in the community. The results of the analysis presented in Table 5.3 showed that there was an improvement in 24 of the 29 areas that were measured. As a result, after the implementation of the community policing program, there appears to be a dramatic reduction in the amount of disorder perceive in the community. There were only five areas in which there was no perception of improvement in the community. These areas include some factors that should be addressable by community policing. These were the areas of noisy parties and bars. Alternatively, the problem of sexual assault is more difficult. Additionally, the problem of abandoned buildings was later addressed by the formation of teams in which code enforcement officials worked with the community policing officers. The problem of gangs in Florida was later addressed at the state level by the creation of county-level Juvenile Justice and Gang Prevention Task Forces that have the intention of fostering integrative community approaches to delinquency and gang prevention.

Table 5.2 Community Cohesiveness

	Amount of Change	Significance
Police Protection	+	.000
Garbage Collection	nc	.419
Street Lighting	−	.000
Fire Protection	−	.017
Public Schools	+	.052
Parks	+	.000
Street Repair	+	.019
Bus Transportation	nc	.476
Health Services	nc	.380
Community Cohesiveness	nc	.095
People Help Each Other	−	.000
People Have Meetings About Problems	+	.000
Do You Feel Part of Neighborhood	nc	.230
Do You Participate in Meetings	+	.000
Participation in Church Meetings	+	.007
Neighborhood	+	.000
Volunteer	+	.000
Satisfaction with neighborhood	−	.014
Likelihood of living here in 1 year	−	.004
Safety outside alone	+	.000
Safety inside	+	.065
Safety inside home	−	.261
Places afraid to go at night	+	.021
Places afraid to go during day	+	.007
Frequency go out at night-N Times	−	.000
In past 6 months crime problem	+	.000
In past 6 months drug problem	+	.000

Evaluation Index:
Adequate
Needs Some Improvement
Needs Much Improvement

COMMUNITY ORGANIZATION

Community policing extensively involves the officers in neighborhood activities. In contrast to the average patrol officer who is mobilized from call to call and has few opportunities to develop a positive relationship with the members of the community, community policing stresses involvement in the community with both individuals and community organizations. These activities include social functions as well as organizations and activities designed to confront problems in the community. There is extensive literature that discusses the relative lack of social organization in communities with significant crime problems. As individuals are driven off the street by the crime problem, their participation in community activities also decreases. In middle and upper class neighborhoods, civic groups and organizations address the wide range of issues and problems which the community confronts. Community policing as one of its goals, works therefore to establish community organizations and to provide legitimacy to citizen groups that require support in their initial formative stages.

Table 5.3 Neighborhood Problems

	Amount of Change	Significance
Dirty Streets	+	.007
Recreation for young	+	.002
Groups Hanging Out	+	.000
Police stopping people without reason	+	.018
Police insulting people	+	.084
Abandoned buildings	nc	.470
Public drinking	+	.048
Poor lighting	+	.006
Police too tough on those stopped	+	.065
Drug dealers on streets	+	.023
Loud parties and noise	nc	.345
Unauthorized parking	+	.022
Speeding and careless driving	+	.002
People being attacked	+	.045
Thefts of property	+	.034
Drug sales by juveniles	+	.054
Drug sales by adults	+	.029
Rape-sexual assault	nc	.208
Breaking/entering homes to steal	+	.000
Abandoned cars in streets/lots	+	.094
Car vandalism	+	.017
Property vandalism	+	.026
Adult drug use	+	.002
Juvenile drug use	+	.030
Prostitutes	+	.002
Gangs	nc	.167
People robbed	+	.000
Neighborhood bars causing problems	nc	.387
Police not making enough contact with residents	+	.000

The results of Table 5.4 indicate that there have been significant efforts with respect to the implementation of community organization efforts in the community policing program area. First, information about meetings is being communicated, secondly, the residents are attending the meetings and third, the police are perceived to be attending meetings of organizations that address community problems and recreational type meetings and events. The response to community policing is in part perceptual. Thus when perceptions are changed, hopefully, changes in behavior will follow as community police officers recognize their leadership responsibility in relation to the community.

Table 5.4 Community Organization Measures

	Amount of Change	Significance
Heard about neighborhood meetings	+	.028
Actual neighborhood meetings	nc	.220
Attended neighborhood meetings	+	.000
Did police attend meetings?	+	.000
Block parties in past six months	+	.000
2Police attending block parties	+	.000

Evaluation Index
Community Organizations: Heard about or participated

Yes
No

NEIGHBORHOOD WORRIES

The professional model of policing is based on the premise that the police presence is a significant deterrent to crime. Research also indicates that while the police respond to crimes, there is little evidence that they can suppress the crime problem in a community. In contrast, in community policing, two interrelated strategies have developed that attempt to affect the crime problem indirectly. Increasingly, community policing officers attempt to ameliorate the fear of crime that in many cases is unrelated to the actual level of crime in the community. While some problems can be dealt with directly, it may be that perceptions of safety may change, but only over a period of time.

Table 5.5 Neighborhood Worries

	Amount of Change	Significance
SO try to rob or steal in neighborhood	+	.002
SO will try to attack you in neighborhood	+	.000
SO will try to break into your home	+	.000
SO will steal things in yard	nc	.140
SO will break into home while occupied	nc	.139
SO will steal car	nc	.290
SO will hurt children	–	.004
SO will try to sell drugs to children	nc	.150
Crime prevents from doing things	–	.000
Do police spend enough time on problems	+	.000

Evaluation Index

Very Worried
Somewhat Worried
Not Worried

This section addresses the perceptions of safety in the community. The questions fall into three areas. The first area deals with the neighborhood, the second with the home, and the third with safety in the home while occupied. The crimes deal with both personal attacks, loss of property, and crimes against children.

This section on the fear or worries about crime indicates that there is a perception that the neighborhood is safer, but that as the questions move closer to home, the perceptions are more difficult to affect. Additionally it appears that crime still prevents residents from doing things. There is one positive indication with respect to the community policing program. The residents believe that the police do spend enough time on the problems. This may indicate that community organization efforts must address multiple dimensions for the quality of life in the community for those perceptions to change, and the residents are satisfied with the efforts of the police. Also, perceptions of personal safety in the home as opposed to community safety may be much more difficult to change, because the residents do not have the option of simply moving to what may be perceived as a safer neighborhood.

INTERACTIONS BETWEEN THE POLICE AND THE COMMUNITY

The riots in Los Angeles, a city with what many had characterized as the model for professional police organizations in the country, indicates that it is not uncommon for professionally oriented departments to lose touch with the citizens who they are supposed to police. At the inception of policing in Britain in the early nineteenth century, the establishment of a positive relationship between the police and the citizenry was a stated principle of policing. Yet the evolution of the professional model has broken that bond between the police and the citizens through the emphasis on 911, the utilization of motorized patrol, and the largely reactive nature of the police function in the community.

The only concession that the professional model has made toward improving the relationship between the police and the community has been the establishment of police-community relations sections in departments. The result is that the community relations sections attempt to undo the damage done by the professional model. The reactive nature of policing within the professional model created few opportunities to interact with the public. The police have become progressively more isolated, resulting in the subculture within police departments that, in some instances, did not interact well with minority cultures. The problem was with the model of policing being implemented, rather than the officer.

The research in this section assesses the interaction of the police with the public. A wide range of activities were reviewed with the residents. The response of those surveyed to the first set of questions in this area, the interactions of the police with the public, are consistently positive. The police are perceived as working with the community, controlling and preventing crime, and making the neighborhood safe. In Table 5.7 the perceptions are that the police are polite and concerned. The one item that indicates that the police have not changed with respect to fairness may indicate that it is difficult to separate community policing from the larger police institution. Additionally, it should be indicated that there were some changes in the assignment of the four officers in the community during the period of the evaluation and that this may explain the lack of knowledge of officer names and the perception that the residents have not seen their community policing officer.

OFFICER VISIBILITY AND PERFORMANCE

The section presented below continues to assess the visibility of the officer in the community. The residents were questioned about whether they had actually seen an officer accomplishing the following elements of interaction with the community.

Table 5.6 Police-Community Interactions

	Amount of Change	Significance
Work with residents to solve problems	+	.000
Preventing crime	+	.000
Keeping sidewalks and streets safe	+	.000
Controlling crime	+	.000
Controlling sale of drugs on street	+	.000
Helping crime victims	+	.000

Evaluation Index

Poor job
Fair job
Good job
Very Good Job

Table 5.7 Police-Community Interactions

	Amount of Change	Significance
Police responsive to community concerns	+	.000
Police-citizen responsible for crime	+	.001
Police time spent on crime problems	−	.001
Police polite	+	.000
Police concerned	+	.058
Police fair	nc	.136
Know names of police in neighborhood	−	.004
Seen officer past 24 hours	−	.000

Table 5.8 Officer Performance in the Community

	Amount of Change	Significance
Seen officer doing following:		
Being social	+	.021
Conducting investigation	nc	.213
Driving through neighborhood	nc	.102
Walking in neighborhood	+	.000
Talking in neighborhood	+	.000
Checking building, houses	+	.080
Giving a ticket	+	.000
Making an arrest	+	.000
Playing with children	+	.065
Helping children	+	.000
Helping neighborhood cleanup	+	.008

Table 5.8 continued

	Amount of Change	Significance
Attending community social events	+	.000
Helping or talking with elderly	+	.000
Working with community groups	+	.000
Evaluation Index		
no		
yes		

In this section, the evaluation criteria ranged from responsiveness, politeness, concern, and fairness and were measured with scales that ranged from low to high. The behavior of the officer is assessed with the residents indicating that they have seen the officers performing a wide variety of roles. In some community policing programs, specific efforts are made to not involve the community police officers with crime-related activities. The belief is that if the officers are involved in investigations and arrests, that will affect their relation with the community. Here it can be seen that in Delray Beach, the entire panoply of police activities are being performed. It is interesting that officers were not observed riding in their cars through the neighborhood. Instead the officers were directly observed walking and talking with a wide array of individuals including children and the elderly, as well as working with community groups.

The consistency of these contacts is significant. One area that is important to assess is the implementation of the community policing program. In some community policing programs it has been reported that the officers receive little training interacting with the public and, as a result, they spend time in "comfortable and familiar areas" such as offices, churches, and so forth to avoid interacting with the public. The information reported here would indicate that the officers are meeting with the entire range of the community and have been observed interacting with them.

INFORMATION EXCHANGES

As community policing evolves, the CPO is increasingly seen as an intermediary or resource person in the community. The research on problem solving and policing (Goldstein, 1990) consistently demonstrates that it is more important to solve underlying problems in the community than to deal repeatedly with the recurring incidents. These incidents incur an inordinate amount of time and resources for police departments. While they generate "productivity" measures for departments, they are frustrating for individual officers and erode the quality of life in communities.

This last section assesses the nature of the interactions of the police with the public. It goes beyond seeing the officer perform a function and addresses whether the officer has had contact with the respondent. The first item shows that the public is interacting verbally with the police, while the second item indicates that a wide range of information on noncrime topics is also being exchanged. These items are critical because they relate to the problem-solving function of the police in dealing with community problems. The community police officers are providing information beyond merely crime-related items. They are making referrals to resources in Delray Beach to deal with problems as they confront the residents of the community. This is important because, due to the lack of resources and organizations, the police are frequently the only governmental representative with whom the citizens come into contact. It is significant that the police officers have come to view themselves as a community resource and in turn view their role in an expanded manner of providing a wide range of services to the community.

Table 5.9 Information Exchanges

	Amount of Change	Significance
Starting conversation-both	+	.000
N Times officer has given you information on		
Social services	+	.000
Government offices	+	.000
Police services	−	.000
Employment opportunities	+	.009
Recreational affairs	+	.186
Community affairs	+	.000
Educational opportunities	+	.000
Rights	+	.000
Responsibilities	+	.000
Police explain response to contact	+	.000
Police polite	+	.018

The final two items relate to the amount of information provided in relation to a contact between the police and the residents. The idea that the community policing officers are explaining their reasons for doing a function and are perceived as polite are significant. The police rely on both legal and moral authority for performing their actions. Legally, they can issue orders and perform functions that require the citizens to comply. If they can accomplish the same functions through the willing compliance of the citizens, then the moral and social functions of the police are enhanced.

THE IMPACT OF COMMUNITY POLICING

Community policing represents a significant decision by the police and community to change the pattern of interaction that has characterized their relationship in the past. The potential for change can range from very nominal, to complete changes in the organization of the department. This means that in some departments community policing is primarily a public relations ploy consisting of the establishment of a small section within the department, new door or fender stickers with COP on them, and little else changing. In other departments, community policing represents a realization that "if you do what you always did, you will always get what you always got." As a result, the departments make a commitment to change, and then implement it. Increasingly, there is the recognition that community policing can represent a rather fundamental change in the orientation of a police department. Some aver that community policing is simply "old wine in new bottles," and that the professional model is too deeply entrenched to result in any substantive change in how policing is accomplished (Sykes, 1990). On the other hand, some departments recognize that organizational change, in reality, represents a rather fundamental reorientation of how they are attempting to perform their mission in the community.

The research reported indicates that in Delray Beach, the second approach to community policing has been implemented. Community policing has been directed at fundamentally altering how policing is effectuated in the community. In first selecting the program areas, an extensive analysis was conducted to determine where the need for community policing was greatest. Next, the department committed scarce resources to allow for an intensive involvement of the officers in the community. The department then committed itself to an objective external evaluation of its community policing program. The results presented here would indicate that there has been a rather substantial change in the community in behavior and attitudes, and in how the community functions as a result of the community policing program.

In the period since community policing was first implemented in Delray Beach, there have been additional developments in relation to community policing programs. First, community policing has been extended to the southeast part of the city. This area represents an even greater challenge than the area in which community policing was first implemented. It is comprised of an area with more rental apartments, more severe physical decay because of the transience of the residents and a more entrenched drug problem because of the above listed factors. The experience gained in the first phase of the community policing program proved to provide an excellent foundation for the new increment of community policing in Delray Beach.

In addition to implementing community policing programs, departments that are serious about community policing must also contend with the issue of how to transform the organization from one oriented to the professional model to a community policing type organization. Organizational change is something that is tremendously difficult to accomplish in private organizations as well as in the public sector. It is made even more difficult in professionally oriented police organizations because of the insistence that police organizations be removed from political influences. This has resulted in the isolation of departments that resulted in their estrangement from the community. Additionally, the isolation makes it even more difficult for the departments to become sensitized to the need for change, and then to implement it. Nonetheless, within Delray Beach, the department has maintained its original momentum and is now directing that energy towards continuing the transformation of the department towards community policing.

6

Dynamics of Community Policing in Small Communities*

Peter C. Kratcoski
Kent State University

Robert B. Blair
College of Wooster

INTRODUCTION

The motives for instituting changes in police organization are varied, but one that is often given is the recognition that the traditional approaches to police work have not produced the results desired. Community-oriented policing became the buzzword around which those who were bent on changing the situation rallied. In addition to the fact that crime appears to be out of control, the movement toward community-oriented policing may be due to a number of factors. The research on citizens' satisfaction with police performance reveals that some groups of people, particularly the poor, minority group members, juveniles, senior citizens, and women are not very satisfied with police performance (Decker, 1981; Hahn, 1971; Skogan, 1978, Rosenberg & Crane, 1994). Those groups that live in the inner city neighborhoods (where the crime rate is highest), are most often the victims of crime, and thus are likely to form definite opinions of the police officers who work in their neighborhoods. Unfortunately, we have a great deal of evidence that the traditional approach to police work has not been effective in controlling and reduc-

*   An earlier version of this paper was presented at the annual meeting of the American Society of Criminology, Phoenix, Arizona, October 1993. This research was supported under the Ohio Governor's Office of Criminal Justice Services grant 92-DG-D01-7277.

ing crime. If we use crime statistics as a measure of effectiveness (UCR, 1993), we see that the amount of crime has continued to increase at a faster rate than the population growth. In addition, the percentage of crimes solved is rather small. For example, in 1992 only 13 percent of burglaries, 24 percent of robberies, 14 percent of auto thefts and 20 percent of larceny-theft crimes were cleared by arrest (UCR, 1993:207). Surprisingly, the crime rate for several specific crimes (rape, breaking and entering, assault) in small cities is also increasing quite rapidly and the arrest rate for these crimes, while higher than that in the large cities, is nevertheless quite low. For example, for cities with a population between 25,000 and 49,999 the percentage of Index crimes cleared by arrest in 1992 was 23.7. For these small cities, 14.2 percent of burglaries, 28.4 percent of robberies, 16.2 percent of auto theft and 23.5 percent of larceny-theft were cleared by arrests (UCR, 1993:209).

COMMUNITY POLICING DEFINED

Depending on the source, community policing has been defined as a philosophy of policing and as a program strategy. As a philosophy of policing, it embodies a number of principles or ideas that guide the structure of policing toward goal attainment. These include using the needs, norms, and special characteristics of the community to decide which goals and services are to be provided and what means are available to determine the effectiveness of the police in providing the services requested (Vera, 1988; McElroy, et al., 1990). For some, community policing appears to be equated with public relations programs, with the main purpose being to improve the image of the police in the community.

When defining community policing, some distinguish community-oriented policing from problem-oriented policing, while others accept the terms as interchangeable. Some definitions are narrow, only recognizing specific problem-oriented or problem-solving strategies (Goldstein, 1990; Eck & Spelman, 1987a), while others accept a wide range of programs or approaches that focus on developing a cooperative approach to problem solving between the citizens and the police. Some look for a department-wide approach to community policing, others accept single program efforts. The difference between community-oriented policing and problem-oriented policing may be more a matter of semantics than of substance. Cordner and Hale (1992:14) find the two concepts compatible and concluded that the combination of COP and POP offers "one of our brightest prospects for improved police effectiveness."

This selection focuses on the dynamics of community policing in small communities. To date, very little of the research has focused on the small community, and none of the research has focused on the dynamics of the community policing programs. Specifically, we will look at the origins of the community policing programs, the manner in which they are structured, the manner in which the officers involved function, and the acceptance of community policing by the officers.

RELATED RESEARCH

The establishment of community policing units or programs in many cities has often been a direct result of the realization by police administrations that some segments of the citizenry were dissatisfied with the performance of the police and with the quality of the services provided by them. Thus, the community-oriented policing projects were often started to counteract a negative public image or to try to solve the specific problem identified as causing the dissatisfaction.

Decker describes two types of variables affecting citizen attitudes toward the police: *individual* variables: age, sex, race, socioeconomic status, and personal experience with the police, and *contextual* variables: crime rates, community beliefs regarding the police, likelihood of victimization, and programmatic innovations designed to improve citizen attitudes. Race, sex, socioeconomic status, and age have been important predictors of attitudes, but *contextual variables* appear to have greater influence on ratings of police than the individual variables (Decker, 1981:83).

Skogan (1978) found that the manner in which the *equality of service* is perceived significantly impacts the formation of attitudes toward the police. He determined that race had an important effect on attitudes toward the police, but the quality of service provided better explained the "polarization of racial attitudes" toward the police. Decker (1981) recognized the necessity of understanding the neighborhood and realizing that it serves as a determinate of attitudes toward the police. This supports the importance of community policing, that is, directing police services at the neighborhood level as a means to improve relationships between police and citizens. Kratcoski and Gustavson (1991) found the satisfaction among the residence of a large city toward police officers identified as community-oriented officers was greater than that expressed toward regular officers who patrolled the neighborhoods of that city. Kelling (1988) found citizens tend to be dissatisfied with the policies and methods of police work if these approaches lead to a distancing and breakdown of communication between the citizenry and the police. Rosenberg and Crane (1994) found that African-Americans and Latinos were less likely to agree that police are respectful, helpful, and fair than were whites.

RESEARCH DESIGN

Community policing programs in three small communities constitute the focus of this investigation. Included are the three small Ohio cities of Forest Park, Kent, and Oberlin. Each city has a population that does not exceed 30,000 citizens, and their police forces vary in size, ranging from 15 to 30 officers. The purpose of the analysis is to delineate the "dynamics" of community policing in these small communities. Our surveys and observations of their police programs yielded three sets of data; the first pertains to features of the community that affect community policing efforts, the second involves the dynamics associated with program origins and implementation, and the third concerns the attitudes and actions of the police officer personnel toward the community policing program operating in the police department in which they were employed.

A standardized interview schedule was developed to tap the areas mentioned above. The questions included in the instrument pertained to the origins of the community policing program or the manner in which the organization was restructured in order to embody the community policing philosophy, the manner in which community policing was implemented, and the administrators', supervisors', and officers' perceptions of the program, including their perceptions of the community's response. The activities of the officers, inquiries on how the program could be improved, and questions pertaining to the personal characteristics of the respondents were also considered. The majority of the administrators, supervisors, and line officers employed in the three cities included in the research was questioned.

DYNAMICS OF SMALL COMMUNITIES

A shortage of crime prevention resources and personnel was cited in all of the cities as a reason for starting community policing. Small cities experience many of the same problems as larger cities. Competition for adequate housing is present and the widening gap between the privileged and the poor is reflected in the alienation of some citizens and the distrust of the public officials, including the police, who are mandated to serve them. The rising crime rates, particularly for violent crime, generate fear among the citizens in small cities just as in large cities. These factors are among the forces that produce—in small communities as well as large cities—an atmosphere of distrust and suspicion, and a growing awareness among police personnel that traditional policing no longer works as an effective strategy for curbing what are perceived as "skyrocketing" crime rates. One city's proposal to start a community-oriented police program was initiated because without it "a crime-free community" would require an "enforcement body . . . twice the size of the community's population." Thus, this community was trying to introduce the same mechanism to control crime that is being employed in the larger cities, that is, community policing. Chief Jones of Oberlin stated that he became interested in community policing when he attended a conference and realized that large and small cities share common problems. He stated, "I first learned about community policing at a NOBLE (National Organization of Black Law Enforcement Executives) Conference in Philadelphia about three years ago. Philadelphia had implemented the program and was telling how successful it was. I came back and drafted a plan for it and began to implement it."

When asked if his plan was based pretty much on the Philadelphia Plan, and if he took into consideration the differences between a large and small community, he responded:

I did take that into consideration because the larger communities where they have mini-stations have officers who are full
time on the job and are being assigned to certain areas every
shift. I did not have enough personnel to work out that plan. I
had to assign each officer to a quad or a section of the town
whereby he would be working and educating the people on
community oriented policing and also doing his regular jobs,
like patrol.

In an article authored by Chief Jones, he noted:

Our city was divided into four quads (zones). Two officers and
one supervisor are assigned to each zone. When a citizen files
a complaint or suggestion and the officer cannot solve the
problem, the program is designed for the officers to meet with
their supervisor and formulate a plan of action to correct the
situation. Keeping the citizens informed of what's being done
is one major element of making them feel a part of the decision making process. Every emphasis should be placed on
teamwork. (Jones, 1993:37)

An officer with 21 years of experience described what he perceived as the
growing erosion of legitimacy of police authority in a small community and why
community policing is needed:

I don't think we're hated, but we're sure as hell losing rapport
with people in the community. We're like Rodney Dangerfield:
we don't get respect anymore. Like with youth . . . it used to
be that when you told them to 'shut up' and go on home,
they'd do it; now when you tell them to do something they
want to argue with you.

One chief stated that community policing was definitely needed in his community and although he received some resistance from his officers, he decided to
try to implement the plan anyway. He noted:

I feel that it was something that I should have done earlier. I
chose this way because I felt it was strongly needed in the
community. I have seen the attitude of the officers. I saw the
changing attitude of the officers in that "we-they" arena. I did
not like it and I thought by implementing this plan and getting
it off the ground as soon as possible, it would be better. I felt
that as time went along their attitude would change. It was a
necessity for me to implement the program as soon as possible.

Police Chief Lillich of Kent informed us that the process there started in 1989. Block grant funds for issues of a nontraditional nature, many of which were law enforcement related, were available from the federal government. The grant was approved in 1991. He stated, "Since there were some serious problems in the Kenwood Courts complex, the program was concentrated in that area." "New management in the housing complex made it a viable project. We were able to deal with a management that was willing to commit." When questioned about the development process, he responded, "Officers were given some initial training and were then thrown out to 'make friends.' They were perceived as an army coming in at first. Residents became involved gradually. The programs helped to change the residents' attitudes. They involved schools and also had a meals program. The residents began to realize that the police cared about their problems." He noted that the scope of the program changed:

> Last year the program was expanded. There was an agreement with the Parks Department. Some of the block grant money was given to the Park Department, and five days a week a recreation program was available to kids who were from the Kenwood Courts. This year the program expanded to include the Summit Gardens two times per week, and the Kenwood Courts three times per week. (Personal interview with Chief Lillich, 1994)

In Forest Park, Lt. McHugh, Coordinator of Community Policing, informed us that, "The crime prevention efforts of the department go back to the 1970s, but a more directed focus and the adaptation of a community policing philosophy within the department occurred in 1990. A goal was to try to tear down the 'us' and 'them' philosophy. Bicycles and bike patrol have been very successful and will be continued. The department also has motorcycles that help to get officers on the street and talking to people. A Cop Shop (a storefront) is used by the police as a place where people can come in and get help with problems. The citizens can see firsthand that patrolling officers are there to help, and are understanding. A shopping center location is used for the Cop Shop."

The police administrators in all of the communities studied claimed that they are paying more attention to how well the resources available to them "actually work" in curbing crime as a result of their attempts to institute community policing. Several police administrators mentioned that they are working with the administrators of other municipal agencies to periodically monitor the health of their communities with work sheets that track indicators of the stability or decline of the "quality of life" in their community. The profiles derived from such analyses assist administrators in distributing resources and targeting areas for innovative policing programs. One dynamic of all the programs we observed was the tendency to introduce the concept of community policing by designating its implementation to control "hot spots" in each community. One program was designed as a pilot project for federally subsidized housing units where crime rates were high and where citizens have been reluctant to report crime incidents to the police.

Another factor that has emerged from the community policing orientation in the small cities studied is the growing recognition that even in small communities there is sufficient diversity among the population to justify efforts to obtain a better "fit" between the homogeneity of subgroups within the population and the policing styles of the officers who serve these citizens. Block Watch programs were among the first such efforts to form a partnership between the police and the citizens in the communities we studied. Block Watch programs were the precursors of more broadly based community policing efforts, and provided the foundations for expanding the community policing concept. These initial efforts tended to develop the "inclination" and "capacity" of some citizens to be involved in cooperative programs with the police. Other "special problem" community policing programs reflected similar efforts to adapt policing styles to the special needs of the residents. One of the three cities has an enclave of "elderly shut-ins" who are contacted once or twice a week by auxiliary police workers. These uniformed volunteer auxiliary workers coordinated their efforts through radio with local police colleagues, and made referrals to other care providing agencies in the area as the need arose. In the other cities involved in the study, community policing appeared to be the most successful when the community policing efforts were tailored to fit the unique settings and needs of the citizens. All of the cities had established police outposts in specified homogeneous population areas, and the officers assigned to these stations attempted to adopt a style of policing that led to an increase in interaction with the residents. One officer referred to it as "the old hue and cry" technique where "we work the beat and get back to the people."

The success of initial pilot projects encouraged the community leaders and administrators of the police departments to explore other ways in which community policing might build on the community support of the police that developed as a result of the initial community policing effort. One officer reported:

> I selected the Southeast quad. It's mostly black and has the biggest percentage of criminal activity. I selected that quad because no one else would. I had good rapport with kids and I knew the problem kids from my work with D.A.R.E. It's like the Old Irish cop idea, and it makes your job simpler. It's taken a while, but now I can go into the "hole" [SE quad] and I know every kid there.

Police administrators, in particular the chiefs, while acknowledging that the politicians and some leaders of the community were favorable to the community policing philosophy and practice and were likely to become involved, nevertheless also recognized that the general citizenry was at best "lukewarm" to the concept. One stated:

We publicized it in the newspaper and I talked with people from different organizations, like the Chamber of Commerce, schools, and ministers. I laid out the plan and asked them for feedback. When we started having our quad meetings, we received very little response and I was thinking that it would take some kind of catastrophe to get the people interested. It is a very slow-selling program both inside and outside of the department.

SELECTION OF COMMUNITY POLICING OFFICERS

The structuring of community policing differed in the three cities included in the research. As mentioned, Oberlin adopted the quad model. In Forest Park, a lieutenant and sergeant were assigned to serve as coordinators of community policing and to provide some training of the officers, but the message presented to the officers was that community policing was to be implemented by all officers, first by their acceptance of the community policing philosophy and secondly by changing their policing styles. Every administrator and officer was expected to embrace community policing.

The Kent Community Policing Program was established to try to solve the problem of increased crime and violence that was reported in a subsidized public housing unit, and a lieutenant was assigned to develop and implement the specifics of the program. The Kent police officers had an opportunity to volunteer for the program on an overtime basis. In Kent, 65 percent of the officers claimed that their primary reason for becoming involved in the program was overtime pay. Gradually, the Kent program was expanded to other parts of the city.

POLICING ACTIVITIES

The community policing officers of the Kent, Forest Park, and Oberlin Police Departments were questioned about the amount of time they devoted to activities directly related to community policing during their tour of duty. In Forest Park, the officers devoted the greatest amount of time to the following activities: completing paperwork, working on priority problems, walking the beat, and responding to requests for assistance. Similar to those in Forest Park, the Kent police officers indicated that completing paperwork, working on priority problems, and responding to requests for help were common activities. In addition, the Kent police officers devoted a significant amount of time assisting the regular patrol officers assigned to the community policing area. Although walking the beat was considered an important activity for community policing by the Forest Park officers, the Kent officers actually devoted a much greater proportion of their time to this form of patrolling. In Oberlin, walking the beat was not employed regularly.

EFFECTS OF COMMUNITY POLICING IN SMALL CITIES

While the long-range effect expected of community policing is a decrease in crime, short-range effects expected are increased policing activities both of a reactive and proactive nature. The reasons for this are the increased interaction of the citizenry with the police, a reduction of citizen reluctance to report crimes and provide information, and an increase in the effectiveness of the police in securing arrests.

The researchers were given access to the Forest Park officers' activity reports for the 1992 and 1993 time periods, and the monthly activity summaries for all police officers were analyzed and compared. Twenty officers patrol the City of Forest Park. They cover three shifts and, as would be expected, the activities for the midnight to 8 a.m. shift are quite different than those for the daytime and early evening shifts. The patrol activities are recorded in terms of the total number of calls and the nature of the activity. There are 21 categories in which any given call could be recorded. These activities can be broadly categorized into those that are of a community policing nature, (attending block watch meetings, preventive patrolling) and those that pertained to more traditional forms of police activity (responding to calls, filing reports, and patrol).

The overall number of calls for 1992 was compared to the number for 1993. The average number of calls responded to by an officer each month in 1992 was 84.5. In 1993, the average was 89.1, a 4.6 percent increase. In 1992, the activities that are specifically considered community police activities were tabulated and the mean number of activities recorded per officer each month was 26.05. This included the activities of attending community-oriented policing meetings, conducting resident surveys of problems in their neighborhoods, attending block watch meetings, walking the beat rather than using motorized patrol, and working with the community on community problem solving (gathering information, assessing the problem, formulating possible solutions). The contacts for 1993 revealed the mean number of contacts for community policing activities to be 41.83, or more than a one-third increase. It should be noted that some officers had virtually no opportunity to engage in community policing activities because they worked the midnight to 8 a.m. shift. Those working the day or evening shift had many more contacts with the citizenry.

In Oberlin, officers were required to log all contacts or communications with citizens in which a follow-up contact was required and "community-oriented police" type of response would be appropriate. This information was given to the "quad officers," who had the responsibility of following up on the matter and recording in the log book the nature of the contact and the type of action taken. The citizen complaints can be categorized into those pertaining to law enforcement matters of a criminal nature, routine auto-related calls (speeding, parking etc.), requests for assistance, and neighborhood disturbance types of calls. In some cases it appeared that the person's only purpose for contacting the police related to letting off steam, that is, "police are not doing their job" or to tell them that "there is no problem, but if I think of one I will call." The larger number of the contacts (40%) pertained to automobile-related problems. These were created in the neighborhood by speeders, those blocking driveways, racing in the streets late at night or having junk cars parked in front of their residence. Closely following in number (28%) were complaints related to neighborhood-nuisance situations such as dogs running loose, children harassing adults, or "kids hanging around" and homes not being properly cared for (lawn not being mowed). Most of the law-enforcement related calls were actually more the result of suspicion of law breaking rather than actual reports of offenses. One noted there were "suspicious people going in and out of the nursing home" and others that they were afraid of all of the drug dealers selling to the kids in the neighborhood. Less than five percent of the contacts were requests for direct assistance. These were generally from elderly persons who needed help "getting to the store" or something of this nature. The larger proportion of all follow-up contacts were with older persons.

Many calls that started as complaints were handled through the community policing officer providing assistance. For example, in one quad where allegedly drug dealers were operating in the area, the officer assisted some residents in starting a block watch group. Some of the complaints were out of the community policing officer's jurisdiction. For example, the officer had to explain to one citizen that he could not force a person to mow his lawn.

Based on an analysis of the officers' reports on these contacts, the citizens generally seemed to be satisfied that something would be done to improve the situation that led to the initial contact with the police. They also seemed to appreciate the "follow-up" contact made by the community policing officer.

ASSESSING THE EFFECTS OF COMMUNITY POLICING

Determining the effectiveness of community policing was one of the objectives of our study. Several questions in our instrument pertained to the perceived effects of community policing. Included were assessments of the overall worth of the programs, and the responses of community members, as perceived by the officers. We also asked the officers to reflect on whether they changed their views of policing, how they evaluate the COP program operating in their department, and the extent to which officers not directly involved in the program are perceived to be changing their attitudes toward community policing. The results presented below must be interpreted with some caution, since two of the departments presented their programs as extending to all officers regardless of their specific assignment, while the other department defined their program more in terms of a specific unit developed to solve specific problems.

Table 6.1 contains comparative data of officer perceptions of community attitudes before and after community policing programs were implemented in their communities. Officers were asked to evaluate how "the people living in the neighborhood . . . felt about the police in general." Twenty-nine of the 54 officers in the three small communities indicated that attitudes of the community toward police in general were either "somewhat positive" or "very positive" at the time community policing was instituted.

Table 6.1 Officer Perceptions of Attitudes of Community Toward Police in General Before and After COP and Toward Individual Officers After COP

	Police in General				Individual Officers	
	Before COP		After COP		After COP	
Very Negative	6	9.3	2	3.7	—	—
Somewhat Negative	13	24.1	2	3.7	—	—
No Opinion	1	1.9	1	1.9	3	5.6
Somewhat Positive	17	31.5	30	55.6	16	29.6
Very Positive	12	22.2	17	31.5	28	51.9
Neither	3	5.6	1	1.9	2	3.7
NA	3	5.6	1	1.9	5	9.3
Total	54	100.0	54	100.0	54	100.0

When asked what they perceive to be the present opinion of the community toward community policing, 47 officers reported that they perceived positive changes in the attitudes of the residents. Similarly, when asked to give their views of how "people on your beat feel about you . . ." most of the officers (44) indicated that they thought they were perceived in a more positive manner than they were before community policing.

The officers were asked to indicate how their own attitudes toward the community have changed since they became involved with community policing in their local departments.

Table 6.2 Officers Attitudes Toward Community Before and After COP Programs

	Before COP		After COP	
	N	%	N	%
Very Negative	1	1.9	—	—
Somewhat Negative	7	13.0	2	3.7
No Opinion	3	5.6	3	5.6
Somewhat Positive	14	25.9	17	31.5
Very Positive	17	31.5	21	38.9
Neither	5	9.3	5	9.3
NA	7	13.0	5	9.3
Total	54	100.0	54	100.0

In Forest Park, approximately 80 percent of the officers reported that the citizens had a somewhat positive or a very positive attitude toward the police before the program and that the citizens' attitudes in Forest Park have risen to about 90 percent being positive. The officers in the city of Kent indicated that, before the program began, only 20 percent of the citizens who lived in the subsidized housing area in which the program operated had a positive attitude toward the police. Since the program has been in effect, the percent of citizens with a positive attitude toward the police has risen to 95 percent. As previously noted, the Kent Community Policing Program was initially limited to one public housing project and other areas of the city were later designated for community policing.

OFFICERS' RESPONSE TO COMMUNITY POLICING

The larger majority of the patrol officers endorsed the philosophy of community policing. In all of the communities, the principle that the community policing philosophy should be the foundation for the entire department and must be integrated into all police was stated, and community policing activity was strongly endorsed by the top administrators. Officers were also asked to reflect on their experiences over the past six months and to judge whether these experiences led them to change their views concerning COP programs. They were also requested to tell us if their experiences over the past six months led them to reassess their "attitude toward being a police officer." As shown in Table 6.3, the results were somewhat mixed for both queries. Nearly twice as many officers (13) developed "more positive" attitudes as those (7) who reported "more negative" views. Several of those who indicated a "negative" change did so because they disagreed with the way the community policing program was implemented. Nearly three-fourths of the officers reported "unchanged" attitudes toward being a police officer, five indicated that their attitudes toward being an officer were "more negative," and six reported "more positive" attitudes.

Table 6.3 Attitudes of Officers Toward Community Policing in Their Department and Toward Being a Police Officer During Past Six Months

	COP Program		Being a Police Officer	
	N	%	N	%
More Negative	7	13.0	5	9.3
Unchanged	31	57.4	40	74.1
More Positive	13	24.1	6	11.1
Not applicable	3	5.6	3	5.6
Total	54	100.0	54	100.0

The officers were asked what they liked or disliked about community policing as practiced in their departments. In Kent, almost 80 percent of the officers assigned to the community policing program indicated that they liked the community involvement, and 70 percent of these officers claimed that they liked to walk the beat. One officer stated that walking the beat provided him with an opportunity to interact with a segment of the population that he would not have an opportunity to interact with if confined to the patrol car. He stated, "I like meeting and talking with people that you would never get to know unless they were the victim of a crime." The regular patrol officers in Kent who were not specifically working with the community policing program were also given an opportunity to respond to questions concerning the use of community policing in their community. In general, the responses of the rank and file officers in Kent revealed an acceptance of the philosophy.

One officer stated, "The information that the public has about the neighborhood is just what the police need to provide better service." Another commented:

> It is essential that the community support the police department. The COP philosophy creates a more comfortable environment for citizens and the police to communicate. It removes the authoritative official type of stigma associated with the police and creates a more personable view. If the community can view the police as caring, sensitive people then they will support us.

Another officer stated:

> Yes, with all the negativity towards law enforcement in the media, I feel a community approach definitely improves relations, and lays groundwork for solving future problems.

Many officers tended to equate community policing with "problem solving." One stated:

> Citizens have to take control of their lives and realize that everyone, police, officials, council, teachers and all facets of our society must work together to solve problems. Simply calling police and then complaining because nothing was done no longer fills the needs.

Indicative of a general acceptance of the community policing philosophy and programs are the responses we received to the question, "Are community-oriented policing programs worthwhile?" Three-fourths of the 54 officers we interviewed indicated that they felt such programs were clearly worthwhile. Several of those who indicated that the programs were not worthwhile qualified their responses with comments about the need to better implement the programs or to change their formats in order to make them more effective. Few officers expressed an outright rejection of the concept.

The comments of one officer in particular are representative of the optimism shared by the large majority of officers in these three small communities:

> The whole COP philosophy could be a source of renewal on both ends [of the age continuum]; for the new guys it could help them get their minds out of TV images; on the other end, the old timers are starting to see that maybe it's time for a change.

Another officer stated, "The neighborhoods have gotten better, there is less crime, and the citizens know us as people and not cops in cars." However, one officer claimed that "if the program were discontinued, the target areas would digress quickly to their original state." Another stated, "I think it has been proved that traditional policing is antiquated. Community interaction and support is absolutely necessary to obtain information to assist the police agency in facing and dealing with problems in a complex society."

In summary, each of the indicators shown in the tables suggests positive sets of outcomes of the community policing efforts in the three small communities studied. Officers report that attitudes of citizens who live in their areas are more positive; they report an increased commitment to their police officer roles, and they have become more convinced of the efficacy of community-oriented policing.

CRITICISMS AND CONCERNS

While the larger majority of the officers and administrators in the three communities surveyed endorsed community policing in principle, many of them expressed doubts about what was actually being accomplished and others were critical of the manner in which community policing was initiated. The comments can be categorized as follows:

1. Community policing is nothing but public relations.

2. Community policing is not needed in small cities because we are already doing it.

3. Community policing should be delegated to a special unit.

4. The manner in which the community policing program was initiated was flawed.

5. The manner in which the community policing program is structured is flawed.

6. Community policing is not "real cop" work.

7. Community policing leads to an increase in work for the officers.

8. The community does not want community policing, so why force it on them?

There is also evidence that some officers do not understand the philosophy of community policing. These officers were likely to equate community policing with public relations. For example, when asked how the program could be improved one officer mentioned:

> If I was in charge, I would do more routine contacts during special events. [For example], during the 4th of July Celebration I would have a booth; I'd have a DARE program booth, and when different community groups have a program, I'd have an officer there to meet and be available to members of the community.

Various comments of the officers illustrate the criticisms and concerns mentioned above. In all communities, there were a few officers who indicated that community policing is just so much public relations rhetoric the administration is using to try to improve its image. One officer stated that the COP philosophy is worthwhile "as long as it is used for the betterment of the community and in ways that actually help the community, not just to make someone look good." Another stated, "COP is nothing but a waste of time and manpower. It is just a dog and pony show to make council and the public think that something is being done about crime. The resources wasted on COP could be put to better use updating training and equipment." One officer stated that trying to involve citizens who don't want to be involved was a major frustration.

Although most officers in Forest Park endorsed the philosophy of community policing, several of them felt that community policing should be done by those officers designated as such. One officer stated "community policing is fine, but the majority of the work should be given to the full-time community policing officers." Another stated:

> Aspects of the COP philosophy are a good step in cities where there are lots of crime and problems. In a suburb such as ours walking the beat or making up monthly problems is stupid. With the size of our department we are automatically acting

within the COP philosophy. The only difference here is that
our administration feels it must prove itself to the public that
we are doing something worthwhile.

And another said, "I think the public in our town have always had high regard
for the police even before we began our COP hype."

In Oberlin, about two-thirds of the officers emphasized the idea that they
know the people in the community, and because they know the citizens, they are
doing COP. One officer mentioned:

There's no need for doing something different if everything is
working OK. We're doing COP already. We know them socially and respond when they need us.

Another stated:

All the people I talk to are OK. The police are OK in this
community. We're being asked to do what we've always been
doing. The guys have good support, except for 20 to 30 people
in town. In a community like ours we still do dog calls and
lockouts.

The feeling that community policing is not real police work is reflected in one
officer's comments that:

A lot of the officers have the feeling that people want us out
catching criminals. We're not paid to be babysitters—chasing
dogs, looking for stray cats, and getting bats out of your
house—the Barney Fife image.

The officers were asked how the community policing program could be
improved. In Forest Park, 25 percent of the officers suggested additional training,
while 20 percent of the Kent officers and 35 percent of the Oberlin officers recommended more training. In Forest Park, several of the officers suggested that
participation in the program should be voluntary. An officer in Oberlin proposed
that COP should include "the indoctrination of all city officials and department
heads from the beginning, otherwise it may be difficult to implement successfully."

Fifty percent of the Kent officers indicated that expanding community policing to other neighborhoods would lead to an increase in the effectiveness of policing in the city. Some Kent officers suggested that "the program should run
throughout the year." Another Kent officer said, "the department should form a
small unit of officers where their whole duty assignment is community-oriented
policing." It was also suggested that Kent's program would be improved "by

involving other agencies, departments, and businesses to assist in improving the quality of life."

There seemed to be agreement that officers and supervisors who were designated for community policing should be out in the community rather than sitting in an office. One mentioned that a way community policing can be improved is to "Make true COP officers that do not work out of an office. Have these COP officers actually work the streets and interact with the citizens of the city."

DISCUSSION AND SUMMARY

The initial successes of community policing motivate communities to expand to additional activities but, unfortunately, efforts to galvanize partnership with community members fail, and the extent to which citizens and local police are willing to try new programs often diminishes. Several officers who predicted sure failure of the police department's latest efforts to implement a community-wide policing strategy traced the reasons for failure to the reluctance of the citizens to get involved. The views of a substantial number of officers are reflected in the frustration expressed by one officer who recounted his disappointment after his efforts to organize block watch programs in several neighborhoods failed:

> I was a crime prevention officer for five years and I tried to set up block watch programs. Only one remains active today. It's in a tight, cohesive area where there's not much turnover in neighborhoods. We would go door to door. The only reason we got anything going in any of the neighborhoods was the rash of burglaries that happened. COP-type programs require community response if they are going to make it. People here just don't want to get involved.

All the cities we studied report some measure of success in obtaining the cooperation of members in the community; citizen acceptance of community policing is especially forthcoming when they begin to notice changes that are easily documented. If crime rates fall, disturbances drop off, troublemakers begin to leave the area, and garbage is picked up, people become more excited about community policing. Many of these changes are documented by the police departments. In one of the cities, a community-oriented officer had to double his investigative and detective work as more and more citizens came forward with information that led to the arrest of offenders. An assessment of one program by its supervisor records the success of the community policing program:

> Now the citizens are starting to interact with us. They now trust us. Officers who used to say, 'nothing could be done with

> that area so why be in all that danger,' are starting to volun-
> teer. City council is underwriting [the program] and we are
> pleased. The success key was the housing management and cit-
> izens coming together with police.

Another supervisor, when asked whether there were any measurable effects of their community policing efforts, responded with the following comment:

> A lot of it is evaluated through the contacts, the comments, the
> types of calls received, the elimination of serious calls, the
> reception that the officers get now. It is a more relaxed envi-
> ronment and is a totally different relationship that we have
> now. We have nothing scientific . . .

From our research, we discovered that while the three communities are similar in terms of population size, they varied greatly in terms of history and culture.
All three of the communities have culturally diverse populations, have a variety of
racial, and ethnic groups living there and extremes in income and housing units
can be found. Two of the communities are dominated by the universities located in
their boundaries, while the other community is a suburb of a large city and, while
racial and ethically diverse, is fairly homogeneous in terms of economics.

The characteristics of the communities constitute one important set of dynamics that are critical to determining success or failure of community policing
efforts. Problems that perplex larger communities have their counterparts in small
cities and these conditions render traditional approaches to policing as superfluous
in small cities as they are in large cities. Initial efforts to become more efficacious
in meeting enforcement needs have led small city police departments to tailor programs to meet special problems; the success of these pilot projects is encouraging.
Now there are signs that these small communities are ready to adopt more pervasive departmental community policing efforts. Innovative police administrators are
defining community policing as both a philosophy and a program, and the rank-
and-file officers of these communities are being asked to join in these efforts.

The manner in which community policing is developed and implemented is
extremely important in determining the degree to which community policing will
be implemented and become ingrained into the culture of the community and the
police culture. As expected, community-oriented police programs vary in the three
communities. First efforts to implement community policing were modest in all
three departments; problems varied and therefore required multifaceted responses.
Typical of how these early programs were implemented are the experiences of two
of the communities who established block watch programs. One or two staff members in two of the communities were designated or volunteered to serve as "crime
prevention" officers. They were sent to the National Crime Prevention Institute for
two weeks of training. Upon their return to their respective departments, they were

charged with the task of organizing block watch programs. Most contacts with the community in these early efforts that pertained to community policing were funneled through these officers. Much of what they did appeared to be public relations work. Gradually, many officers and some citizens demanded that the community policing program have more substance.

Providing appropriate training in community policing and indoctrinating officers to accept the community policing philosophy are factors that are still problematic in community policing, especially in small cities. Small communities cannot afford to send all their officers to training programs; thus a variety of other training alternatives have been tried. One city used a local theatrical group to assist in the training for community policing by structuring role-playing situations that are designed to increase cultural and racial sensitivity. Another department purchased videotapes, and all the offices have had brief discussions of the community policing concept in department meetings. In general, the training appeared to be too abbreviated and superficial to provide the necessary resocialization that is required for a department to build its program on the goals and objectives implicit in the philosophies of community policing that appear in the mission statements of the departments studied. When asked if he had the chance to do it all over again, and if there was something that could be done to make the officers more receptive to the program, one chief responded, "I would have had more training in the area of community-oriented policing. Being that it was a new field, there was little training going on. I had to take the chance of going on with the program." While this chief acknowledged that special training in community policing is not provided in his department, he did state that, "It is going to be my decision that for any new officers I will definitely set up a format for them to obtain X amount of hours in community policing. I would send them off-premises, maybe to a different state, so they can get some exposure to what other departments are doing and feel that it is not just pushed down their throats here."

Another dynamic of community policing programs in small cities is that most of the programs are introduced through administrators who hear about it from professional contacts outside the local community. In two of the communities, the supervisors attempted to implement their programs through departmental directives. Officers tend to interpret top-down implementation as heavy handed, even when some effort was made to discuss the concept in an open meeting. In two of the communities, grant monies helped to motivate officers to participate. As one supervisor suggested, "Grant monies help to sweeten the pot, since they function as inducements for getting officers to volunteer for innovative programs." One might question what will happen to the program when the grant money is discontinued.

It appears that the acceptance of the notion that community policing embraces a philosophy is gradual, and the willingness of the officers to accept the necessary structural changes in the organization also comes along gradually. Some of the factors that appear to be critical for successful implementation of a department-wide community policing concept include the extent to which the programs are clearly articulated in the department's mission statement, and the extent to which local police administrators can set the agenda for gradual change and offer strong leadership. Of particular importance is their ability to articulate a clear and concise definition of community policing. In our study, it appears that a few supervisors equated community policing with public relations.

The information obtained from the questioning with 54 community policing officers revealed that administrators interested in implementing community policing must recognize the central role of the patrol officer. If the concept is going to work in small communities, it will be the officers working the neighborhoods who will get the job done. Whether these officers endorse the program and strongly promote it will be determined by a number of factors. They include the manner in which the program is introduced and portrayed, the support given by the upper administration, and the types of rewards granted for those involved in the community policing endeavors.

How programs are introduced and implemented in small departments is as critical for their success as the nature of the programs. It takes strong leadership at the top to pull it off; moreover, middle managers must get involved and function as mentors and on-the-job trainers.

The receptivity and support of the programs by the citizenry will be shaped by historic antecedents that include the amount and quality of previous relationships with law enforcement agents. Departmental administrative styles and quality of follow-through on program implementation are also important factors that determine the success or failure of COP programs in small communities.

The community policing concept is new, and has only recently been introduced in small communities as both a philosophy and program. Hence its implementation is uneven, understandably piecemeal, and necessarily experimental. Where it has been introduced, there is evidence that it "works," although the indicators for judging "success" tend to be loosely documented and based on qualitative data. Departments that do use more rigorous documentation procedures report lower crime rates and more community/police cooperation as indicators of success.

Section III

RECRUITMENT AND TRAINING OF COMMUNITY POLICING OFFICERS

Part III examines some stereotypes, and myths about police officer personalities are discussed with implications regarding selection, matching to community, training, and job satisfaction. The literature is now beginning to converge to produce a clearer description of community policing and the community policing officer.

The data suggest a subpopulation of police officers distinct from the general population of officers. Community policing officers in major cities tend to be older with more time on the force and more experience in other units on the force than the "typical" officer. In smaller suburban and rural communities, however, these officers tend to be younger than the average age of the force. More important, though, is the fact that community policing officers diverge from the "profiles" of the "typical" officer personality.

The literature on the personal characteristics of police officers is quite detailed. In this literature, police officers tend to be more aggressive, controlling, extraverted, and conservative. They are typically authoritarian, suspicious, courageous, cynical, conservative, loyal, and self-assertive. They place much lower value on concepts such as social recognition, pleasure, and a world of beauty. Police trainees have been found to have a high need for achievement, exhibition, intraception, dominance, and heterosexuality.

Negative outcomes associated with the job and these personality characteristics include greater incidences of stress, suicide, heart disease, ulcers, alcohol abuse, chronic depression, family strain, and marital problems.

We found neither these personality characteristics nor the negative outcomes associated with them in the community policing officer. In fact, we found quite the opposite. The community policing officer appears to be a well rounded, caring and dedicated career officer who is fulfilled in his/her work.

The effectiveness of community policing is directly associated with qualities of the police officer. Furthermore, it is clear from initial comparisons with officers in programs in other cities that the "ideal" officer profile is strongly related to the way the city's community policing program is constructed.

It appears that community policing works very well. One effect of this is that the community policing officer is better adjusted and has greater job satisfaction than the average officer. More research needs to be done in the specialized topic of community policing personality, however, for two major reasons. First, we believe that many of the effects that we documented are the product of the department and the structure of the program, as well as the neighborhoods within which the community policing program was located but these hypotheses require testing.

Second, just as psychological testing has become important in the employment of police officers, research in community policing should become more important in developing and implementing effective policing for the community. As a result, political and administrative decisions were made that have dramatically altered the effective program described here.

Effective police work is essential in modern society; and this work can demand much from the officer. Hence, it is imperative that police administrators emphasize the importance of police forces comprised of officers who are psychologically healthy and suited to the tasks at hand; mainly, police officers should have the ability to adapt to daily stressors, communicate effectively with each other and build rapport, cooperate as an integrated team, and cope with the conflicts which arise from the complicated nature of the subculture of policing and the criminal justice system. Not only is the selection of recruits who are well-adjusted and who have good coping skills important, and not only is the screening out of applicants with diagnosable psychopathologies and depression problems vital; but, the regularly administered psychological tests (i.e., MMPI, PVS, etc.) should be used to seek out officers who have the ability to adapt to unusual demands. Officers must be willing to expose themselves to danger on a daily basis and must be able to confront life-threatening circumstances in an instant. Therefore, it is only natural that one should be concerned with "the police personality." Unfortunately, when the preliminary data from this study were offered to a city official at a time when policy decisions were being made about this program, we were told that "you are only doing research; this is politics."

7

Community Policing and Its Implications for Alternative Models of Police Officer Selection

Eric Metchik
Salem State College

Ann Winton
John Jay College of Criminal Justice—City University of New York

INTRODUCTION

The present era is one of considerable change regarding the public's view of police and the functions they should serve in our society. In particular, the enthusiasm with which the community policing movement has been embraced, especially by the highest strata in both police and civilian hierarchies (Walker, 1992), connotes a profound shift in the way police functioning is conceptualized: from a reactive, crime-fighting stereotype to a more proactive, socially involved ideal. This change in turn has important implications for how we select police recruits from typically large pools of applicants. In particular, past and present practice has focused on screening out unsuitable candidates; i.e., those with inabilities to tolerate stressful situations, systematic biases against special interest groups (such as ethnic minorities, homosexuals, women, and the homeless) or other psychological problems, including poor interpersonal relationships, judgment or impulse control, and disordered thought processes. This approach will henceforth be referred to as the "screening out" model. We argue that the new conception of community policing requires a reevaluation of past practice, and the development of more positively oriented (i.e., prosocial) selection criteria and procedures.

We first discuss the traditional, "screening out" model of police recruitment and evaluate its positive and negative features. Following this, we define community policing and present its goals, along with their implications for changing to a prosocial model of police officer selection. A model of key community policing psychological selection criteria is presented. Methods of implementing the model are discussed, with special emphasis on the potential contribution of assessment centers as part of a new approach. Finally, we make some projections concerning future sets of psychological selection criteria.

THE "SCREENING OUT" MODEL

The predominance of a negative orientation (i.e., screening out "undesirable" applicants) can be traced to the initial awareness among police administrators concerning the importance of personality assessment in recruitment. This orientation is hardly surprising when we evaluate psychological screening in light of other components of the selection process. Applicants to a police force initially take a civil service examination that assesses their ability to read and interpret simulated situations they may confront as officers. They are asked to exercise their best judgment in picking the most appropriate response. A cutoff score is established below which no applicant will receive further consideration. This first step serves to screen out illiterate applicants and those with poor judgment or inadequate critical thinking abilities.

The other stages in the application process, character, and medical evaluations also serve to eliminate candidates with problematic legal records or height, weight, or medical conditions. These assessments may occur at the same time as the psychological screening but ideally are made beforehand, so that expensive psychological evaluations can be reserved for candidates who are viable in all other respects. A constant theme characterizing the entire process, however, is the drive to discover and eliminate applicants who clearly do not meet the various minimal standards. It is quite the exception to find any articulation (much less validation) of ideal or even desirable physical and psychological characteristics shared by officers with the best prospects for optimum job performance.

Psychologists employed by police departments to evaluate candidates typically review and integrate several different sets of data. Decisions regarding what information is collected are guided by the extent to which the data help to detect a candidate's weaknesses. For example, applicants usually report on a biographical form information concerning school and employment history, military service, and psychological treatments. Their achievements are not the focus of this inquiry, instead, they are expected to explain their failure to complete a school program and the reasons for leaving each job. Similarly, for military service, an explanation for anything less than honorable discharge is required. Psychological treatment can be seen as indication of a possible ongoing problem that may seriously weaken a candidate's job performance. Any such report is carefully scrutinized.

Psychologists screening applicants for police positions also review the results of paper-and-pencil psychological tests administered earlier in the application process. The most commonly used instrument is the Minnesota Multiphasic Personality Inventory, or "MMPI" (Dwyer, Prien & Bernard, 1990). Developed in 1943 by Hathaway and McKinley and normed on a psychiatric population, the MMPI was designed to diagnose major psychological disorders. Among its 10 psychopathology scales are depression, paranoia, schizophrenia, and mania. Psychologists evaluating MMPI profiles typically scan the scale scores for elevations that differ significantly from the norm. If time allows, they may examine the individual item responses that produced the scale elevation and then direct their questions in an oral interview to seek confirmation of the test indications.[1] The structure and output of the MMPI are highly compatible with the "screening out" model, since the instrument's focus is the discovery of psychological deviation.

EVALUATING THE EFFECTIVENESS OF THE "SCREENING OUT" MODEL

The individual components of the "screening out" model (biodemographic and psychological test data) have generally been evaluated separately in the literature. The two foci of these studies are performance in the police academy (during a training period lasting from several weeks to six months) and the actual work record. A problem with the former is that the quality of performance in training has not generally been shown to predict actual job effectiveness (Burkhart, 1980). In particular, the most quantifiable aspect of training performance, course grades, has not been systematically related to the qualities of drive, perseverance, or assertiveness that can be critical for success on the job.

Furthermore, job performance has traditionally been difficult to monitor and evaluate in most police agencies. Performance evaluation forms may be overly broad or inherently vague. In addition, supervisors often have limited contact with or knowledge of the hourly activities of their field officers. Secondly, strong police subcultures and face-saving tactics may dissuade supervisors from giving detailed and truthful evaluations. Rating a supervisee too low may be perceived as disloyal to a "brother" officer, while giving too high a rating exposes the evaluator to review and possible reprimand if the supervisee does not meet later expectations.

A third methodological issue in evaluating the effectiveness of the "screening out" model concerns possible restriction of range when independent variables are measured using populations of police academy recruits or new patrol officers. The potential performance of those rejected during the screening process remains unknown. In addition, the predictive validity of various biodemographic and psychological test data from rejectees is tested.

With these caveats in mind, the elements of the "screening out" model will each be examined to determine their predictive utility in the selection process.

Studies evaluating the potential of biographical data to predict police officer firings have differed in their conclusions. For example, Levy (1967) found that the severity of the prior criminal record and the length of previous jobs significantly differentiated police failures from successes. Cohen and Chaiken (1972), studying a similar set of factors, failed to replicate these findings. Spielberger, Spaulding, Jolley and Ward (1979) defined their biographical variables in a broader way and the results can be used to reconcile some of the contradictions from other studies. Regarding prior employment, they found that terminated officers felt more need for job encouragement and had lower achievement or public service motivations than those who were not terminated. It is possible that job confidence and the strength of conventional, middle-class goals are more telling predictors than the mere amount of time spent at previous jobs.

Other more specific behavioral items have been strong predictors of problematic police performance. These include the frequency and recency of motor vehicle violations and the number of previous job firings. They are consonant with a rebellious orientation toward societal authority and support the proposition held by many that the best predictor of future behavior is past behavior.

The results from research involving the MMPI have been equally mixed. Some researchers found individual scales significantly differentiated officers with problematic work histories from those without evidence of problems. The argument is then made that the MMPI can be an invaluable adjunct in making the initial hiring decision (Hiatt & Hargrave, 1988; Beutler et al., 1985). This approach is questionable in several respects. For example, statistically significant differences between MMPI scale means do not necessarily have substantive importance. This is especially the case when the differences between the means of the problematic and nonproblematic groups do not exceed their standard deviations (see Hiatt & Hargrave, 1988) or when the means of each group are all within the range of what is deemed "normal" for this test (Saxe & Reiser, 1976).

While the basic orientation of the MMPI (to diagnose pathology) fits in well with a "screening out" model, it is often used by psychologists with little or no formal training in the test's interpretation. A cursory review is made for individual scale elevations and when none are detected, the MMPI profile is largely ignored. More telling predictions might well be made from consideration of *patterns* of configurational variation across several MMPI scale scores. The reliability and validity of configurational interpretations is likely much greater than that of individual scale readings since the former are based on larger sets of independent test items.

If the "screening out" model had no reliability or validity problems such as those discussed above, its advantages would be fairly obvious. In the short term, it could greatly reduce the danger to the public posed by armed, unsuitable officers. Of course, even assuming an extremely rigorous selection system, we might well not detect severe instances of pathology that develop only years after the officers join the force. This can be seen in the invariably fruitless attempts to review posthumously the files of police officer suicides for any signs of disturbance that should have been identified by the "screening out" process when they applied to the force.

In the long term, elimination of problematic candidates can improve the public's evaluation of officers as effective crime fighters. More specifically, officers with poor stress tolerance, prejudicial attitudes, or impaired judgment, thought processes, and interpersonal skills could well be at a distinct disadvantage in terms of the aggressive yet controlled activities required to apprehend and safely manage criminal suspects. Of course, this potential advantage must be evaluated in light of the fact that crime fighting actions usually comprise only a small proportion of the typical officer's work schedule (see Lefkowitz, 1977; Bennis & Cleveland, 1980; Renner & Barnett, 1984).

One of the main disadvantages of this model is the "false positives" dilemma. For every candidate legitimately excluded from further consideration, there are many others also rejected who might have made fine officers. This is an issue in nearly all selection systems, but is exacerbated when prediction criteria are inexact and the behavior predicted (in this case, officers who will have problematic records) is relatively infrequent.

The demand characteristics of the interview are also very high, since applicants know that psychologists actively seek criteria that can be used to exclude them from further consideration. Candidates take an understandably defensive stance and it can affect their candor. This may be especially problematic when assessing such sensitive areas as prejudicial attitudes or stress tolerance. The interview can quickly degenerate into an inquisition, with adversarial sides in active confrontation. The psychologist in such a situation may lose his or her objectivity and provide a less than dispassionate review of behavior related to the selection criteria. For example, instead of focusing on the candidate's age and maturity level at the time of a past criminal offense, the psychologist evaluating his present capacities may summarily reject him. This in turn increases the "false positives" problem mentioned earlier.

Perhaps the biggest drawback of the "screening out" approach is its failure to distinguish between mediocre and outstanding job candidates. After eliminating the most problem-prone applicants (along with many others, as mentioned above), we retain a conglomerate of candidates with widely varying abilities and attitudes. This system does not allow us to identify and give specialized assignments to the most promising applicants. The loss of efficiency is tolerated since the focus of concern is the exclusion of potential officers who might otherwise prove to be an embarrassment to the department. This narrow barometer of "success" serves to institutionalize the status quo and engenders a conservative spirit, impervious to many forms of innovation and experimentation needed in today's society that is an integral part of policing.

The officers chosen through many current "screening out" procedures are those who will conform most easily to the paramilitary, authoritarian organizational structure that characterizes many police departments in the United States.

Applicants who do not fit desired social stereotypes are quickly eliminated. Unfortunately, this may include some who have matured after tumultuous or rebellious periods of adolescence. These candidates might best be able to understand and deal with similar behavior from youths on their beats. Given the increasingly complex nature of policing in the 1990s, recruits selected through the traditional procedures can hardly be expected to deal efficiently with their daily tasks, no matter how rigorous or extended the training period.

COMMUNITY POLICING: IMPLICATIONS FOR THE SELECTION OF PATROL OFFICERS

The community policing movement represents a fundamental philosophical shift in the conception of police work. Instead of the police being the "thin blue line" between the public and crime, community policing in its broadest interpretation proposes a partnership between the police, the community and other public/private agencies and groups. The shift is from viewing police as exclusively a professional crime-fighting organization to seeing them as a community–oriented group with a proactive, problem-solving focus.

Wilson (1976) suggested that traditional policing practices were classifiable either as fitting a law enforcement or service-oriented model. Law enforcement, however, has attracted the lion's share of media attention. "The pop image of the police is one of constant action. In cop movies and TV shows, station houses are crawling with snarling felons and their victims, and every tour of duty in a radio car is a non-stop series of emergencies" (*New Yorker*, June 1993:4). This powerful image contrasts with the daily experience of most police officers. In addition to "down time" that is often accompanied by a sense of alienation, most of the work police officers perform on a daily basis is service-oriented. Patrol officer job analyses indicate that there is an enormous range in duties performed. Law enforcement and crime-related tasks comprise only about 10-15 percent of total police time. The largest amount of time is spent in administrative and social service functions (Lefkowitz, 1977). Bennis and Cleveland (1980) asserted that only 3-10 percent of police time is spent in crime-related work. Others (Reiss, 1971; Renner & Barnett, 1984) report various figures ranging from 3-20 percent of time spent on criminal matters. Therefore, most police work involves non-crime-related activities that are initiated by citizens. It is clear that the vast majority of police time is spent with law-abiding citizens. In these interactions, the normal social rules are expected.

Wilson and Kelling (1982) described sentiments experienced by both police and citizen groups. Police officials believed they should deal with serious crime but recognized that their efforts were largely unsuccessful. While citizens believed crime to be a problem, they were very much concerned with smaller matters that disrupted and frequently destroyed daily neighborhood life. The community policing movement seeks to broaden the traditional law enforcement model, giving prominence to citizens' "quality of life" priorities. In particular, it envisions the empowerment of communities to participate with the police in problem-solving and decisionmaking about the delivery of a wide variety of services.

The community policing movement attempts to widen patrol officers' conception of their duties, making it more proactive. For example, some crime is assumed to be caused by ongoing, continuous problems within a community such as a disorderly milieu (Goldstein, 1987). This assumption may require nontraditional policing techniques. Moore and Trojanowicz (1988b) have suggested that in a community policing program, officers need skills in negotiation and conflict-resolution. This would facilitate the resolution of interpersonal disputes before assaults occur and without immediate recourse to criminal law, arrest, and prosecution.

A very common and frustrating situation for officers is the call to intervene in a domestic dispute. More than likely, this conflict is nothing new for the couple involved, their neighbors, or the police. The police try to restore the peace, sometimes by separating the couple. They might encourage them to go for counseling or, if violence has occurred, they may arrest the perpetrator. Goldstein (1987) recommends more training in mediation techniques so that the police can become problem-solvers in these types of situations. It is important to note that this approach is not social work. Rather, a primary police function remains the enforcement of the law. The officer's intervention is short-term and focused on the problem. His role, for example, might be to gather information and help develop or mobilize services such as a crisis intervention team.

The community police officers become one of many neighborhood groups responsible for improving the quality of life. Local residents are their active partners and important allies. In many cities, citizens and police have developed night patrols, cleaned up vacant lots and organized activities bringing families into neighborhood parks. Other civil agencies have also been mobilized, including the housing authority, the sanitation department, and human resources. In this way, community policing emphasizes not only crime control, but maintenance of civil order and fear reduction. The partnership between the police and the community includes families, local merchants, schools, and churches.

This close working relationship is the essence of community policing. Patrol officers are given relatively long-term assignments to a beat, with steady tours. Programs are implemented that increase interactions between police and neighborhood residents. For example, police may consult on crime control issues at neighborhood meetings or knock on doors, getting to know the people who live in an area. They may also be assigned "caseloads" of households with ongoing problems. Most significantly, police are encouraged to respond to the feelings and fears of people that result from a variety of social problems and types of victimization. People are encouraged to bring their problems directly to beat officers or the precinct. Kelling (1988a) has written that the role of the police is to gather information about citizens' wants, diagnose the nature of the problem, and devise possible solutions. In addition, the police determine which segments of them can best be served by the police and which can best be served by other agencies and institutions.

While community policing models vary from city to city, they all share some common assumptions. The return to foot patrol is prominent in every program. Underlying this is the notion that an officer walking his or her beat learns the unique characteristics of a neighborhood and its residents. Citizens watch the police perform their jobs with more understanding and sensitivity to the community and this in turn increases community trust in law enforcement. Neighborhood residents' definition of a problem and appropriate police interventions becomes important. Community policing tasks stress the patrol officer's social and interpersonal skills. This goes beyond the technical application of procedures to situations, whether dealing with crime, disorder, or other social problems. There is an emphasis on respect for the citizenry at all levels of operation.

GOALS OF COMMUNITY POLICING

There are many, varied goals in community policing. One of the most important is a change in the manner in which police service is delivered. The traditional model of policing is largely reactive. The focus has been on developing effective means of responding to criminal incidents and citizens' complaints. A major goal of the community policing model is to develop a proactive, problem-solving orientation. Brown (1989:9) writes that "community policing is an operating style. The community policing model envisions broadening the available repertoire. In the past, the police responded over and over to the same problems, but in adopting a proactive stance, the police become problem-solvers."

Another very important goal in the community policing model is the expansion of the role of the patrol officer. In fact, the success of community policing depends on the work of the neighborhood patrol officer. By giving him greater discretion and more varied duties within a less rigid hierarchical administration, it is hoped that tedious periods of "down time" on patrol will be much less frequent, benefiting both police and citizens. Moore and Trojanowicz define the domain of community policing as "anything that is named as a community problem" (1988b:12). Furthermore, the patrol officer "seeks to handle the problem with any means available—not simply arrest and prosecution" (p. 12, op. cit.). The officer is expected to see beyond seemingly unrelated incidents, widespread community fears or persistent crime problems, understanding and dealing with their deeper roots.

The role of patrol officer is to have increased status, becoming more dynamic and rewarding. Rather than simply following a set of rules and being evaluated on the number of arrests made or positive citations awarded, she is seen as a flexible thinker. The officer helps to identify problems and is encouraged to be creative and innovative in formulating their solutions. Given more permanent assignments instead of the traditional rotating shifts, police officers become part of the community. The traditional patrol job has been structured around random patrols and response to service calls. Police officers respond "by the book," carrying out policies as directed in a mechanical fashion. Under the community policing model, the officer first learns the needs of the community and then is given the authority to try creative solutions in a fair and just manner (Riechers & Roberg, 1990). The job becomes less routinized and boring, which in turn should increase job satisfaction.

A third goal of community policing is broadening the responsibility for and effectiveness of crime control and prevention (Goldstein, 1987; Wilson & Kelling, 1982). This is no longer seen as solely the job of the police, but is rather addressed by the police and the community as active partners. Neighborhood residents possess significant information that the police can effectively use in solving and preventing crime. The riots of the 1960s and the more recent riots in 1992 continue to reveal the price of having a "police department backed by the power of the law, but not the consent, much less active support, of those being policed" (Williams & Murphy, 1990:3). Community policing operations are to be more public, leading to better officer accountability and increased respect for their efforts.

Finally, another important goal for community policing is the reduction of the public's fear of crime. There has been little consideration of fear as a problem, separate and distinct from crime and criminal activity. However, communities respond to their fears in varying ways. Some have adopted defensive, individualistic solutions to protect themselves. This has led to the collapse of more marginal areas and often reduced the number of people on the streets. In turn, the risks of actual criminal activity may also increase. The community policing model proposes that citizens and police together cope with the fear of crime and victimization in a manner which can ultimately strengthen the community. The expanded role of patrol officers increases police visibility and helps to reduce the public's fear of crime. The research findings on foot patrol suggest that increased police presence is noticed when police presence was previously low (Cordner, 1986). Moore and Trojanowicz (1988a) conclude after reviewing several studies that increased foot patrols and closer contact between officers and neighborhood residents does indeed reduce citizens' fear.

These goals viewed together as a set underline the importance of numerous psychological characteristics shared by officers who will most successfully implement the community policing model. Many of these have not been actively considered in "screening out" systems. We next propose a model that groups these factors in specific skills categories.

SELECTION

Traditional models of police recruitment, especially the "screening out" system discussed earlier, do not select for the qualities that are most important for the community policing patrol officer. Instead, the "screening out" model focuses on eliminating those police recruits who are perceived as being a detriment to the public and to the police organization. The issue, however, is not to discard this system completely but to modify it, adding a prosocial component. As community policing expands the role of patrol officers, it becomes critical to hire applicants whose psychological profiles best fit the new job requirements.

PSYCHOLOGICAL CHARACTERISTICS AS CRITERIA IN A PROSOCIAL SELECTION MODEL

Any discussion of specific psychological traits is preliminary until job assessments and further research are conducted. However, we now present some of our preliminary ideas about relevant psychological traits to be assessed in a prosocial selection model. These are based on the community policing goals discussed earlier.

Cognitive Traits

Two goals described previously, changing to a proactive model of police service and expanding the role of the patrol officer, essentially serve to redefine this position. The patrol officer is now to be a *problem-solver*. Selection would favor those who are interested in creating solutions rather than applying previously learned rules. Furthermore, there is an emphasis on practical intelligence (i.e., the ability to quickly analyze key elements of a situation and identify possible courses of action to reach logical conclusions).

It is evident that certain cognitive traits overlap and interact with each other so that it is difficult to neatly delineate separate problem-solving elements. However, these elements must include an analysis of the situation and an awareness of the environment. They may additionally include fact finding, planning, and organization of relevant data. A patrol officer might witness, for example, neighborhood youth painting graffiti on a wall. The officer has to analyze the situation and define the problem. He also has to search for the possibility of a deeper cause and how to address that most effectively. This may or may not include the arrest and prosecution of the offender. The officer must be sensitive to the needs of the community as well as responsive to the youthful offenders themselves.

Another scenario is a patrol officer assigned to a beat in which automobile windows are smashed and vandalized each night. In order to formulate the best response, the community policing officer must define the problem and address the motivations of the offenders.

The two examples cited are commonplace in many urban communities where the police have often abdicated responsibility. The community policing officer would be expected to work with the local residents to address these problems and help develop solutions, perhaps using negotiation and conflict resolution skills.

Under the community policing model, the patrol officer is expected to recognize when old methods are inadequate and new and different solutions are needed. The officer is now expected to display many of the skills demanded in higher-level personnel such as detectives. The optimal patrol officer is not only interested in problem-solving but also *open to experience;* that is, able to assimilate and apply new information and to welcome the participation of others. Another aspect of this would be *cognitive flexibility and creativity.* Cognitive psychologists speak of functional fixedness or the inability to think about use of common items except as concretely defined (Zimbardo, 1992). The patrol officer needs to be open to possible changes in a given situation and to changing societal values as well. There may be a need to modify his or her style accordingly. The community policing officer is expected to be creative and innovative in his or her approach to neighborhood problems. Two other important cognitive characteristics are the abilities to work independently and maintain self-discipline. This is because under the community policing model, individual officers are not functioning in a rigid hierarchy. They instead exercise increased discretion and make independent decisions concerning the use of administrative resources.

Communication Skills

Communication skills are vital. Brown (1989) stressed that the community policing patrol officer is expected to work with local residents and focus on problems defined by them. This requires not only the ability to work cooperatively with others to solve problems but also the ability to listen. He reported that during the implementation of Houston's community policing program, it was found that neighborhood concerns were different than police officers assumed they would be. "For example, before listening to citizens' concerns became routine, officers assumed that the public worried most about major crimes such as rape, robbery and burglary. After talking with the people who live and work in their beat, officers found that the community's main concerns were quality-of-life issues such as abandoned cars and houses, loud noises and rowdy youngsters" (Brown, 1989:8).

Implementation of community policing changes many aspects of the traditional model. There will need to be more integration and communication laterally within various segments of the police department. The patrol officer becomes the link between various groups, both within the police department and outside in the community. Aspects of communication that may be especially important include a willingness to be observed, self-presentation style, and effectiveness in communicating ideas in both verbal and nonverbal formats.

We also need to consider the interactional effects between cognitive traits and communication skills. Mischel's work on situation-person interactions indicates that how a person encodes and categorizes both the self and the situation is important and somewhat stable. For example, if a person encoded others in a general way in terms of their hostile threats then he is sensitive to the possible attempts to challenge, manipulate, and control. In most situations, this person would be vigilant to threats and be primed to defend him or herself. This is significant for a patrol officer out on the street. Does this officer encode an innocent gesture or a shove in a crowded place as an affront or violation? People develop distinctive encoding strategies and then selectively seek out and attend to different information (Bower, 1981; Miller, 1987). Does this have practical implications? Forgas' (1983) research, for example, indicated that persons with poor social skills tend to encode situations in terms of the degree to which they feel self-conscious or self-confident in them. People who are more socially skilled encode the same situation using different dimensions such as how interesting or pleasant they might be.

In the community policing context, an officer with limited social skills may approach working with a group of rebellious teenagers as a threatening assignment. He will likely employ a strict, authoritarian orientation in this assignment. Another officer with more finely tuned social acumen may interpret the youths' defiant acts as an attempt to empower themselves and achieve their own version of social legitimacy. His tactics would likely be more conciliatory than confrontative. This underlines the importance of interpersonal abilities to be discussed next.

Interpersonal

One of the basic tenets of community policing is that a close, working relationship will develop between the beat officers and the people living and working in that area. The officer is assigned a permanent beat and is expected to learn about every facet of life in his neighborhood. Input from the community becomes an important additional resource in crime-prevention and law enforcement. Neighborhood residents are seen as allies, not adversaries. This involves empathy, respect for others and listening sensitively to residents' concerns. The patrol officer cannot be defensive about his or her role. She has joined the force not for the spirit of adventure but from an interest in service and helping others.

This model of policing broadens officers' roles and jurisdictions so that they are less isolated from the community and have broader contacts than ever before with mainstream, law-abiding civilians (not just the negative, antisocial elements of society). This makes interpersonal abilities such as tolerance and sensitivity especially important. Integrity and assertiveness are also psychological traits with important prosocial components. One aspect of community policing emphasizes handling some matters including certain domestic disputes without invoking the criminal justice system. This requires a personal sense of integrity and assertiveness, without resorting to threats of authority. It also means accepting personal responsibility for mistakes.

The last category overlaps with many of the other qualities already discussed. This is *self system or intra-psychic characteristics*. These psychological traits include positive self-esteem, integrity, stress tolerance, and self-discipline. Stress tolerance is the ability to maintain one's composure and perform effectively while under stress. Currently, much of patrol work is time spent waiting, a problem frequently mentioned in police literature. While community policing specifically hopes to lessen the waiting time, there are many stresses inherent to the job, such as coping with hostility from those you are supposedly helping or from many teenagers and young adults who need to maintain a tough image in front of their peers. The police may consequently experience their authority challenged. Wright and Mischel's work with children (1987; 1988) indicates that there is a relationship between stress and aggressive behavior in this population. Stress tolerance may be increased by more opportunities for problem-solving and greater job satisfaction. Another self system characteristic is both interpersonal and intrapsychic flexibility. By definition, the community policing patrol officer must be even more flexible than those in traditional departments since he will frequently encounter unpredictable events without standard, textbook responses available. One has to be prepared for danger, and yet alert to other possibilities.

All of the above psychological characteristics together constitute a preliminary model of prosocial, "screening in" selection. The question now becomes how best to measure and incorporate them in a valid, reliable hiring process.

Implementation

The main goal is to integrate the desired psychological characteristics for community policing in an alternative selection model that stresses *inclusion* (i.e., hiring) the best candidates, as opposed to excluding problematic applicants. Paper-and-pencil psychological tests are not adequate in and of themselves to measure even a limited number of "screening out" criteria. They can hardly be expected to accurately predict a wider range of skills involved in community policing. Instead, the direct measurement (and comparison across candidates) of concrete, job-related behaviors seems to offer a more complete and objective alternative. We suggest that the rise of the assessment center movement is highly consonant with a reorganization of selection priorities that clearly reflects a community policing model. Assessment center exercises can be developed that arise directly from situations community patrol officers may be expected to handle.[2]

An assessment center consists of a series of exercises in which several observers rate candidates' behaviors in a variety of job-related, simulated tasks (Wendel & Joekel, 1991). In the police context, these might include any or all of the following:

1.   an in-basket exercise requiring applicants to prioritize and respond to a series of agency tasks;

2.   a leaderless group discussion focusing on issues related to community policing, the use of firearms or other current controversies;

3.   candidate ratings of videos depicting adaptive and nonadaptive police responses in such tasks as domestic violence intervention, witness probing, and press conference briefings. Applicants might also be asked to role-play these latter situations.

The exact content of the tasks would depend on a particular department's priorities, recent crime trends in the area and job analyses conducted by industrial psychologists for specific titles in that department. Those creating an assessment center need first to develop ideal profiles of behavior for each task and then train the raters to evaluate how well individual candidates meet the ideals (Pynes & Bernardin, 1992; Coleman, 1992; More & Unsinger, 1987). Before candidates begin the assessment center exercises, it is suggested that they rate themselves on effectiveness in a variety of interpersonal situations. For example, how confident is the candidate that he/she could approach a group of strangers at a social gathering, make an appropriate introduction and join in the conversation? Personality research has suggested that a person's expectations and beliefs concerning personal mastery of a situation is an important component of success (Bandura, 1982). The self ratings can then be compared with ratings by others from similar assessment center exercises.

Assessment centers were used earlier in this century in a military context. The Germans used them in the 1930s to select officers with leadership abilities and the British also used them in World War II for the same purpose. Assessment centers have been extensively used in private industry, including a 20-year longitudinal study by American Telephone and Telegraph started in the mid-1950s (Wendel & Joekel, 1991). In this study, applicants were rated on 25 characteristics of successful managers and the likelihood of promotion to middle management within ten years. Assessment centers used in policing were found to have significant predictive validity with regard to the training academy record and later on-the-job performance (Pynes & Bernardin, 1989, 1992).

The major advantage of an assessment center as the centerpiece of a prosocial approach to police selection is the development of an ideal behavioral model against which actual activities of candidates can be assessed. Using candidate behaviors in well-chosen, structured exercises increases the chance to achieve maximum reliability and validity, compared with paper-and-pencil tests. The latter assume stable, measurable personality traits which express themselves across all situations. Assessment centers, on the other hand, allow for the possibility of unlimited trait-situation interactions.[3]

A related advantage is that the assessment center is easily customized to reflect a particular department's most frequent and important on-the-job problem situations. For example, management in a small police force may place great importance on the ability of patrol officers to simultaneously handle multiple problems and shift gears rapidly from one task to the next. Reflecting this, assessment center designers may include a role-play that involves candidates in a routine house break-in investigation, interrupted by an emergency call for police presence at the scene of a riot.

A disadvantage of this approach is that assessment centers are time-consuming and expensive to develop and use. Their implementation usually requires all-day workshops that include orientations for both evaluators and participants, running candidates through the exercises themselves and later conferencing among the raters. The use of multiple raters, while desirable in terms of checking ratings reliability, also allows disparate evaluations of similar candidates. Training staff properly is critical in order to assure the maximum convergence of ratings.

In terms of a development strategy, both formal and informal job analyses are required. As mentioned earlier, we would also want to assess local crime trends and seek a consensus regarding department enforcement priorities. Although insufficient by themselves as predictors of prosocial police behavior, certain paper-and-pencil tests may nonetheless be quite useful in designing assessment centers. Tests that measure adaptive elements of the "normal" personality, as opposed to those designed to detect and diagnose various forms of psychopathology, can help to clarify the psychological attributes of the model officer, including many of the qualities mentioned above with reference to community policing. Profiles of such attributes can be used in turn as reference points for the selection and development of assessment center exercises.

The exercises themselves should each reflect one or more of the psychological characteristics discussed earlier. For example, an in-basket exercise might require applicants to prioritize and respond to a series of tasks that will confront them on a typical day. The tasks could include developing a community newsletter designed to provide accurate crime information, establishing a park program to reduce vandalism and increase park use by local residents, meeting with school personnel and parents to design a program reducing truancy, setting up a radar check on a busy road, enforcing disorderly conduct laws at the request of a community group, and providing more visible foot patrol in response to concerns of local merchants. This exercise would allow a candidate to demonstrate cognitive flexibility in how the tasks are handled. It also measures how well the candidate can work independently and assume responsibility. Finally, ratings would reflect the ability to organize and plan time effectively, as well as analyze and bring some practical problem-solving techniques to bear on situations faced during a typical day.

In the leaderless group discussion, the candidate is evaluated on his/her ability to listen to and work effectively with others, communicate ideas and negotiate differences. Another trait that can be assessed in this exercise includes openness to experience (i.e., accepting the participation of others and assimilating and applying new information). One discussion topic especially relevant for community policing would be a review of how mentally ill, homeless people are being handled in a residential neighborhood. Candidates would be informed that complaints were filed claiming these street people menaced children and the elderly. They would then be asked to suggest interventions and ways to garner support for them from all sectors of the police department.

A different type of exercise would have candidates rate videos depicting adaptive and nonadaptive police responses in such tasks as domestic violence intervention, witness probing and press conference briefing. This would again tap candidates' analytic and problem-solving skills. The ideal candidates would also demonstrate creativity and innovation in the solutions they propose. These situations could be recreated as live role-plays, using confederate actors as necessary. Raters would focus on candidates' assertiveness in both comfortable and unpleasant or dangerous circumstances.

Candidates can be rated on their communication skills in oral presentation exercises. These exercises can be developed in the context of police-community meetings or requests for help within the department. Raters judge the candidate's interpersonal style and effectiveness as well as his ability to organize and give presentations. Another idea is to present a short tour of a neighborhood and ask the applicant to prepare a talk on what he or she thinks the problems are. The applicant will then listen to taped interviews with selected neighborhood residents discussing their actual problems, after which he or she will again prepare a talk on the relevant issues. This not only taps listening ability, but also encoding skills and flexibility.

Certain exercises may combine elements of more than one of the specific types described above. For example, candidates may be told that patrol officers have noted a large amount of graffiti around the neighborhood, along with increased complaints about it from local residents. The officers have also noticed that there is little foot traffic in the evening hours and people are afraid to sit outdoors, even in warm weather. Candidates are asked as a group to suggest within a 15-minute period as many solutions as possible, as well as ways to implement them. Everyone must then rank these ideas according to their effectiveness and ease of implementation. Finally, each candidate is asked to make an oral presentation of his ideas to a community group.

Assessment center exercises can also measure stress tolerance, how effectively anxiety is handled, and the candidate's understanding of his own abilities, strengths, and weaknesses. The possible choice of exercises is virtually limitless. It should be guided, however by the results of formal and informal job analyses as well as the policy priorities of the police and neighborhood residents in specific jurisdictions.

A NOTE ABOUT THE FUTURE

The future development of police officer selection systems will be heavily influenced by the impact of the community policing movement. If departments fail to adopt this philosophy on a wide scale, we will remain in a quagmire of conflict between the unrealistic but traditional "crime fighting" model of policing, a more accurate but unsatisfying model with routine patrol as its centerpiece, and the community service model embodied by community policing. Each individual police department will develop its own variation of "screening out" or "screening in" (i.e., prosocial) criteria, depending on its overall philosophy. This assumes, of course, that each department has a strong, clearly articulated guiding philosophy. A confusing, disparate collection of selection criteria will be an inevitable by-product of the failure to achieve consensus concerning an ideal policing model.

On the other hand, if community policing becomes the dominant style of the 1990s and beyond, we can expect to see more uniform selection systems that increasingly emphasize direct behavioral measures. As confidence in assessment center data increases, the approach will evolve from an adjunct source of supplementary information to a graded part of the formal selection process. The developmental methodology will become more standardized, including a prominent role for personality questionnaires as part of a validated basis on which to choose and develop the behavioral exercises. While the exact nature of these exercises may vary greatly across departments, all will reflect a clearer conception of the way model community policing officers handle their positions and responsibilities.

NOTES

1   This represents a responsible, if limited, application of the test results within the confines of the "screening out" model. Sometimes, however, candidates are eliminated solely on the basis of test findings without the oral interview component. It is our opinion that this is a most regrettable and even reprehensible state of affairs in these jurisdictions. It represents a serious abuse of the test data, which were meant to guide thoughtful decisionmaking instead of replacing it.

2   It might be argued that entry-level candidates know little about police procedures and this makes the use of assessment centers less valid. We are selecting, however, for certain psychological characteristics and not knowledge of the job per se. Assessment center exercises must be structured to measure these qualities and not require the display of detailed procedural methods that are taught during academy training or learned later in the field.

3   Personality psychologists have long struggled with the question of the stability of personality traits across situations and through the life span. The current view of Mischel and others (Mischel, 1990; Small, Zeldin & Savin-Williams, 1983) is that a person's behavior is sometimes cross-situationally consistent and sometimes situationally specific. Wright and Mischel (1987, 1988) have suggested that traits be viewed as clusters of conditions or behavioral contingencies. For example, they have studied the interaction of stress and aggressive behavior in children. They found that if a child is subjected to a high stress situation, the child acts aggressively. If the child is not subjected to stress, then he or she is not likely to act aggressively. Therefore, they suggest that there are certain types of situations that engender high trait/behavior correlations and others that do not. For assessment center development, this suggests a promising approach. There are several possibilities but since stress appears to be an important characteristic of any police work, it is crucial to delineate the types of situations that encourage high trait/behavioral correlations. For example, is a person's ability to be an effective problem-solver affected by situational variables? If so, how can these best be reflected in the specific assessment center exercises that are chosen?

8

Training for Community-Oriented Policing

Vance McLaughlin
Savannah Police Department

Michael E. Donahue
Armstrong State College

INTRODUCTION

Community policing, in its idealized form, is said to constitute a break with incident-driven policing. With community policing, police officers are encouraged to incorporate, if not outright co-opt, the assistance of neighborhood residents to act as "co-producers" of public safety. Beyond that, several features of community policing are said to be necessary for its success. These include empowerment, partnership, problem solving, and accountability (Portland Police Bureau, 1990). Training must be a precursor before any of the above features can be accomplished.

The recent proliferation of literature on community policing is reminiscent of other research on police strategy, always fashionable for a time and then forgotten for the most part (e.g., team policing in the early 1970s, directed patrol in the late 1970s, and foot patrol and differential police response in the early 1980s to mention but a few). With each of these topics, evaluation research showing even limited effectiveness is hard, though not always impossible, to find in the literature. It is the same with community policing.

For all the accolades bestowed on this "new" form of policing, there is good reason to be skeptical of its effectiveness, if for no other reason than the limited empirical evaluation that has been done to date. In fairness to proponents of community policing, however, this is due as much if not more than anything else to the difficulty in technically defining "effective" police work. In addition, complicating any analysis of community policing is the claim by its proponents that traditional measures of effectiveness may not be suitable to assessing either the tangible, much less the intangible, benefits that accrue from a community's implementation of community policing. But the fact of the matter is that no one, at least at this writing, knows how well—or poorly—it serves the communities in which police have applied it—whether in terms of police performance or quality of service delivery. But beyond this evaluation of community policing there is an even more fundamental barrier to understanding COP and its implications for practice.

That second defect, and one which is addressed in this chapter, concerns training police to become community oriented. In fact, very little is written with respect to how a department goes about implementing it. Moreover, virtually nothing in the literature informs us on how effective, if at all, this training has been for departments or the communities they serve.

If police are going to be co-producers of public safety with the community, it would seem axiomatic that community policing cannot thrive in an autocratic or otherwise rigidly hierarchical environment. But the fact that police departments are precisely this way, and are not likely to change in any substantive fashion, presents undoubtedly the greatest impediment to its potential usefulness as a policing strategy. Therefore, any training must accept this very real condition as fundamental and incontrovertible, if the training has any chance of influencing street-officer behavior. One could hardly imagine anything more counterproductive than providing police training founded on an inaccurate conception of the nature of police bureaucracy. And yet, some departments commit this egregious error when they promise street officers autonomy in identifying problems and solutions and then do not provide the structure empowering them to do so.

Preparing police officers to become community oriented also assumes that recruitment and selection practices are congruent with the overarching principles of COP. If they are not, one can hardly expect much from even the most thoroughly grounded COP training regime. This is *not* an issue with which this chapter deals. Suffice it to say, however, that with or without qualified personnel, training in COP becomes reorientation to a new way of doing policing, albeit under the same, virtually immutable structures and processes that govern it. And yet, it is not simply a rehearsal of established training regimes in a new context. There are ways in which community policing training is very distinct from traditional training. There is, however, no blueprint from which departments can build a COP training program to fit all or even most environments they police.

What this chapter attempts to do is quite modest. It briefly describes the content and substance of the training modules that, for the moment, appear to apply quite well in the Savannah Police Department, a Southeastern department of roughly 500 employees. If some find our efforts—and our mistakes—profitable, then our objective has been met.

CHALLENGES

COP must filter from the top down. This means that those who oversee the process must understand and support its goals. This means that politicians (i.e., county commissions, city councils, and mayors), appointed officials (i.e., city managers, chiefs of police), and high-ranking police managers must have a firm grasp of COP and its application. These leaders usually "delegate" responsibilities of the "nuts and bolts" running of the police department, and as a practice, rarely attend training.

COP training is different from traditional police training, such as firearms, defensive driving, executing search warrants, and effecting arrests. Most police training is rigid, evolving as it does from law, policies, and procedures to which the law enforcement agency must conform. COP is also a philosophy that is not likely to be embraced by officers and their supervisors, unless they believe that the administrators are committed to its implementation.

Savannah Police Department staff developed feedback mechanisms so that the curriculum would constantly be upgraded to maintain relevancy. An instructor was placed in each of the four precincts, and the three bureaus (staff services, special operations, and investigations) to teach COP modules. These seven instructors attended special training sessions and were encouraged after they taught the current modules to communicate proposed changes in the curriculum in writing. The department training director also regularly solicited feedback from these trainers throughout the several months over which these modules were administered. Last, staff requested participants to complete anonymous evaluation forms for each of these modules. Information from these were useful in reformatting instructional material.

A second challenge was to define the components of COP training and develop appropriate lesson plans. Of course, a review of current COP literature and copies of other departments' curricula provide a reasonable starting point. No doubt, these must be adapted to specific community needs, considering factors influencing the likelihood for success. For example, a department in southern California may feel it is important to include a course on basic Spanish for its officers, to facilitate communication between officers and Latinos. Knowledge of Spanish may not be of any help to a department that has no Latino community within its jurisdiction.

Another challenge is determining whether supervisors and officers are using the COP training, and if so, whether a measurable improvement in performance results. At this time no official mechanisms exist at the Savannah Police Department to make this determination. Informal interviews with management, supervisory, and line personnel, however, clearly indicate that more formalized measures must be developed not only to enhance quality control but to demonstrate management's commitment to community policing.

Provided these challenges are met, the most difficult may be to maintain a strong and vibrant COP philosophy, without it becoming just another law enforcement "fad." Some have characterized it as "soft policing," where law enforcement skills are subsumed to public relations concerns. In some jurisdictions COP officers are even known as the "grin and wave squad" and "lollipop cops" (Trojanowicz & Bucqueroux, 1990). Ultimately, the challenge of maintaining department enthusiasm about COP belongs to the community's political leaders and the Chief of Police. The fear of "soft policing" is discussed in each module. In addition, concurrent with COP classes, we continue to emphasize training in officer survival skills. For example, the same training staff is moving the department to .45 caliber semiautomatic handguns and the department has added a three-day police driving course for officers.

THE SAVANNAH EXPERIENCE

The Savannah Police Department's transition to community policing evolved from a broader effort to address the systemic conditions fostering crime, and a local movement to form collaborative efforts to ameliorate these conditions. Collaboration among criminal justice and noncriminal justice agencies, among private and public sector organizations, and across all levels of government typified this movement. Community policing was an integral component of this effort, receiving ample political and fiscal support for its implementation.

The Savannah Police Chief assigned the Staff Services Bureau the task of designing and implementing COP training. This Bureau is responsible for providing staff and logistical support for the entire department, including training, personnel administration, planning, research, budgeting, computer applications, quartermaster, vehicle purchase and maintenance, and criminal records. The Bureau Commander and Training Director jointly authored, designed, and supervised the administration of all COP training modules. At the outset, the developers adopted a "philosophy" that addressed some of the challenges mentioned above.

TRAINING MODULES

Of the seven modules comprising the Savannah Police Department's COP training regimen, five have been finished at this writing. The remaining two are planned for 1994. All new recruits are trained in the modules like the rest of the department, before they are assigned to a precinct. A discussion of each module follows.

Module I–Participatory Decisionmaking and Leadership Techniques for Management, Supervision, and Street Officers

The first module was designed for administrators and managers. It previews the six succeeding modules, thus giving administrators an overview of COP and what is to be taught to their employees. Participants in this training are encouraged to attend later modules offered to their commands to identify concepts that their officers find difficult or confusing. Participants were given a bibliography of articles and books that were available through the Staff Services Library. Local elected and appointed officials were invited to attend the training seminar.

Module II–Community-Oriented Policing

The second module consists of three segments and was designed to give the employees of the Savannah Police Department an overview of COP. First, each employee is given the Executive Summary of the "Comprehensive Community Crime Control Strategy."

This document explains the rationale behind the department's new precinct system, an important feature of the COP program. Completed in 1990, by police and community planning personnel, it examined a number of variables hypothesized to foster crime and social disintegration. The document's writers collected baseline and secondary data from criminal justice and social services agencies on variables. These included reported crime (e.g., crimes against persons, crimes against property, public disorders, and other disturbances), environmental factors (e.g., dilapidated housing, unmaintained property, and dwelling fires), and socioeconomic factors (e.g., youth unemployment, teenagers giving births, and child abuse and neglect). Crime was classified into 21 categories, environmental data into 12, and socioeconomic data into four categories. Each of the city's 12 service zones were then ranked across all of these categories. Spot maps indicating geographical distribution of these conditions also formed part of this document. Descriptive analysis clearly described what spot mapping made abundantly evident: areas with high crime also had the worst environmental and socioeconomic problems.

Based on these findings, the Savannah Police Department divided patrol operations into four different precincts. Although the geographic areas and populations patrolled by each precinct varied sharply, each contained similar distributions of environmental, socioeconomic, and crime problems.

The second phase of this module consists of providing to and discussing with the participants three handouts:

1. Module II Notes–which answer the student performance objectives. These objectives are:
   a. Name the document that was the basis for the formation of precincts and the adoption of community-oriented policing.
   b. List the four elements of community-oriented policing.
   c. List four of the eight principles of community-oriented policing.
   d. State how much of the community-oriented policing plan has been implemented at this time.

e.   Identify in writing the main role of each of the following:
(1) manager
(2) supervisor
(3) police officer

2.   "Broken Windows" by James Q. Wilson and George L. Kelling from the *Atlantic Monthly*, March 1982.

3.   *Crime and Policing* by Mark H. Moore, Robert C. Trojanowicz, and George L. Kelling published by NIJ, June 1988.

These handouts clarify and reinforce difficult aspects of the class. Emphasis is on the concept that the public should be seen as co-producers of safety and order with the police. Differences between police-community relations and COP are also enumerated. Instructors also underscore that COP departments tend to have many of the following elements in common: community-based crime prevention, reorientation to patrol activities, increased police accountability, and decentralization of command (Skolnick & Baley, 1988). Last, a videotape on COP from our Law Enforcement Television Network (LETN) library is shown.

The third segment of Module II focuses on the Savannah Police Department itself. This portion of the instruction informs the participant that the SPD has completed the first phase of COP. It emphasizes the implementation of specific programs designed to bring officers into more frequent contact with the citizens, such as mini-stations, Neighborhood Watch, Project Shield (increased police presence in public housing), horse patrol, and bicycle patrol. These projects illustrate the importance of citizen support and involvement to the success of COP. At this point, the importance of the precinct concept to SPD's COP program is made clear: decentralization of patrol operations places officers closer to the residents they police, geographic accountability becomes paramount, and officers are the immediate decision-makers on the means and types of police services they make available to citizens.

Instructional staff also emphasizes that the second phase, full acceptance of COP, by the police and the community will take several years. In this context the roles of managers, supervisors, and officers are discussed. Managers' roles are to ensure cooperative interaction among all parts of the police department to produce planned results. Supervisors are to provide resources, encouragement, and decision-making authority to officers so that they can accomplish their tasks. Officers are cast as problem solvers.

Module III–Problem-Oriented Policing (POP)

The third module focuses on problem-oriented policing (POP). Much of the literature on POP and COP confuses these terms. For the SPD COP program, however, POP is defined as an actual project that addresses a specific problem. The participants in this module are given three handouts:

1. Module III Notes–which answer the student performance objectives. These objectives are:
    a. What does problem-oriented policing emphasize over efficiency?
    b. List the four steps of the problem-oriented policing process.
    c. List the four attributes a problem must have to be considered for the problem-oriented policing process.
    d. List the five solutions that problem-oriented policing may produce.
    e. List the four forms concerning problem-oriented policing, that are used in the Savannah Police Department.
    f. List the three main themes of problem-oriented policing.

2. *Problem-Oriented Policing* by William Spelman and John E. Eck published by NIJ, January 1987.

3. "What is Problem-Oriented Policing?," furnished by PERF.

The steps in problem solving are reviewed in detail: scanning, analysis, response, and assessment (SARA). It is noted that during the scanning process, to warrant police attention, the following four conditions must exist: (1) a problem must involve a group of incidents; (2) two or more problems similar in nature must exist; (3) the problem is causing harm or has the potential to cause harm; and (4) the public expects the police agency to handle the problem. Sources of information for identifying problems are also presented.

This module also reviews the second step of POP—analysis, or the actual investigation of the problems. Included in analysis is the generation of a number of different solutions to this problem. These solutions may be simple or complex, depending on the degree of difficulty the problem presents.

The third step, response, is the actual selection and implementation of a solution. These solutions may produce the following impacts: (1) totally eliminating the problem; (2) reducing the number of incidents the problem creates; (3) reducing the seriousness of the incidents the problem creates; (4) designing methods for better handling the incidents it creates; or (5) removing the problem from police consideration. Each of these receives considerable attention in this module. A solution is then selected based on a number of factors including cost, legality, and likelihood of success.

Staff also covers the fourth step, assessment, in which the effectiveness of solutions is evaluated. Instructors show that the problem is solved, reduced in scope, or becomes larger. Staff teaches that a number of measurements may be used for evaluation, including calls for service, citizen satisfaction, and numbers of complaints. Instructors also stress that each project requires an assessment tailored to it.

The last phase of Module III consists of reviewing several forms designed to facilitate officers' efforts to undertake POP (These are included in the appendix.). The first is a "Request to Open POP Project." This form provides a basic overview of the problem and allows the officer's direct supervisor to approve the beginning of the project. The second is a "POP Data Sheet," which lists the criminal justice and social service agencies and phone numbers which the officer contacted in the POP process. A third form, the "Officer's Log," gives a written diary of the officer's actions. The last form is the "Narrative Summary," which is to be written by the officer after he has completed the project. These forms provide officers with a consistent, easily followed method for identifying and solving problems.

The final portion of this module presents a videotape, made by the Fort Myers Florida Police Department depicting an innovative response to problems created by transients. Finally, the module deals with problem-solving exercises furnished by the Tempe Arizona Police Department. Completed Savannah Police POP projects are also added to this repertoire to emphasize relevance to the Savannah community.

Module IV–Referral System, Materials, City Ordinances

The fourth module examines the importance of a good referral system and how to use specific city ordinances in dealing with subjects. The students are given the following four handouts:

1. Module IV Notes–which answer the student performance objectives. These objectives are:
    a. List three of the six benefits that a good referral system provides a police agency.
    b. State in writing three elements of a good referral.
    c. State in writing the one reason why First Call for Help is the most important number to remember.
    d. State three sources of obtaining materials to give to citizens explaining referral services.
    e. What one brochure should officers have at all times?
    f. Where can an SPD officer get a City Code Manual to refer to?
    g. List three city codes that have been used successfully in the past to charge offenders.

2. Referral Agencies in Chatham County

3.   Toll-Free Numbers of National Hotlines

4.   City Ordinances

This module focuses on the importance of referrals. Good referrals include pertinent information (i.e., address, phone number), what is expected from the referral, and how contact by the citizen with the officer is made for more information. The officer is encouraged to visit the subject a few days after the referral is made to ascertain whether the responsible agency is working with the resident to solve the problem.

Officers are provided with a key telephone number which is available 24 hours a day that refers the officers to all available agencies. Training participants are also given a list of phone numbers of all the referral agencies in Chatham County. A book, *Community Services Directory*, which is produced in conjunction with the United Way, is presented. A copy of this book is located in each precinct and explains the type and scope of services each agency offers. A second list of national hotline phone numbers is given to each participant. This list includes numbers to Poison Control, Cocaine, and the Fair Housing Commission.

Three films are shown in this module: the Savannah Police Department's response to Domestic Violence (LENET #4, cassette 9), Police Response to Seizures and Epilepsy (Police Foundation), and Police Response to Alzheimer's. These are intended to introduce officers to different types of situations where referrals may be appropriate. The parallel is drawn that just as POP projects try to solve problems in the community for the long-term, referrals are used to try to solve long-term human problems. Preparing officers to act as conduits for aid to a person or family, may prevent future criminality arising from these problems.

A number of specific materials generated by helping agencies are distributed to the officers in this module. It is suggested that they carry examples of each in their briefcases to distribute to those who need information.

The last part of the module concerns city ordinances. These are laws that the city council has passed that are enforceable only within the city limits. The staff developed a document of the ordinances applicable and successfully used in the past by the department. This acquaints the officers with conduct that they may not know is illegal and provides them with authority to investigate certain actions by citizens if appropriate. An actual case, where city ordinances are used, is presented.

Module V–Developing Sources of Human Information

This module is the best received by the officers, who refered to it as the "real" police work module. It is also the most controversial among supervisors and city attorneys. It stresses that all contact with people is important and explains this contact on the basis of a continuum, from that causing the least intrusion to that causing the most intrusion. This module addresses the "gray" areas in the law and examines those police-citizen contacts that cause the most controversy and cause officers the most problems. Handouts for this module consist of:

1. Module V Notes–which answer the student performance objectives. These objectives are:
   a. Define the "GAP" problem in listening.
   b. List 4 ways to enhance active listening.
   c. List 4 barriers to effective listening.
   d. List the 5 areas a citizen can be affected (internal checklist) by contact with a police officer.
   e. List the 4 areas on which a field interview may be based.
   f. List the 2 additional reasons, over and above a field interview, an investigative detention requires.
   g. The "threshold inquiry" during an investigative detention is limited to 4 questions. List them.
   h. Define the topics of each of the following 3 Georgia Statutes:
      (1) 16-11-36
      (2) 16-10-24
      (3) 16-10-25
   i. List 5 areas which may motivate an informant.
   j. Name the S.O.P. that covers informants.
   k. In what ways does developing sources of human information properly promote COP?

2. "Specific Occupations Providing Useful Information," SPD Staff.

3. "Types of Police-Citizen Contacts," SPD Staff.

The first part of the module deals with how officers can enhance active listening. Because they are problem solvers, they must gather information as part of that process. Developing good interpersonal communications, particularly active listening skills, is essential to the COP process.

The second portion stresses that no incident in police-citizen contact is trivial. There are five outcomes to all police-citizen contact: (1) The citizen's problem is either solved or unsolved; (2) He feels either better or worse about the situation; (3) He has more or less respect for the police; (4) He is either more or less likely to call the police again; and (5) He is either more or less supportive of the police. Instructors also emphasize that after the contact with the police officer, the citizen is either more or less likely to: (1) give the police the benefit of the doubt when listening to rumors; (2) discuss order maintenance concerns with the police; (3) supply information to the police because he feels that the officer is concerned with the neighborhood and the people who live there; and (4) feel that the officer will treat all citizens as if they are important.

The instructors stress that at one time or another most people have information about a crime. If citizens trust the police, they will share this information. Instructors discuss occupations that, because of their nature, have numerous contacts with other people and thus have the potential of providing police with important crime information.

The focus of this module is on four types of contacts police can have with citizens: Daily police-citizen contacts, field interviews, investigatory detentions (including pat-downs), and informants. Distinction between field interviews and investigatory detentions is somewhat controversial.

The instructors show that field interviews are entirely voluntary on the part of the subject. The officers stop the subject for the expressed purpose of acquiring identifying information. The subject can tell the officer that he does not want to cooperate or, at any time during the field interview, decide to end it. The stop may be based on criminal activity in the area, previous criminal record of the subject, the person's behavior, or hour of the day or night.

The instructors show the investigatory detention may or may not be voluntary. This stop may be based on the same factors as a field interview but, in addition, there must be a substantial possibility that the person has committed a crime or that criminal activity is afoot. The threshold inquiry is limited to the following information: name, address, what the subject is doing, and where the subject is going.

Because this module deals with "gray areas" in the law, in this case, the distinction between field interviews and investigatory detentions, officers and managers found it confusing and controversial. For example, many officers believe that if a person did not cooperate during a field interview, that made the subject a candidate for an investigative detention.

Formulating this module was not without problems, and although staff consulted with veteran police officers, prosecutors, and judges, being careful to articulate these "gray areas" with as much precision as possible, there were divisions among the cadre of experts consulted. Many believed, for example, that the differentiation between field interviews and investigatory detentions served little purpose, and would only "raise questions" for which answers would be difficult to derive. SPD training staff concluded, however, that the "gray areas" of police work are what cause the most divisiveness in the community. As part of COP, police must candidly and forthrightly address those areas of controversy and include them in the training.

The last portion of the module deals with informants. Trainers review the historical significance of informants to law enforcement, what motivates them, what questions they ask police officers, and some general rules for interacting with them. Module V integrates training on developing information sources, training traditionally reserved for quasi-experts (investigators), into SPD's COP repertoire. Line officers enjoy it and begin to understand the relevance of information sources to COP, and more importantly, see COP as the proper context in which "real policing" can be done.

Module VI–Neighborhood Meetings, Survey of Citizen Needs, Tactical Crime Analysis

At this writing, Module VI is being designed. Its objectives are to show patrol officers how to conduct neighborhood meetings, surveys of citizen needs, and tactical crime analysis. The common thread to these is that each requires face-to-face contact of police with citizens.

The section covering neighborhood meetings consists of showing officers how to organize and facilitate them. It includes identifying types of groups that may exist in different precincts. For example, some groups form around specific problems and dissolve once they are solved. Other groups have long-term concerns or are part of a larger organization that wants continuing contact with the government and the police. Officers will be taught how to organize, coordinate, and assist neighborhood group meetings to provide a forum for the exchange of ideas and to identify solutions to neighborhood problems.

Conducting citizen surveys will cover formulating questions, pre-testing the questions, gathering data, and analyzing the results. The Savannah Police Department's research and planning unit will provide guidance in the development of this part of the module. The department has a history of joint efforts by its research analysts and sworn personnel in the development, administration, and analysis of survey instruments. This was accomplished in the areas of bike patrol surveys and public housing policy.

The last portion of this module, tactical crime analysis, is designed to show officers how to organize and interpret crime data to obtain accurate daily pictures of crime trends in their beats, precincts, and citywide. Emphasis will be placed on detecting and analyzing characteristics and methods of operation, contextual conditions precipitating victimization, and victim characteristics. Analysis and description of patterns (geographic distribution) and trends (temporal distribution) will be directed at prevention and apprehension. Last, the staff will discuss the urgency for timely (daily) dissemination of these data to patrol and investigative officers.

Module VII–Crime Prevention Home and Business Surveys

This module will discuss crime prevention in the context of COP. Although the Savannah Police Department has crime prevention officers assigned to each precinct, this module will stress that crime prevention is every officer's job. The roles of patrol, investigations, special operations, and staff services in crime prevention will be discussed. In addition, strategies linking police and private business efforts to prevent crime will be presented.

An important part of this module will be training officers on how to conduct security surveys of homes and businesses. Upon completion of this module, every officer will know what to look for in terms of improving environmental design and physical security.

A summation of all the previous six modules will conclude Module VII. The purpose of this summation will be to integrate the previous instruction into an organic whole. It is also meant to reinforce the notion of COP as a dynamic, fluid concept or philosophy that may dictate changes in policy, strategies, and tactics over time to accomplish the department's mission.

CONCLUSION

This chapter presents a training paradigm that may be useful to departments engaged in the planning and administration of community policing. Although these seven modules are distinct and separate, they are designed to be integrated and presented over the long term.

Module I serves to introduce management to the overarching principles of community policing and the critical nature of its role in implementing it. This module stresses the creation of an environment in which patrol officers are made to feel confident of their new role as decision-makers and problem-solvers. Because COP will fail without this environment, this becomes perhaps the most critical phase of training. Reluctance on the part of management to relinquish centralized control of vital police functions generates nothing. Any reservation on the part of mid- and upper-level managers to support community policing must be negotiated here, otherwise the succeeding modules are largely superfluous.

Module II is designed to give rank-and-file employees an overview of community policing, the context in which it arose in Savannah, and the expectations of line officers, supervisory personnel, and managers. Module III is dedicated to a thorough treatment of problem-oriented policing (POP) and the procedures and forms to complete it. Considerable attention is paid to the SARA model, with specific direction on how to conduct a POP project. POP is characterized as an essential element complementing the larger, overarching concept of community policing.

Community-specific strategies and tactics are addressed in Module IV. Here, particular city ordinances and referral systems unique to the jurisdiction, are covered. Module V shows officers how to develop sources of human information, an essential skill to both problem-solving and developing valuable linkages with community residents. Unique to this module is its innovative use of the intrusion continuum to teach traditional policing skills dealing with the "gray areas" of criminal law and procedure. Modules VI and VII, while still in the design stage, present formalized instruction in proactive policing. Areas not generally considered part of traditional patrol work will be explored in detail. Officers will be taught how to organize and manage neighborhood meetings, conduct formal surveys of citizens' needs, perform tactical crime analysis, and conduct business and residential security surveys. In addition, patrol officers will be trained in counseling residents on improving crime prevention tactics and strategies.

Feedback loops are, of course, built into the training cycle; consequently the content and substance of the modules may vary somewhat from one set of administrations to another. This is as it should be for it accurately reflects the nature of communities in transition, communities with quality-of-life and public-safety needs that are subject to change over time. As a result, community policing is a dynamic style of policing and, by its nature, offers few templates to govern its implementation, particularly in the area of training.

In traditional police training, course titles and content, beyond the point of definitive criminal and case law, were designed to reflect the peculiarities of the police subcultures in which they were administered. With community policing, the equation is further complicated by the necessity to factor in the specific values and expectations of the communities being policed. And, of course, these values vary across a city's communities as well as within the same community over time. The Savannah Police Department, after a two-year analysis of the conditions fostering crime in the city, has succeeded in hypothesizing what it believes to be the approach uniquely fitted to its jurisdiction (Donahue, 1993). Contained in these pages may be some very general guidance to other departments with respect to initiating or revising COP training. Our only admonition to the reader is to pick and choose judiciously, testing the relevance of this training regime to the specific needs of the community in which COP is be practiced.

Section IV

ADMINISTERING COMMUNITY-ORIENTED POLICING PROGRAMS

What are community police officers supposed to do? What, in fact, do they do? The article by Walsh (Chapter 9) describes the expectations that have evolved for community police officers in recent years. Based on data collected from sergeants in the field, Walsh summarized supervisor's expectations and reported problems they encountered. Most important, however, is the list of recommendations that Walsh provides for departments beginning community policing. The answers to the second question we had to seek out in original research as reported in our article in this section (Chapter 10). We reviewed Duty Logs, conducted direct interviews with Neighborhood Police Officers and made site visits to local neighborhoods. This gave us a perspective for understanding the quantified data produced from the Duty Logs.

To our surprise, we found that time use by neighborhood police officers was much like that reported by many researchers during the past two decades for district officers with the notable exception that time is dedicated to communication with citizens. Like their fellow officers serving the district, the majority of time is spent in administrative matters. One-half of the officers spent almost four hours of the day in administrative matters and one-third of the officer-shifts were comprised of 60 percent to 80 percent administrative work.

A principal charge of the neighborhood police officer is to provide a personal link between the citizenry and the police department. Nearly an hour and a half is spent each shift (on average) in direct communication with citizens, but this distribution is skewed. The bottom quartile of officer-shifts had no contact at all with citizens while the top quartile ranged from more than two hours to seven and a half hours. The average time spent on citizen-related communication over all officer-shifts is slightly under 21 percent.

Slightly less time is devoted to patrol than to direct communication with citizens, just less than 19 percent of the total Duty Log time. Just under 20 percent of the officer-shifts involved no patrol at all and nearly nine out of 10 officer-shifts are characterized by less than 40 percent of the shift devoted to patrol activity.

Time in responsive law enforcement and number of arrests and citations account for 3 percent of the shift. The mean time spent towing cars and issuing citations per neighborhood police officer shift is less than 13 minutes. Of the 97 shifts during which the neighborhood police officer responded to a law enforcement situation, on 77 shifts the incident took less than 20 percent of his/her time. On 50 percent of the shifts no warrants, citations, or arrests are made. The majority of actions occur in 25 percent of the shifts and when they do, they often occur in quite a flurry. Only 3 incidents during this research period resulted in a neighborhood police officer initiating and completing an arrest; another 5 incidents occurred in which an officer served as backup for a district officer.

Community police officers spend limited, if any, time in traditional law enforcement pursuits. This is consistent with the charge for their units to be oriented toward crime prevention. They are to be accessible, informative, and helpful to citizens in the neighborhoods. This "presence" in the neighborhood appears to work when the officer has found the "right mix" of time in his/her Duty Log for the neighborhood.

Community police officers can feel quite beset by their "open-ended" duties to the neighborhood. Perhaps the most obvious form of conflict is to be at once available to all while also dealing with specific and individual problems in depth greater than district officers are able. We found that all community police officers relied upon technology (telephones and answering machines) to help them circumvent this conflict. They structured their time to allow this technology to help them.

The community police officer's use of time to respond either with a phone call or a visit to the home of a resident with a problem has helped to produce an atmosphere of closeness to the police that has not been felt in many neighborhoods for decades. "Patrol" is also a part of this closeness; great personal contact is made on foot patrol, but in today's police department, the neighborhoods to be covered are often quite extensive, necessitating car patrol.

For reasons discussed in this chapter, it is our conclusion that the time spent by neighborhood officers communicating with citizens and patrolling the neighborhood serves the community and the department very well.

In "An Assessment of Police Officers' Acceptance of Community Policing" (Chapter 11) by Peter Kratcoski and Susan Noonan, the results of a survey of police officers working in two large cities are given. While the response to community policing by the patrol officers employed in these cities is generally positive, it is apparent that many do not understand or accept the community policing philosophy and others equate community policing with police-community relations.

9

Analysis of the Police Supervisor's Role in Community Policing*

William F. Walsh
University of Louisville

INTRODUCTION

During the last decade, we have witnessed a purposeful shift in policing to community-oriented, problem-solving operational strategies (Skolnick & Bayley, 1986; Kelling, 1988; Goldstein, 1990; Moore, 1992, Kennedy, 1993). It is estimated that as many as two-thirds of the police departments serving communities of 50,000 population or more in the United States have embraced this new concept or plan to do so shortly (Trojanowicz & Bucqueroux, 1992). Community-oriented policing incorporates both a managerial and operational orientation that aspires to redirect police resources toward the substantive problems associated with the root causes of community crime and disorder (Wilson & Kelling, 1982; Kelling, 1988; Skolnick & Bayley, 1988; Goldstein, 1990; Skogan, 1990). This objective is to be achieved by the employment of differential patrol strategies through which it is hoped the community and the police department will form a mutual self-defense effort against crime, fear of crime and neighborhood decay (Skolnick & Bayley, 1988; Trojanowicz & Bucqueroux, 1990). Skogan (1990:91-92) summaries the guiding principles of underlying this movement as follows:

1. Community Policing assumes a commitment to broadly focused, problem-oriented policing.

---

* This article is a revision of a paper presented at the Academy of Criminal Justice Sciences Meeting, Kansas City, Missouri, March 1992.

2.   Community Policing relies upon organizational decentralization and reorientation of patrol tactics to open informal, two-way channels of communication between police and citizens.

3.   Community Policing requires that police be responsive to citizen demands when they decide what local problems are, and set their priorities.

4.   Community Policing implies a commitment to helping neighborhoods help themselves by serving as a catalyst for local organizing and education efforts.

In the majority of police departments now experimenting with community-oriented policing, individual officers designated as community police officers (CPOs) are either assigned to a defined neighborhood foot-patrol beat or to a community-based team operating in a specific area. These officers are instructed to develop a greater familiarity with the residents on their beats, identify crime and order maintenance problems, and function as communications links between beat residents, the police department, and other municipal services (Farrell, 1988). In addition to the traditional law enforcement activities of observing, reporting, citing or arresting, they are expected to develop nontraditional responses to beat problems that enhance the safety and security of their area (Skolnick & Bayley, 1988; Trojanowicz & Bucqueroux, 1990).

Conceptually, community policing is a bottom-ups organizational strategy that places emphasis on the CPO's ability to use judgment, wisdom, and expertise in working with neighborhood residents to fashion creative approaches to contemporary problems (Trojanowicz & Bucqueroux, 1992). In order to accomplish their mission, COPs are expected to undertake a number of specific proactive activities on a daily basis that include, but are not limited to:

1.   Operating neighborhood substations.

2.   Meeting with community groups.

3.   Analyzing and solving neighborhood problems.

4.   Working with citizens on crime prevention programs.

5.   Conducting door-to-door surveys of residents.

6.   Talking with students in school.

7.   Meeting with local merchants.

8. Making security checks of businesses.

9. Dealing with disorderly people (Mastrofski, 1992:24)

These activities are intended to put the officer in direct contact with community residents and enhance his or her opportunity to obtain information regarding neighborhood problems. Their ultimate goal is to make the community police officers more responsive to the quality-of-life concerns of community citizens and to assist them in developing ways to create a safer, less crime-prone neighborhood.

This mode of operation, however, necessitates that the community police officer be granted autonomy from the demands of the police radio, time, resources, and support to work on community problems. Departments experimenting with community-oriented strategies usually free COPs from the 911 response system or assign them to non-emergency service calls emanating from their neighborhood beats. It is hoped that these efforts will not only enhance the quality and quantity of citizen police contacts but also assist in addressing the needs of specific neighborhoods with the resource capabilities of the department and the local community.

This form of policing necessitates that police administrators adopt a flexible, decentralized management style that enhances the autonomy and responsibility of the community police officers. This administrative redirection, however, represents a serious challenge to mainstream police managerial philosophy that espouses the maximization of efficiency, rational decision making, cost-effective procedures, and accountability at all levels of policing (Lynch, 1986; Sheehan & Cordner, 1989; Swanson, Territo & Taylor, 1993). Police administrators traditionally favor the centralization of managerial control, uniformity of procedures and policy, strong discipline and efficient use of personnel and technology. This value system favors an organizationally centered style of management that views a community and its residents as part of its problem-generating environment. It has created police organizations in which community problems are treated as single incidents to be addressed by standard operating procedures and rapid response of patrol units (Wilson & McLaren, 1977; Sheehan & Cordner, 1989; Bennett & Hess, 1992; Swanson, Territo & Taylor, 1993).

The community-oriented policing movement's advocacy of the expansion of the police mission beyond crime control to decentralization and personalization of police services and empowerment of line officers as problem solvers is the antithesis of this traditional police management orientation (Murphy & Muir, 1985; Weisburd, McElroy & Hardyman, 1989). It casts the community policing officer in a community social activists role similar to that advocated by the late Saul Alinsky and the founders of the community organization movement in the famous Chicago School of Sociology during the 1920s and 1930s (Broderick, 1990). Many police traditionalists view these activities as "soft policing." It is feared that community policing will lead individual officers to act more like politicians than police officers, thus violating the political neutrality of the police (Short, 1983). While some warn that in solving community problems the police might exceed the legal limits of their authority and revert to "street justice" (Manning, 1984; Walker, 1984; Klockars, 1985b; and Sykes, 1986). If these critics are to be taken seriously then the supervision of community policing operations is a critical factor in the success of this movement.

However, as more and more police departments commence community-oriented policing operations, supervisors are finding themselves in command of community policing units with limited preparation and organizational support for this demanding assignment. This analysis focuses on the forces shaping the supervisor's role in community policing and offers some recommendations relative to that role and the management of community-oriented operations.

THE POLICE SUPERVISOR'S ROLE

Police supervisors, like their counterparts in all organizations, serve an oversight function controlling line operations for management. They are responsible for seeing that police officer performance complies with organizational policy, procedures, and legal standards of behavior. Supervisors constitute the major link between a department's management and line personnel; policy and practice (Thibault, Lynch & McBride, 1986; Walsh & Donovan, 1990). They are an officer's primary contact with the department. As such, the quality of an officer's daily work day is heavily dependent on how well the officer satisfies the expectations and demands of his or her immediate supervisor (Ericson, 1982; Goldstein, 1991).

In order to fulfill their organizational responsibilities, supervisors must have a clear understanding of management's expectations as well as an awareness of the competence and commitment of their subordinates. These demands require that supervisors keep current on the changes that take place in the law, policy, procedures, and management practices that affect them and their officers. In turn, the decisions made by supervisors regarding the utilization of their subordinates to meet operational directives and workload demand affect not only the individuals involved but the department's performance objectives, effectiveness, and financial liability as well (Sheehan & Cordner, 1995).

Police supervisors usually hold the rank of either Sergeant, Corporal, or in some smaller departments, Acting Supervisor. They perform their control function by maintaining a day-by-day follow-up over their officers' routine activities, not only to ascertain the suitability of their officers' work product, but also to ensure that the department's behavioral standards are followed in contacts with citizens. The supervisor is the one member of the department's management team who is in the best position to prevent a situation that could lead to embarrassment and or liability for an officer and the department. This is because their role places them in close proximity to officers on a daily basis which permits them to directly observe officers and detect performance problems or misbehavior (Gaines, Southerland & Angell, 1991).

Police supervisors operate in an increasingly complex litigious world that structures their authority. Supervisory action is governed by the Law of Contract, Collective Bargaining Agreements, Civil Law, Federal Regulatory Law, Administrative Law, State Law, Court decisions governing employment and basic Constitutional Rights. Supervisors have an affirmative legal duty to take appropriate action when subordinate behavior is inconsistent with law or departmental policy and procedures. Failure to perform this duty may subject the supervisor to a charge of negligence and possible liability (del Carmen, 1991:227). As a result, both management and the law exert pressure on police supervisors to be control oriented.

However, the effective supervisor not only monitors and guides officer performance but also must find a way to balance the need for structure and authority against the need for creativity and discretion (Bieck, Spelman & Sweeney, 1991). This can be especially problematic in traditional police organizations where the interaction between management and line personnel is often adversarial. Supervisor find themselves caught between the pragmatic value system of the street patrol officers coupled with the need to avoid second-guessing their officers, and the demands of law, department policy, and the values of police managerial professionalism (Brown, 1981; Reuss-Ianni, 1983). This is particularly true in community-oriented police operations when supervisors find themselves caught between the control orientation of their organizational managers and the discretionary needs of their COPs. These competing demands can create a classic conflict position for community police supervisors. Most supervisors will attempt to strike a balance between these competing demands. However, the resolution of this dilemma is often difficult because the final authority and review of a supervisor's role performance rests with management.

COMMUNITY-ORIENTED POLICE SUPERVISION

Community-oriented policing operations require that supervisors shift managerial styles from a control orientation to one that accounts for the officer's knowledge of and involvement in the community and the adequacy of their problem-solving activities (Weisburg, McElroy & Hardyman, 1989). Supervisors are expected to employ a participative style of supervision in which they are to function as facilitators, problem solvers, resources and conduits for the community officers and their community (Payne & Trojanowicz, 1985; Ward, 1985). Goldstein (1990:158) claims that they must shield their officers from peer pressure to revert to traditional policing tactics while sustaining the community police officers autonomy, creativity, flexibility, and ingenuity. In addition, they are required to become involved with their officers in diagnosing community problems, organizing community residents and developing strategies to address community needs. At the same time, however, they are accountable that department-level concerns are effectively integrated and addressed in their unit's planning and operational functioning.

In short, the community-oriented policing movement is asking supervisors to take on duties and risks that were unimagined in their organizational training and development but are now considered vital to the success of this innovation.

THE STUDY

These thoughts prompted an examination of the community-oriented policing supervisor's role during a series of seminars in 1992. Seminar participants were members of police departments presently engaged in or about to commence community police operations. The subjects of this analysis are 60 police sergeants who function as supervisors in medium to large police departments (i.e., 50-150 sworn personnel). Although, they do not constitute a random sample of all community policing supervisors, they do represent a convenient sample of positional informants from which information can be drawn about community-oriented operations in second-tier smaller municipal departments presently engaged in this organizational change. The sergeants are employed in 18 municipal police departments located int he Northeastern part of the United States.

The average police supervisor participating in the study is a white male 27 years of age, with 16 years in the police service and five years in rank as a supervisor. The average educational attainment of the study group is less than two years of college with four participants having attained a four-year college degree. During the initial seminar contact, the participants were asked to identify the supervisory related problems they were experiencing with community-oriented policing and record these problems on paper. Their responses were collected, analyzed, and incorporated in a group problem-solving sequences during the seminar. Data reported here were drawn from the problem identification and solution identification sessions. Some of the key problems identified are shown in Table 9.1.

Table 9.1 Summary of Sergeant's Responses

Problem	Frequency *	%
Lack of support and understanding from patrol supervisors and officers.	50	83
Minimal managerial support.	46	77
No job description for C.P. supervisor and COPs	43	72
No policy or directives regarding community policing program.	39	65
Evaluation process statistical oriented does not reflect COP's duties.	39	65
Limited and/or inadequate training	37	62
Lack of input in CPO selection	31	52
C.P. Supervisor's authority limited.	28	47

*Supervisors frequently listed more than one problem.

FINDINGS

A major finding is that 85 percent of the supervisors (N=51) disclosed that intra-organizational difficulties were their main concern, not operational or personnel control. This subject became a major discussion topic in the problem-solving sessions. The most frequently reported problem, 83 percent (N=50), is a lack of support and understanding from patrol supervisors and officers. In addition, 77 percent (N=46) claim they received minimal managerial support. These two problems were jointly reported by 40 supervisors. In the discussion sessions, participants continually voiced the opinions that operational personnel considered community-oriented policing as "soft-policing" or not "real police work while managerial support among mid-level managers was limited or nonexistent.

One supervisor stated that during his chief's introduction of the program at a department training session he made the remark that, "There is nothing new about this, we performed foot-patrol thirty years ago, it's a costly form of policing but now we are going back to its thanks to the federal government." The sergeant interpreted this as evidence that the chief had little understanding or support for community-oriented policing. In this department the development of the program and funding was accomplished by the Captain in charge of the operation's division. Another supervisor stated that when he attended a roll-call to inform the patrol officers of his unit's operational efforts, the shift commander remarked, "I understand all the assholes are now called customers," clearly indicating hostility for the community-oriented program.

In addition, many seminar participants felt their programs lacked legitimacy because their department's policy did not set forth the programs purpose, personnel authority, and duties. The discussants claimed that these were established in the grant application used to obtain funds for the program but were never incorporated in the department's directive system. Thus, contributing to a feeling among the supervisors that the program is temporary and will be disbanded when the funding ends. Also, the lack of procedural guidelines has caused problems for some supervisors who have been questioned by senior-level managers regarding the appropriateness of the activities of the community policing officers.

Many of the supervisors claimed that they were placed in their operation role with little or no prior training. They were selected on the basis of prior performance or given the task because they had crime prevention training. More than one-half of the participants stated that their role preparation consisted of a generalized introduction to the philosophy and purpose of community policing with an emphasis on community outreach rather than supervisory requirements of this new style of policing. Training programs containing inspirational talks and war stories by apostles of this movement are not sufficient to prepare a department for the transition from philosophy to operational reality. In addition, many resented their lack of input in the selection of their CPOs.

However, 15 percent of the sample (N=9) offered a different perspective of their programs. These supervisors belong to four different municipal police departments in which the chief's leadership is the driving force behind this organizational change. All these supervisors claim that community policing has reduced service calls and has gained significant support throughout the department and the community. In each of these departments, the chief established external political and community support for the program prior to establishing it. Once the program was commenced each of these chiefs worked closely with the program supervisors to insure that it became established properly.

For example, in one municipality, the chief first sought support and funding from the local business community before attempting to institute the program. He started the program on a few beats and after positive results were obtained, the program was expanded with additional funding from business and community organizations. This program cost the department in personnel resources only; equipment, office space, and officer overtime were paid for by business and community funding.

A secondary finding resulting from the discussion sessions is that many of these supervisors were having problems balancing their traditional control orientation with the autonomy needs of their officers. This problem is more of a factor in those departments in which the supervisors are facing a general lack of support from management. Some participants noted that although administrators in their department voice support for team building and employee participation, their actual behavior is control oriented. This concern for control was reinforced by several individuals who expressed fear that the COP's familiarity with community members and operational freedom may lead to deviations from their department's standards of behavior which would give management an excuse to end the program.

DISCUSSION

Community policing is attempting to change reactive organizations into proactive ones. The successful implementation of this change necessitates that line supervisors whom for the majority of their careers have operated as reactive problem solvers in control-oriented bureaucratic organizations become proactive leaders of innovation. This demanding role requires individuals with special abilities, training, education, and commitment to their mission. These skills include problem conceptualization, synthesis and analysis of information, ability to develop complex plans, conduct evaluations, and communicate with diverse groups within and without of the department (Riechers & Roberg, 1990). It may be argued that to a greater or lesser degree some police supervisors possess these skills and perform these tasks already. This should be true for the skill level of supervisors in those departments than have made higher education a promotional requirement but for the vast majority of police departments, it is not (Carter, Sapp & Stephens, 1989;

Riechers & Royber, 1990). In addition, most supervisors have little experience with the diverse public they will be called upon to interact with in community-oriented policing.

Community policing supervisors will require a great amount of organizational support to ensure that they and the officers who work for them are able to fulfill their mandate while at the same time establishing a basis upon which this operational philosophy can be spread throughout the department. If the leadership of their departments fail to provide vision, inspiration, support and a climate of organizational cooperation this reform will fail as did Neighborhood Team Policing (Sherman, Milton & Kelly, 1973). Organizational support must not be in the form of "lip service" designed to obtain initial funding to increase department resources as some of the subjects of this analysis believe has happened in their departments. It requires the operationalization of community-oriented policing through policy and practice that clearly define roles, functions, duties, and responsibilities of program participants. Administrators need to establish criteria by which they can identify qualified officers to serve as COPs and supervisors as well as what constitutes appropriate training for these individuals. It is apparent from this analysis that little attention has given to these matters.

These findings further suggest that researchers of community-oriented policing programs specifically examine the dual issues of how community police units are integrated into their department's organizational structure, as well as how the culture of the department contributes to or hinders this operational reform. If there is to be true reform in policing, the last thing we need is for the unit's to develop into what Toch and Grant (1991:65) termed "innovative ghettos" isolating the people who are in them. This was often the case with previous community-oriented reforms in policing (Greene, 1989). When this happens the program officers will, as some of our participants indicated, become labeled as individuals who are not real cops and who are not doing policing.

Many believe that a department should put its "best" supervisors in charge of these units. However, the best sergeants will not be able to function over a long period of time in an organization that is offering limited support to them. A major challenge for advocates of this reform movement lies in systemically changing the traditional police managerial culture to one more conducive to what is needed for this reform to succeed.

This movement, however, does represent a serious commitment on the part of many police executive officers to redirect their departments toward a more positive response to the needs of their diverse communities. It encourages an organizational philosophy dedicated to providing quality service that has renewed commitment on the part of line officers involved in community programs while at the same time enhancing their job satisfaction (Trojanowicz & Banas, 1985). A positive accomplishment for any police executive. It has enhanced debate and revitalized operational experimentation. It also has helped to create in policing an innovative, creative, and more responsive executive leadership. Although, the resourcefulness of the individuals selected to engage the community with these new police strategies and the willingness of police administrators and department rank-and-file to support their efforts are the important variables in the successful implementation of community-policing.

RECOMMENDATIONS

In light of this analysis, the following recommendations are suggested for departments about to engage in community-oriented policing:

1. Policy and procedures should be established that define the mission and objectives of the community policing program.

2. Job descriptions should be developed identifying the authority and duties of the community policing supervisor and COPs.

3. Departments should develop a characteristic profile upon which to base the selection of CPOs and supervisors.

4. Task-specific training should be given to community policing unit members that will prepare them for their specific function.

5. Departments should establish evaluation criteria upon which to assess the accomplishments of the community policing program and its members.

6. Community policing supervisors should be included in the department's operational planning.

7. Lastly, if the department is serious about community-oriented policing it should develop an operational plan for moving beyond the experimental stage, to a department-wide integration of this proactive style of policing.

CONCLUSION

Community-oriented policing represents a shift from a professional insularity to an orientation that sees the community and its police working together in an active partnership. First-line supervisors are crucial players in the operational success of community-oriented policing programs. Although the Sergeants' principal responsibility is still that of supervision, their success will depend upon their organizational support as well as their ability to facilitate creativity and innovation in themselves and their officers. The successful implementation of community-oriented operations will necessitate a change in the traditional police managerial culture from the domination of bureaucratic professionalism to a more facilitating management style accompanied with a normative system emphasizing community service. The validity of these observations are currently being tested in the police departments through out the United States. Time will tell whether these new operational methods will change policing or the traditional police organizational culture will win out.

10

Activity Time Allocations
of Community Policing Officers*

Peter C. Kratcoski
Kent State University

Duane Dukes
John Carroll University

INTRODUCTION

Researchers, policy-makers and police practitioners have recognized that some groups, youths, and minorities in particular, are not satisfied with the police (Sparrow, 1990; Goldstein, 1990). In response to this, there have been various attempts to provide different types of policing that is more sensitive to the needs and problems of these special groups. These specialized programs, while taking many forms, are often given the label community policing.

Studies show that at least 76 percent of all police activity is citizen initiated (Decker, 1981). Attitudes toward the police are often used as measures of the effectiveness of policing activities. What residents and organizations think about local policing and what newspapers or interest groups publicize can be significant in determining police policies for local communities (Sherman, 1986). Community attitudes can restrict or enhance cooperation with the police in the achieving of their crime control objectives in the community as shown by Hahn (1971) who revealed that citizens who are dissatisfied with the police fail to report crime (Hahn, 1971).

---

* An earlier version of this paper was presented at the annual meeting of the Academy of Criminal Justice Sciences, Pittsburgh, Pennsylvania, March 1992. This research was supported by a grant (90-DG-D01-7098) from the Ohio Governor's Office of Criminal Justice Services.

Scaglion and Condon (1980) found that personal contact with the police explained more than 30 percent of the variance between those who viewed the police in a favorable manner and those who viewed police in an unfavorable manner when effects of differential evaluation of police service were controlled. While race was next in explaining the variance, it only accounted for six percent of the difference.

In another study of personal contact with the police, respondents who spoke with police officers "informally but officially," as in seeking directions, were more likely to have better opinions of police than those who did not have these contacts (Scaglion & Condon, 1980:488). In this study 93.7 percent of the respondents reporting informal, official contacts indicated that they were satisfied with police service (Scaglion & Condon, 1980). They conclude that "socioeconomic factors such as race, age, and income appear to have little direct effect on attitudes toward the police (Scaglion & Condon, 1980:493)." They also suggest that police-community relations programs designed to educate the public by featuring favorable aspects of the police role should include personal contact between the officer and the citizen or suffer limited success (Scaglion & Condon, 1980).

Trojanowicz (1986) observed that "the special interaction and close communications fostered between foot patrol officers and community residents allowed trust to build, regardless of the race of the officer involved." Further he observed that residents began assessing the officers' performance independent of the race of the officer.

Another variable influencing attitudes toward police discussed by Decker (1981) is neighborhood culture. "The effect of neighborhood, a contextual effect, of generating and reinforcing negative attitudes toward the police has been noted in other research. Schuman and Gruenberg (1972) concluded that the primary dimension which with satisfaction and dissatisfaction varies in the neighborhood." (Decker, 1981:83). Personal contact with the police is relevant to culture.

COMMUNITY POLICING

Community policing has as its core an "interactive process" by which the police and community jointly solve problems (Hartman, et al., 1988). It is characterized by organizational values that stress community involvement and key concepts such as decentralization, neighborhood police having responsibility for handling problems in the neighborhoods, problem solving, and respect for the community being policed (Hartman, et al., 1988). The goals of community policing are generally defined in terms of controlling crime, reducing the fear of crime, maintaining order, and improving the quality of life in the neighborhoods.

The research showing that neighborhood culture and personal contact with police can determine attitudes toward the police supports the fundamental idea of community policing. Efforts to direct individualized police service to the neighborhood is one way to improve citizen satisfaction.

The origins of community policing can be traced back to when policing was rooted in the neighborhoods with officers walking a beat and being charged with the responsibility of keeping the neighborhoods safe and free from crime (Sparrow, 1988). Although the early system through the turn of the century was criticized for its corruption and politics, officers were well integrated into the neighborhoods. In retrospect, police experts saw that they did much good (Sparrow, 1988).

While there are several definitions of community problem solving currently being utilized, some distinguished neighborhood-oriented policing from problem-solving policing, while others accept the terms as interchangeable. Some definitions are narrow, only recognizing specific problem-oriented or problem-solving strategies (Goldstein, 1990); others accept a wide range of programs that focus on the neighborhood. Some look for a department-wide approach to community policing; others accept single program efforts. Most community policing programs now in place are special units of tactics aimed at improving levels of citizen satisfaction of reducing neighborhood crime.

Community policing is also an umbrella term applied to a wide range of specialized programs, such as mini-stations, store fronts, or foot patrol, which are incorporated in police departments across the country. Although the programs differ in specific features, they share many of the following operational and organizational principles:

1. Permanently assigning officers to specific neighborhoods or beats.

2. Developing a knowledge base about problems, characteristics, and resources in the neighborhoods.

3. Outreach to business and residents, making the police more visible in the neighborhoods.

4. Involving the community in identifying, understanding, and prioritizing local problems, and in developing and implementing plans to solve them.

5. Delegating responsibility to community police for creating solutions to crime and order maintenance problems.

6. Providing information to the community on local crime problems and police efforts to solve them.

7. Opening the flow of information from the community to the police to assist with making arrests and developing intelligence on unlawful activities in the community (Vera Institute of Justice, 1988; McElroy, et al., 1990; Goldstein, 1987).

Personal contact with the community is the foundation of community policing practice (Trojanowicz, 1988). Community policing puts officers in daily face-to-face contact with residents and businesses in the community. Many researchers and practitioners suggest that it is the close personal contact between the community and the police that accounts for the current popularity of the community model as an alternative to conventional police practice (Scaglion & Condon, 1980; Decker, 1981; Dunham & Alpert, 1988).

RESEARCH GOALS

The literature on community policing emphasizes the importance of close personal interaction of the community police officers with the residents of the communities in which they work, the purpose of this study is to contrast the activities of the officers who were assigned to the Cleveland Mini-Station program with regular patrol officers. Since the job descriptions of the Mini-Station officers specifically calls for community involvement, even in areas not traditionally considered police work, it is expected that the amount of time devoted to such service activities as attending community crime prevention meetings, talking with youth in the schools, conducting home safety inspections, and conducting follow-up calls with victims of crime would be much higher than that reported in the research on time studies of regular patrol officers.

Greene and Klockars (1991:199) report that the studies of police activity completed in the 1960s and 1970s concluded that 80 to 90 percent of police work is "service related" and approximately 10 percent of police work is "crime-related." They qualify this assertion, however, by mentioning that the results from some of these earlier works may be misleading in that accurate methods to measure police activity were not available and the researchers were often forced to rely on the recollections of police on how they spend their time, or by recording patrol officers' activities while riding along with them, or by analyzing calls that come into the dispatchers. For the latter, these calls only record the times when the officer may be actively engaged in responding to the call and not the numerous hours devoted to patrolling, goofing off, paperwork and other activities. These hours are generally thrown into the service category, thus inflating these functions. Cordner (1979) concludes that a great deal of police officer time is not committed to either law enforcement or assisting citizens, but the essence of the police workload is primarily determined by the citizens and it is reactive rather than proactive. Cumming, Cumming and Edell (1965) examine dispatch calls and conclude that about 10 percent of radio calls were law enforcement related, 30 percent order maintenance, 22 percent for information gathering and 38 percent for services. Bercal (1970) concluded that 16 percent of the calls could be classified as crime- and law-enforcement related.

Reiss (1971) using Chicago Police dispatch records concluded that 83 percent of patrol calls were noncriminal matters, but service-related activities accounted for only 14 percent of the officers' time. Most if the patrol officers' time was spent on regular patrol. From self-reported time studies and observational studies (riding along with the police) it was concluded by O'Neill and Bloom (1972) that only 5 percent of officers' time was devoted to crime-related activity and the larger amount of time devoted to patrolling. Kelling et al. (1974) stated that 60 percent of the patrol officers' time was over-committed and Cordner (1978) found that 55 percent of patrol officers' time was over-committed.

Mastrofski (1983) concluded that 71 percent of police activities were devoted to services that did not involve crime activity. Greene & Klockars (1991) using data obtained from a computer-aided dispatch system in Wilmington, Delaware, concluded that patrol officers devoted 29.35 percent of their time to general patrol, 15.09 percent investigating situations which were crime-related, 8.07 percent being involved in order-maintenance activities, 6.49 percent meal breaks and under 3 percent for all other crime-related activities. Direct service-related activities (such as medical emergency, opening car doors and helping motorists in distress) were very low, less than 10 percent (1991:278-279).

The author of this research concluded that regardless of the measures used "nearly half the time they (patrol officers) are doing police work they are dealing with criminal activity" (1991:281). They also concede that police work may have changed since the earlier studies in the 1960s and 1970s and police work of today as experienced by the patrol officer, particularly in the large cities, is more oriented toward crime control and crime-related activities.

We expected that officers who are involved in "community policing" would devote a considerably larger amount of their time to service-related activities than regular patrol officers as has been found in the research mentioned. The very essence and underlying philosophy of community policing is service to the community and if the community policing officers are performing in accordance with the mission to which they are charged, an analysis of community policing activities should reveal that the service function permeates all other activities.

The mini-station program in Cleveland, the subject of this research, is administered as a separate unit within the Cleveland Police Department. Officers operate independently of the basic patrol units. Cleveland's mini-station program was started in 1984. The purpose of the program is to provide more personal police protection to the neighborhoods. The mini-stations expanded the police capacity to respond to complaints and conduct preventative patrol in low and moderate income areas and to interact more directly with citizens through community organizations and crime watch meetings. The program emphasizes crime prevention.

Mini-Stations were established in 36 neighborhoods located throughout Cleveland. The mini-station staff includes one captain who is responsible for the overall operation of the unit, a lieutenant who oversees daily operations, six sergeants responsible for direct supervision, and 36 patrol officers assigned to the

36 neighborhood bases. Many mini-stations shared facilities with auxiliary police headquartered in churches, storefronts, apartment buildings, and office buildings.

The officers' fundamental duties include handling walk-in complaints, making reports; performing foot or car patrol in their assigned area; maintaining contact with neighborhood and business organizations; attending community meetings to encourage participation in the crime watch programs; conducting crime watch training to assist the community in crime prevention; providing crime prevention training to neighborhood residents is also a major program component of their mission; maintaining an active presence in the schools, and attempting to prevent the development of youth gangs, delinquency, and drug abuse problems; conducting safety programs for the elderly to enhance their street and home safety; identifying and correcting hazardous conditions in the neighborhood such as poor sanitation, abandoned cars and trucks, and working toward eliminating poor street lighting or housing code violations in that such conditions could cause disorder or contribute to neighborhood crime; and conducting follow-ups on crime-related incidents after a district police officer has filed a complaint. Mini-station officers train residents in neighborhood or "block watch" home security, auto theft deterrence and child protection.

Mini-station officers did not respond to radio-dispatched service calls. However, citizens could request service for neighborhood problems by calling the mini-station directly. Presently, the mini-stations are staffed by one officer who rotates his/her time schedule from 8:00 a.m. to 5:00 p.m., Tuesday, Thursday, and Saturday to 12:00 a.m. to 8:00 p.m. on Monday and Wednesday.

RESEARCH METHODOLOGY

As part of a larger research project evaluating the effectiveness of neighborhood policing, we collected Duty Log data on neighborhood police officers during the weeks of March 1, June 12, and October 23, 1990. These three weeks yielded data on a total of 430 "officer-shifts."

The Duty Log is a simple record of the events on the shift. Some of the vital information is quantified on the Log and we directly recorded it into our own databases. For the most part, however, information in the Log is given at the officer's own discretion. This fact required us to engage in an additional data coding step which is qualitative; a sample of records was read and a coding scheme devised which would be meaningful for this research. Important to this phase of the research is the fact that all members of the research team were involved in the other aspects of the research. We all conducted direct interviews with Neighborhood Police Officers and site visits in the local neighborhoods. This gave us a perspective for understanding the quantified data produced from the Duty Logs.

From this database we created six summary variables: LOGTOT, ADMTOT, COMTOT, PATTOT, ACTTOT, AND LAWTOT. In all but LAWTOT we measured the time (in minutes) that the officers indicated they spent on various tasks. LOG-TOT is the total amount of time reported on the Duty Log.

ADMTOT is intended to be the amount of time spent "Reporting in, Out, and Conferring" with other officers, "Filling Out Reports," and eating "Lunch." To this we added "Other;" 95 percent of which is comprised of "Office Duties," "Washing-Fueling-Repairing Auto," and the "AIM Test." (No more than 5 of the more than 450 entries refer to each of the following activities: "Response to Traffic Incident," "Assist Another Officer," "Process-Follow Up Arrest," and "Youth Resource.")

COMTOT is intended to reflect the amount of time spent by the neighborhood police officer in direct contact and communication with citizens in a preventive, mediating, facilitating, or diversionary manner. These include "Answering Telephone Messages," " Response to Citizen Complaint," "Response to Council Complaint," "Met with Citizens' Groups," and "Provided Information or Advice."

PATTOT is the amount of time spent by the neighborhood police officer in active patrol. We included both "Car Patrol" and "Foot Patrol." We separately recorded, because the officers quite often separated out, the "Special Attention Patrol."

ACTTOT is the amount of time spent in responsive law enforcement; in other words, the data we have under "Issue Citations" and "Towed Auto." ACTTOT is complemented by LAWTOT, the reported number of "Felony Arrests," "Misdemeanor Arrests," "Traffic Citations," "Moving Misdemeanors," "Parking Tickets Issued," "Summons Issued," and "Radio Calls."

The data for ADMTOT, COMTOT, PATTOT, and ACTTOT are reported in minutes and as percent of the total time on the log (PADMTOT, PCOMTOT, PPATTOT, and PACTTOT.) The percentage data are recoded and reported as RPADMTOT, RPCOMTOT, RPPATTOT, and RPACTTOT so that the distribution of time use is more evident.

DATA ANALYSIS

The range in total number of minutes reported (Table 10.2) is probably a product of two independent factors: (1) variation in actual shift length and (2) some variation in reporting "styles." Apparently not all officers felt equally compelled on all days to account for every minute of their behavior.

Table 10.1 Total Log Entries

Percentile	Value	Statistic	(NLOGTOT) Value
Minimum	1.000	Mean	9.533
25th	8.000	Median	9.000
50th	9.000	Mode	10.000
75th	11.000	Std dev	2.534
Maximum	18.000		
Valid cases	430	Missing cases	0

Despite this the majority of time on the shift is accounted for in the Duty Log. Table 10.1 shows that every Duty Log had at least one entry (which is appropriate if the work for the day is an assigned detail or if a particular response took the entire day) and averaged 9 entries.

Table 10.2 shows that these logs accounted for an average of nearly 7 hours of the day; since the brief transition time between duties and the time that it takes to use the restroom are not accounted for, the "lost" hour can be "found" by simply projecting 5 to 10 minutes for the 9 entries.

Table 10.2 Total Log Minutes

Percentile	Value	Statistic	(TLOGTOT) Value
Minimum	165.000	Mean	416.302
25th	375.000	Median	405.000
50th	405.000	Mode	405.000
75th	430.000	Std dev	86.558
Maximum	1020.000		
Valid cases	430	Missing cases	0

Table 10.3 Total Time Spent in Administrative Duties (in Minutes)

Percentile	Value	Statistic	(TADMTOT) Value
Minimum	20.000	Mean	239.070
25th	178.750	Median	230.000
50th	230.000	Mode	210.000
75th	290.000	Std dev	101.202
Maximum	890.000		
Valid cases	430	Missing cases	0

To our surprise, we found that time use by neighborhood police officers was much like that reported by many researchers for district officers during the past two decades with the notable exception that time is dedicated to communication with citizens. However, like their fellow officers serving the district, the majority of time is spent in administrative matters.

Table 10.4 Administrative Time as % of Total Time

		(PADMTOT)	
Percentile	Value	Statistic	Value
Minimum	.043	Mean	.577
25th	.428	Median	.585
50th	.585	Mode	1.000
75th	.726	Std dev	.205
Maximum	1.000		
Valid cases	430	Missing cases	0

Table 10.3 shows that all officers spent at least 20 minutes of the day, but that one-half of the officers spent almost four hours of the day in administrative matters. As Table 10.4 shows, this is approximately 58 percent of the day. The overall distribution of time (Table 10.5) shows that one-third of the officer-shifts were comprised of 60 percent to 80 percent administrative work while nearly another third were comprised of 40 percent to 60 percent administrative work. (Not shown here is the fact that very little of this time is actually devoted to lunch; many officers on many shifts logged 10 minutes or less for this and, as noted above, time for other personal reasons was not logged.)

Table 10.5 Administrative Time as % of Total Time (Recoded)

		(RPADMTOT)			
				Valid	Cum
Value Label	Value	Frequency	Percent	Percent	Percent
1% to 20%	1.00	13	3.0	3.0	3.0
20% to 40%	2.00	77	17.9	17.9	20.9
40% to 60%	3.00	138	32.1	32.1	53.0
60% to 80%	4.00	142	33.0	33.0	86.0
80% to 100%	5.00	60	14.0	14.0	100.0
	Total	430	100.0	100.0	

Mean   3.370   Median   3.000   Mode   4.000   Std dev   1.027
Valid cases   430   Missing cases   0

A principal charge of the neighborhood police officer is to provide a personal link between the citizenry and the police department. Elsewhere, we document the considerable effectiveness of this effort. This is all the more impressive considering the limited amount of actual time remaining to communicate with citizens.

Table 10.6 Total Time Communicating with Citizens (in Minutes)

		(TCOMTOT)	
Percentile	Value	Statistic	Value
Minimum	.000	Mean	86.174
25th	.000	Median	70.000
50th	70.000	Mode	.000
75th	140.000	Std dev	85.982
Maximum	450.000		
Valid cases	430	Missing cases	0

Table 10.6 shows that nearly an hour and a half is spent each shift (on average) in direct communication with citizens, but this distribution is skewed. The bottom quartile of officer-shifts had no contact at all with citizens while the top quartile ranged from more than two hours to seven and a half hours.

Table 10.7 shows that the average time spent on citizen-related communication over all officer-shifts is slightly under 21 percent. One-half of all logs sampled showed no more than 17.7 percent of the officers' time was spent in citizen-related communication; in three-quarters of these logs, no more than 35.7 percent of the time was spent in citizen-related communication.

Table 10.7 Time Communicating with Citizens as % of Total Time

		(PCOMTOT)	
Percentile	Value	Statistic	Value
Minimum	.000	Mean	.205
25th	.000	Median	.177
50th	.177	Mode	.000
75th	.357	Std dev	.193
Maximum	.767		

Table 10.8 Time Communicating with Citizens as % of Total (Recoded)

Value Label	Value	Frequency	Valid Percent	Cum Percent	Percent
		(RPCOMTOT)			
None	.00	114	26.5	26.5	26.5
1% to 20%	1.00	117	27.2	27.2	53.7
20% to 40%	2.00	119	27.7	27.7	81.4
40% to 60%	3.00	64	14.9	14.9	96.3
60% to 80%	4.00	16	3.7	3.7	100.0
		Total	430	100.0	100.0
Mean 1.421	Median 1.000	Mode 2.000		Std dev 1.139	

Table 10.8 shows that more than 25 percent of all logs sampled reported no citizen-related communication at all. Only 18.6 percent of the logs indicated that more than 40 percent of the time was spent in citizen-related communication.

Table 10.9 Total Time on Patrol (in Minutes)

Percentile	Value	Statistic	Value
		(TPATTOT)	
Minimum	.000	Mean	78.186
25th	25.000	Median	65.000
50th	65.000	Mode	.000
75th	115.000	Std dev	72.110
Maximum	450.000		
Valid cases	430	Missing cases	0

In interviews with neighborhood police officers that we conducted as a part of this study, officers often indicated that they spent "half the day" on patrol. In fact, slightly less time is devoted to patrol than to direct communication with citizens. About 78 minutes on average (Table 10.9) is spent on patrol, which is just less than 19 percent of the total Duty Log time (Table 10.10).

Table 10.10 Patrol Time as % of Total Time

		(PPATTOT)	
Percentile	Value	Statistic	Value
Minimum	.000	Mean	.188
25th	.065	Median	.159
50th	.159	Mode	.000
75th	.275	Std dev	.163
Maximum	.957		

Table 10.11 shows that just under 20 percent of the officer-shifts involved no patrol at all, while just over 60 percent involved less than 20 percent of the log time. Finally, nearly nine out of ten officer-shifts are characterized by less than 40 percent of the shift devoted to patrol activity. It would seem that the neighborhood police officer, perhaps like other officers, "mentally subtracts" the administrative hours before calculating the balance of time spent between other duties.

Table 10.11 Patrol Time as % of Total Time (Recoded)

		(RPPATTOT)			
Value Label	Value	Frequency	Valid Percent	Cum Percent	Percent
None	.00	81	18.8	18.8	18.8
1% to 20%	1.00	181	42.1	42.1	60.9
20% to 40%	2.00	124	28.8	28.8	89.8
40% to 60%	3.00	35	8.1	8.1	97.9
60% to 80%	4.00	8	1.9	1.9	99.8
80% to 100%	5.00	1	.2	.2	100.0
	Total	430	100.0	100.0	

Mean	1.328	Median	1.000	Mode	1.000	Std dev	.950

These three variables, ADMTOT (administrative time) COMTOT (time communicating with citizens) and PATTOT (time patrolling) combine to account for 97 percent of the time spent on the average officer-shift. Our last variables, ACTTOT (time in responsive law enforcement) and LAWTOT (number of arrests and citations) account for the remaining 3 percent of the shift.

Table 10.12 shows that the mean time spent towing cars and issuing citations per neighborhood police officer shift is less than 13 minutes. While the maximum time spent reacting to an offense was 44 percent of the shift, this was the only shift on which more than 40 percent of the time was so spent; of the 97 shifts during which the neighborhood police officer responded, 77 took less than 20 percent of his/her time.

Table 10.12 Total Reactivity Time (in Minutes)

		(TACTTOT)	
Percentile	Value	Statistic	Value
Minimum	.000	Mean	12.872
25th	.000	Median	.000
50th	.000	Mode	.000
75th	.000	Std dev	30.429
Maximum	195.000		
Valid cases	430	Missing cases	0

Table 10.13 Reactivity Time as % of Total Time

		(PACTTOT)	
Percentile	Value	Statistic	Value
Minimum	.000	Mean	.030
25th	.000	Median	.000
50th	.000	Mode	.000
75th	.000	Std dev	.070
Maximum	.440		
Valid cases	430	Missing cases	0

The "average" time shown in Table 10.13 are is somewhat deceptive, as Table 10.14 shows; more than 75 percent of the shifts are characterized by no such activity at all.

Table 10.14 Reactivity Time as % of Total Time (Recoded)

		(RPACTTOT)			
				Valid	Cum
Value Percent	Label	Value	Frequency	Percent	Percent
None	.00	333	77.4	77.4	77.4
1% to 20%	1.00	77	17.9	17.9	95.3
20% to 40%	2.00	19	4.4	4.4	99.8
40% to 60%	3.00	1	.2	.2	100.0
	Total	430	100.0	100.0	

Mean .274 Median .000 Mode .000 Std dev .550
Valid cases 430 Missing cases 0

The amount of time spent responding to crime is borne out in the LAWTOT data (Table 10.15) which show that on 50 percent of the shifts no warrants, citations, or arrests are made. On another 25 percent from 1 to 3 such actions are taken. The majority of actions occur in 25 percent of the shifts and when they do, they often occur in quite a flurry.

Table 10.15 Total Law Enforcement Entries

			(NLAWTOT)
Percentile	Value	Statistic	Value
Minimum	.000	Mean	1.937
25th	.000	Median	.000
50th	.000	Mode	.000
75th	3.000	Std dev	3.413
Maximum	34.000		
Valid cases	429	Missing cases	1

The shift on which 34 citations were issued involved a well-grounded citizen complaint regarding parking, to which the neighborhood police officer responded by ticketing the street. Only 3 incidents during this research period resulted in a neighborhood police officer initiating and completing an arrest; another 5 incidents occurred in which an officer served as backup for a district officer.

SUMMARY

The limited amount of time spent by neighborhood police officers is consistent with the charge for their unit. They are intended to be "proactive" and not "reactive." They conduct Crime Watch training sessions, organize community block organizations and youth groups, meet the people of the neighborhood and work with the elected officials in the ward. They are accessible, informative, and helpful. Their work, as we have reported elsewhere, has resulted in improved citizen-city relations, greater feelings of safety in the neighborhood, and higher rates of crime reporting.

In some cases it also appears that the long-term effects of their presence is to reduce crime in the neighborhood. But this effect is complex and highly qualified. It appears that some neighborhoods are very responsive to the policing tactics outlined here, while other neighborhoods are significantly less so. It also appears that, where neighborhood policing is working, it works exactly because the officer has found, among other important ingredients, the "right mix" of time in his/her Duty Log. Our experience with neighborhoods and neighborhood police officers is that an important match must take place between the person who is the officer and the community that is the neighborhood.

In terms of Duty Logs, this means that there is no single "right" balance of time. Although not intended to answer radio calls, every officer we interviewed had backed up a district officer and/or answered a call as the first car within the last 12 months. In short, while neighborhood police officers tend to be older and more prevention oriented, they still intend to exercise from time to time their general charge to enforce the law. And, they will support their fellow officers as they enter high-risk situations.

To fulfill their charge to prevent crime through the development of community relations, perhaps the single greatest contribution that neighborhood police officers make is in their availability. Every officer we met had installed an answering machine in the mini-station so that they would not miss calls while they were away. Of course, every machine's message began with a phrase equivalent to "If this is an emergency, hang up now and dial 911 immediately." But the machine means accessibility and the neighborhood police officer always dedicated the first part of his shift to taking messages from the machine and responding either with a phone call or a visit to the home of a resident with a problem. This produces an atmosphere of closeness to the police that has not been felt in many neighborhoods for literally decades. One officer is so respected for this that people come from other neighborhoods to his mini-station to report crimes.

Finally, the patrol would seem to be indispensable as a part of neighborhood policing. We joined more than one officer in walking a "beat" where they were greeted on a first name basis by residents and retailers alike. Greatest personal contact is made on foot patrol, of course, but this is possible in only some neighborhoods. In today's police department, the neighborhoods to be covered are often quite extensive; the shear area and the need to be responsive necessitates a car. Of course, the vehicles that are relegated to neighborhood policing are those that have been taken out of district service; these were neither reliable nor impressive machines but they allowed the officer to patrol the neighborhood.

The importance of this patrol capability should not be lost on the reader. On one sunny summer day as we rode through a particularly rough neighborhood in a police district with more than its share of crime, we asked the neighborhood officer regarding the strength of the force on that shift. He indicated that, effectively, there were only three zone cars on the shift; the radio had been busy that morning so we knew but hesitated to ask the next question, "How many cars are on the street right now?" His answer was, "Counting this one, just one." During another "ride-along" one of the authors of this paper witnessed a neighborhood police officer who was flagged down on patrol regarding a domestic disturbance; he kept the scene reasonably quiet until his request for backup could be answered by district officers. Within a half hour, he passively backed-up an officer with a suspicious moving violation (without request).

It is our conclusion that the time spent by neighborhood officers communicating with citizens and patrolling the neighborhood serves the community and the department very well.

11

An Assessment of Police Officers' Acceptance of Community Policing*

Peter C. Kratcoski
Kent State University

Susan B. Noonan
Cincinnati Human Relations Commission

INTRODUCTION

The research described here focused on police officers' response to a community-oriented policing program. The research was completed in Cleveland, Ohio and Cincinnati, Ohio. In order for community-oriented policing to be effective, the cooperation and support of the entire community is needed. This includes the residents of the community, the politicians, the business establishment, service agencies, police administrators, and the rank-and-file police officers. It is critical that the police officers accept the community-oriented policing philosophy.

To interpret the officers' responsibilities, it is important to know how police departments are traditionally structured and how community oriented policing differs from traditional policing.

Although the research is scarce, there is some evidence that the current emphasis on "community policing" may be partially a result of concerns with the traditional policing models raised within the policing establishment and partially a result of concerns with the effectiveness of policing raised by the residents of the

*   A version of this paper was presented at the annual meeting of Academy of Criminal Justice Sciences, Kansas City, Missouri, March 1993. This research was funded by the Ohio Governor's Office of Criminal Justice Services—Grant Number 92-DG-D03-1277-Evaluation of Community Policing.

communities which are being policed. It is not clear whether the movement in American policing toward community policing is a result of changing values among the rank-and-file officers or a reflection of innovations made at the administrative level (Brown, 1984).

In spite of the billions of dollars spent each year to deal with the problem of crime, a large proportion of the population believes that the problem is getting worse rather than better (Gallup, 1992, cited in Bureau of Justice Statistics, 1992:185). The movement toward community oriented policing may be due to the recognition that the traditional approach is not working, as evidenced by the rising crime rates and low percentage of crimes solved, or to the fact that the research on citizens' satisfaction with police performance reveals that groups that live in the inner city areas, particularly the poor, minority group members, juveniles and senior citizens, and women, are not very satisfied with police performance (Decker, 1981; Hahn, 1971; Skogan, 1978).

Zhao, Lovrich and Gray (1994) note that community-oriented policing and team-policing place "a high priority on the assumption that police organizational structures ought to change from a paramilitary and hierarchical model to a much more decentralized and participatory ("employee empowerment") form (1994:4). In order to facilitate this form of structural change, the Washington State Police developed a program designated TEAMS. With the implementation of this community policing approach, drastic changes in traditional patrol were made. Operational decisionmaking moved from a centralized format to a format in which the decisions came mainly from the TEAMS. Contrary to what might be expected, the upper administration and middle managers were very receptive to this decentralized approach to policing and they tended to endorse it without reservations. The first line supervisors and patrol officers were more cautious in their assessment of the positive effect this new structure would have on policing.

Alpert and Moore (1993) note that community policing encompasses four major themes. First, the residents of a community must be involved in working toward the elimination of the crime problems in the community, with the police and citizens becoming partners and working toward common goals. Second, police work must be perceived in a much broader context than reducing or eliminating serious crime. Third, police officers must change the way they visualize their work, as well as their methods. A fourth theme involves changes in internal working relationships, with police seeking ways to guide officers toward the most appropriate use of discretion through professionalization of the police experience (1993:116-117). According to Alpert and Moore, "Police should become pro-active, interactive, and preventative in their orientation, rather than rely solely on reacting and control" (1993:117).

If these four themes are incorporated into police work, many aspects of community life that were formerly ignored or given minimal attention by the police are now given considerable attention. These include seeking community satisfaction with the performance of police as service providers, working closely with community leaders, both those who serve in official capacities and those who have assumed informal leadership positions in the community, and assisting the community in organizing to prevent crime and improve the quality of life. This function involves providing service to victims of serious and less serious crimes, and exerting efforts to control and eliminate other community problems that have a negative effect on the citizens' welfare. These problems include substance abusers loitering in the neighborhoods, youth gangs harassing adults, vehicles speeding through residential areas, abandoned houses, violent incidents in and around the schools, and lack of appropriate recreational activities for youths.

It appears that the potential for a community-oriented policing program to succeed is closely tied to the rank-and-file officers' acceptance of the community policing philosophy concepts and the four community policing themes mentioned above.

THE CLEVELAND MINI-STATION PROGRAM

The Mini-Station Program in Cleveland is administered as a separate unit within the Cleveland Police Department. It was started in 1984 as a response to complaints of inadequate police protection in lower class and lower-middle class neighborhoods. The mini-stations expanded the police capacity to respond to complaints and conduct preventive patrol in these areas and to interact more directly with citizens through community organizations and crime watch meetings.

The mini-stations were originally established in 36 neighborhoods. The staff included one captain, who was responsible for the overall operation of the unit, a lieutenant to oversee daily operations, six sergeants responsible for direct supervision, and 54 patrol officers assigned to the 36 neighborhood bases. The number of mini-stations was reduced to 24 in 1992. One staff member at each station was assigned to work directly with the citizenry. The officers' fundamental duties included:

1. Handling walk-in complaints.

2. Making reports.

3. Foot patrol or car patrol in their assigned areas.

4. Maintaining contact with neighborhood and business organizations.

5. Attending community meetings to encourage participation in the crime watch programs.

6. Conducting crime watch training to assist the community in crime prevention.

7. Maintaining an active presence in the schools, with an eye on youth gangs, delinquency, and drug abuse problems.

8. Conducting safety programs for the elderly to enhance their street and home safety.

9. Identifying and correcting hazardous conditions in the neighborhood such as poor sanitation, abandoned cars or trucks, poor street lighting, or housing code violations.

10. Follow up on incidents after the district police have filed a complaint. (Both district police and mini-station officers work in the same neighborhoods (Kratcoski & Gustavson, 1991:7).

Providing crime prevention training to neighborhood residents is also a major program component. Mini-station officers train residents in neighborhood or "block watch" home security, auto theft deterrence, and child protection.

In Cleveland, the mini-station officers, along with the citizenry, representatives of the Mayor and City Council, business organizations and community welfare organizations, have worked to develop crime watch programs throughout the city, to implement school resource officer programs in which mini-station officers collaborate with school officials to prevent crimes from occurring in the schools and the surrounding area, to gather intelligence on gang activity, to speak with students on the ill effects of alcohol and drugs, and to be available for general counseling. Again, in Cleveland they have worked with the citizenry in the neighborhoods to identify crack houses, and, along with other city departments, such as sanitation and building, have sought to close such houses. They have removed junk and abandoned cars, and have assisted in having summer educational enrichment programs for youths in low public rental housing implemented, occasionally using the mini-station facility as the location for a program. Surveys of the citizens of Cleveland have revealed that the mini-station officers are regarded very highly and those in the mini-station neighborhoods believe it would be beneficial to have more officers there. The politicians, in particular the city council members, realizing that the community has reacted positively to this program, have endorsed it wholeheartedly and have been supportive of the officers' activities.

CINCINNATI COMMUNITY POLICING TEAMS

The Cincinnati Community-Oriented Policing (COP) was started in 1991, with 31 officers assigned to five districts. These officers worked in 11 neighborhoods within the districts. The boundaries of the neighborhoods in Cincinnati were mapped out by the Cincinnati City Planning Department. The characteristics of the populations residing in the neighborhoods seemed to be racially and ethnically diverse, but generally a neighborhood had a population that was homogeneous in terms of socioeconomic class level. The COP officers working in each district had a sergeant who served as the immediate supervisor. A lieutenant coordinated the entire COP program.

At the time of our study, the officers and supervisors included 16 white males, nine black males, two white females, and four black females. All of the COP personnel volunteered for the program. Their educational backgrounds ranged from high school diploma (or GEDs) to Master's degrees, and their lengths of experiences extended from three to 24 years.

Each police district has one or two neighborhoods in which the COP operates. These neighborhoods tend to vary demographically. For example, one neighborhood, located near the University of Cincinnati, had a fairly high transient population because of the number of students residing there. Considerable renovation of housing was taking place, and more professionals were moving into the area. Another neighborhood was experiencing a considerable population decline, and a third neighborhood exhibited population stability and cohesiveness among its residents.

The COP officers are under the direct supervision of the district commander. Their specific assignments for each shift are given by the district commander, but COP officers can be given special assignments from time to time that may take them out of the neighborhood in which they generally work. Normally, the COP coordinator will take responsibility for planning and implementing the specialized activities.

While on duty, the COP officers generally patrol on foot and have great latitude in the activities they pursue. The COP team for each district, which includes the supervising sergeant, meets to identify the problems and concerns in the neighborhoods and to develop appropriate strategies for solving the problems. Although two or more neighborhoods may have similar problems, the strategies developed by the COP teams to solve these neighborhood problems may differ. The COP officers are constantly being reminded that the characteristics of the community and of the residents must always be considered when strategies for eradicating problems are developed. What works in one neighborhood may not be effective in another because the neighborhood cultures differ.

All COP officers tend to perform similar types of duties, regardless of their specific neighborhood assignments. These duties include:

1. Crime prevention activities, which involve meeting with community leaders and citizens, assisting with efforts to organize crime prevention activities, and working on priority problems in the neighborhoods;

2. Patrolling the neighborhood on foot and making special efforts to interact with the residents, especially with specific groups such as senior citizens and students;

3. Providing assistance to those in need of services, and informing citizens of the methods for securing the assistance of city agencies;

4. Completing normal police activities, including occasionally responding to 911 calls, the apprehension of criminals, traffic patrols, and investigating crimes;

5. Assisting with citywide special events or programs, particularly those focused on youth;

6. Assisting regular district officers when help is requested; and

7. Completing security inspections for citizens making such reports.

The general focus of their activities is toward reducing or eliminating the problems of the neighborhood, which include such matters as noise, traffic violations, or dealing with intoxicated persons, substance abusers or dealers, or youth gangs.

RESEARCH DESIGN

Hundreds of police jurisdictions throughout the United States have endorsed the community policing philosophy and goals and have established community policing programs. Unfortunately, the programs are often created and staffed without any consideration being given to the training of the officers in the community-oriented policing method. Often, the officers selected for the program are instructed to go out and do "community policing" and must rely on their own ingenuity to determine how the tasks are to be accomplished. Many of the underlying policies of community-oriented policing are difficult for some officers to accept, since they seem to be contrary to training and practices they have experienced.

As mentioned, the purpose of this research was to determine if the rank-and-file patrol officers in Cleveland and Cincinnati are knowledgeable of the community police programs operating in their departments and if their attitudes toward the program are generally positive or negative.

To accomplish this goal the authors obtained permission to distribute questionnaires to the officers assigned to the operations divisions of the Cleveland Police

Department and the Cincinnati Police Department. In Cleveland, after a discussion with the Deputy Chief on what methods would be likely to elicit the greatest response, it was decided that the questionnaires would be distributed during the roll-call period at the beginning of each shift. All districts were included, but only those officers working the first and second shift were surveyed. A letter from the Deputy Chief, in which the research was endorsed, was inserted in each of the envelopes containing the questionnaires. Anonymity was guaranteed. The officers were instructed to complete the questionnaire, place it in the envelope, seal it, and return it to their immediate supervising officer.

In Cincinnati, a similar process was followed. However, at the request of the Police Chief all members of the Department were included in the survey, including the detectives, administration, and support staff.

In Cleveland, approximately 600 questionnaires were printed. While it cannot be determined how many were actually distributed, 255 completed questionnaires were returned. They were representative of officers from all shifts and districts. No attempt was made to complete a follow-up to determine the characteristics of the officers who did not complete the questionnaire. In Cincinnati, approximately 800 questionnaires were distributed and 679 were returned completed. Of these, 453 were from patrol officers, and these were used for this facet of the research.

RESULTS

Table 11.1 gives the characteristics of the officers who completed the questionnaire. In Cleveland, the profile is of an officer in his/her early 30s with less than five years experience and having had some college education, but not being a college graduate. Approximately one-third of the respondents were African-American or Hispanic and less than 15 percent of the respondents were female. No attempt was made to determine if the respondents were comparable to the entire patrol officer population. One might suspect that this group was somewhat more educated (53.6% having some college and 20.9 having a college degree or above) than the larger patrol division population. The Cincinnati district officers were very similar to the Cleveland officers in age (mid 30s). More than one-half of them had five or less years experience, and approximately one-fourth were African-Americans or a race other than Caucasian. More than 85 percent of the Cincinnati officers were male, a figure almost identical to that of Cleveland. Almost two-fifths of the Cincinnati officers had college degrees, a figure almost twice as high as that in Cleveland.

Table 11.1 Characteristics of Police Officers Who Completed the Questionnaire

	Cleveland (N=256)	Cincinnati (N=453)
Mean Age	34.4	36.2
Median Age	33.0	32.4
Experience		
Less than 1 year	8.1	6.3
1 to 5 years	48.0	31.8
5 to 10 years	15.4	9.9
10 to 20 years	19.0	29.7
More than 20	9.0	22.4
Race		
African-American	28.2	19.3
Caucasian	65.3	77.3
Hispanic	4.2	.8
Asian/Other	1.8	.3
Sex		
Male	85.3	85.6
Female	14.7	14.4
Education		
High School or less	25.5	15.0
Some College	53.6	46.7
College Graduate +	20.9	38.3

The officers in each department were asked how important the community policing program was to the overall success of their respective departments. As indicated in Table 11.2, almost two-thirds of the Cleveland respondents stated that the Mini-Station Program was important to the Cleveland Police Department, and 60.6 percent of the Cincinnati officers' indicated that the Community Policing Program was important to the Cincinnati Department. The difference in their responses to this question was not statistically significant.

Table 11.2 Perception of the Importance of Community Policing to the Officers' Success of their Department

Community Policing Important	Cleveland		Cincinnati		Total
	N	%	N	%	
Yes	79	36.7	162	39.4	240
No	134	63.3	249	60.6	383
	212		411		623

$p < .05$

In Cleveland, the district officers patrol the same neighborhoods in which the mini-stations are located, and the officers assigned to regular patrol are likely to be aware of the location of the mini-station in their area. Likewise, in Cincinnati the district patrol officers are likely to observe the community police officers "walking the beat." However, some officers are more likely to come into contact with mini-station officers than others, since the Mini-Station Program operates on a 8 a.m. to 4 p.m. schedule for three days and a 12 p.m. to 8 p.m. schedule two days of the week. This is also likely to be the case in Cincinnati, since the COP teams do not work in every neighborhood in the city and do not work during the late evening or nighttime shifts. The officers were asked to recall how they felt about the success of the community policing program, when it first started, and how they feel about it now that it has been in operation for some time. A large proportion of the officers stated that initially they didn't have much knowledge of it, and thus could not offer an opinion about its effectiveness (41.6% for Cleveland and 35.1% for Cincinnati). In Cleveland, 48.5 percent and in Cincinnati, 49.1 percent of the officers thought the program operating in their city was either somewhat or very successful when they first obtained knowledge of the program. When asked if their opinion changed after learning more about the program, the percentage of "no opinion" responses dropped to 32.6 percent for Cleveland and 16 percent for Cincinnati.

Table 11.3 reveals the responses of the officers to a series of questions on the success or failure of COP in eliminating or reducing community problems. The range of available responses included "not successful," "somewhat successful," or "very successful." As shown in Table 11.3, the larger majority of patrol officers in both Cleveland and Cincinnati agreed that their community policing program increased police visibility, increased the involvement of the residents in crime prevention activities, and was effective in working with the communities on school related problems. The responses of the officers from the two cities on the question of involving the citizens in crime prevention were not significantly different, but a significantly higher proportion of the Cincinnati officers claimed that the community policing program was successful in making the police more visible in the community. A higher proportion of the Cincinnati officers (75%), compared to the Cleveland officers (66.2%), stated that the community policing programs were somewhat successful or very successful in reducing or solving school-related problems.

Table 11.3 Patrol Officers' Opinions of the Success of Community Policing Programs. Perceived Success in Reducing/Eliminating Specific Problems

Problem	Cleveland				Cincinnati				Sig.
	Not Successful	Somewhat Successful	Very Successful	Total	Not Successful	Somewhat Successful	Very Successful	Total	
Providing Police Visibility	28.0	41.0	30.8	211	12.4	46.9	40.8	429	>.000
Involving Residents in Solving Community Problems	22.1	45.2	32.7	208	17.0	58.1	24.9	418	>.01
Solving School Related Problems	33.8	48.8	17.4	207	25.1	57.5	17.4	414	>.05
Developing New Recreational Activities	44.3	39.4	16.3	203	26.6	55.3	18.0	394	<.001
Solving Community Drug Problems	53.1	39.7	7.2	209	41.3	44.1	14.6	426	>.003
Dealing with Street People	57.2	32.7	10.1	208	48.9	35.5	15.5	425	<.05
Helping Solve Youth Gang Problems	62.8	29.0	8.2	207	48.0	43.8	8.1	406	>.001
Controlling Drunks in the Neighborhood	35.1	29.9	33.3	208	52.3	37.3	10.5	421	<.05
Securing Abandoned Buildings	54.4	34.0	11.7	206	51.0	38.5	10.5	410	<.05
Getting Trash/Junk Cars Removed from Streets	64.3	26.1	9.7	207	64.5	30.2	5.3	414	<.05

However, less than one-half of the officers in both departments stated that the community policing programs were successful in working with the community in areas that could lead to an increase in "quality of life," such as reducing or eliminating problems in the neighborhoods related to having street trash removed or boarding up abandoned buildings, dealing with street people or street noise, and dealing with dangerous people.

A significantly larger proportion of the Cincinnati officers, compared to the Cleveland officers, believed that the COP program operating in their city was successful in handling youth gangs, but a large proportion of the officers in both cities were not convinced that their community policing program was succeeding in controlling youth gangs. Almost two-thirds of the Cleveland officers and one-half of the Cincinnati officers stated that the community policing program operating in their city was unsuccessful in curtailing youth gang activity. The same conclusion was reached with regard to reducing or eliminating the drug problems in the neighborhoods. More than one-half (53.1%) of the Cleveland officers and 41.3 percent of the Cincinnati officers stated that community policing was unsuccessful in this area. A larger proportion of the Cincinnati officers (55.3%), compared to the Cleveland officers (44.3%), stated that COP was successful in developing more recreational programs for young people.

As previously mentioned, the Cleveland Mini-Station Program was set up as a separate unit within the Cleveland Police Department, while the COP officers in Cincinnati work out of the districts under the supervision of the district commanders. Thus, in Cleveland the mini-station officers report to their mini-stations, which are located in the various districts throughout the city. The district officers patrol the same areas being served by the mini-station officers, with the district officers normally responding to the 911 calls. The community policing officers only respond to 911 in emergency situations. The amount of contact between mini-station officers and district officers depends on the relationships and communication that have been established between the two sets of officers. Since the mini-stations are only open from 8 a.m. to 4 p.m. three days a week and 12:00 p.m. to 8:00 p.m. three days a week, those district officers working the late evening and night shifts are not likely to have opportunities to interact with the mini-station officers. A similar situation exists in Cincinnati, with the COP teams patrolling during the day and early evening only. Assuming that interaction and communication between the two sets of officers would lead to a greater appreciation for and understanding of the role of the community policing officers, the responses of the officers who had contact with the community policing officers were analyzed and compared to the response of the patrol officers who did not have such contact with regard to their assessments of the success of the program in the two cities.

In Cleveland, the nature of interaction between the patrol officers and the mini-station officers varied. Interviews with the mini-station officers revealed that the most common forms of interaction were:

1.   Assisting with accidents and occasionally with domestic incidents.

2.   Taking low priority requests for service when the district patrol officer was involved with a high priority request.

3.   Completing follow-up interviews/investigations with victims.

4.   Providing information to specialized police units (drugs, vice, gangs).

5.   Providing information on "trouble areas" (schools).

6.   Unofficial conversation not necessarily related to police work.

Almost two-thirds of the district patrol officers reported that they never had contact with the mini-station officers.

As shown on Table 11.4, a high proportion of the officers (68.8% in the no contact category and 86.8% in the contact category) agreed that the program was successful in involving the residents of the community in problem solving. The larger majority of the respondents in both categories (65.5% in the no contact and 79% in the contact) believed that the program provided greater police visibility in the community.

Table 11.4 Cleveland Police Assessment of Mini-Station Program Success with Solving Community Problems by Contact with Mini-Station Officers

Community Problem	Respondents' Mini-Station	Stating Success	Significance Difference
	Contact No %	Contact Yes %	(.05 level)
Involving Residents in Solving Community Problems	68.8	86.8	S
Providing Police Visibility	65.5	79.0	S=.06
Solving School Related Problems	57.9	74.7	S
Solving Community Drug Problem	44.5	59.0	NS
Obtaining New Recreational Opportunities	54.7	56.2	NS
Dealing with Street People	35.2	50.5	S
Controlling Drunks in the Neighborhood	39.2	46.0	NS
Securing Abandoned Buildings	45.3	45.4	NS
Helping Solve Gang Problem	32.4	41.8	NS
Getting Trash/Junk Cars Cleared from the Streets	33.0	38.1	NS

These are areas that encompass the job description of the mini-station officers, and it appears that there is considerable agreement by the patrol officers that the program was successful in accomplishing these goals. On the other hand, there are community-related problems that both categories of officers stated that the mini-station officers were not very successful in eliminating. These included getting trash and junk cars cleared from the streets and alleys, helping solve gang problems, solving the drug problems of the community, controlling drunks in the neighborhood and securing abandoned buildings. Several of these activities are within the scope of the mini-station officers' duties and it would be appropriate to research these matters in more depth to try to ascertain why the majority of the respondents did not see the program as accomplishing these goals. A larger proportion of the respondents who had contact with the Mini-Station Program than of those in the no contact group stated that the program was successful in helping to solve the drug problems in the community (59% for the contact group compared to 44.5% for the no contact group) and a larger proportion of the contact group (41.8% compared to 32.4%) stated that the mini-station program was successful in helping solve gang problems. Perhaps some of these respondents who asserted that the program was successful in these areas (gangs and drugs) were aware of the importance of the mini-station officers' role in obtaining information from the residents on gang activities and drugs and feeding this information on to the more specialized police units which have direct responsibility to control these problems.

There were statistically significant differences between the contact and no contact groups on the questions pertaining to the mini-station program's success in helping to solve school related problems and in dealing with street people. Almost three-fourths of the officers who had contact with the program stated that it was successful with helping to solve school-related problems, compared to 57.9 percent of the no contact group who believed the program was successful in this area. More than 50 percent of the officers who had contact stated the program is successful in dealing with street people, compared to 35.2 percent of those in the no contact group. In Cincinnati, the type of contacts between the district police and the community policing officers consisted of the following:

- Assisting with investigations of all types, particularly drugs, homicide, robberies
- Passing along to other police units information obtained from residents
- Providing follow-up on calls
- Providing "back-up" disturbance calls
- Assisting with domestic cases involving children
- Assisting patrol officers with identifying suspects
- Engaging in crime prevention activities
- Occasionally relieving district patrol officers
- Engaging in school related programs

More than three-fourths of the Cincinnati district patrol officers reported having contact with the community policing officers.

As shown in Table 11.5, the proportion of Cincinnati officers who stated that the community-oriented policing program was successful in reducing or solving community problems was significantly higher for those officers who have had contact with the program than for those officers who did not have contact for all community problems except controlling drunks in the neighborhood and getting trash and junk cars cleared from the streets. The district patrol officers who had contact with the community policing officers stated that the program was most successful in providing police visibility, involving residents in solving community problems, obtaining new recreational opportunities for the youth, solving school-related problems, solving community drug problems, dealing with street people, and helping solve youth gang problems. They considered the COP least successful in matters pertaining to the physical improvement of the community, such as getting trash and junked cars cleared from the streets and securing abandoned buildings. Race was also considered in the analysis. African-American (74.1%) and Hispanic officers (100%) were more likely to state that the community policing program was an important part of the Cleveland Police Department than were Caucasian officers (61%). Race did not differentiate the response patterns of the officers on any of the items relating to the mini-station program's success in solving community problems.

Table 11.5 Cincinnati Police Assessment of Community-Oriented Police Success with Solving Community Problems by Contact with Community-Oriented Police Officers

Community Problem	Respondents' Mini-Station Contact No %	Stating Success Contact Yes %	Significance Difference (.05 level)
Providing Police Visibility	84.0	90.6	S
Involving Residents in Solving Community Problems	79.7	87.9	S
Solving School-Related Problems	66.4	76.9	S
Obtaining New Recreational Opportunities	63.9	73.5	S
Solving Community Drug Problem	50.0	65.7	S
Dealing with Street People	46.9	58.2	S
Helping Solve Gang Problem	42.6	57.1	S
Controlling Drunks in the Neighborhood	48.0	52.7	NS
Securing Abandoned Buildings	41.2	51.4	S
Getting Trash/Junk Cars Cleared from the Streets	32.5	36.8	NS

Male patrol officers were much more likely to have had contact with the mini-station program than were female officers (47.4% for male compared to 18.8% for females). However, the responses of male and female officers did not differ significantly on any other question. Their responses were markedly similar on questions pertaining to the importance of the mini-station program and the success of the program in helping to solve community problems.

The educational level of the patrol officers appears to have little effect on their perceptions of the importance of the mini-station programs, likelihood of having contact with the program, or perception of the success of the program in helping to solve community problems, with the exception of helping to solve school-related problems. Those officers with a high school or less education were more likely to state that the program was successful in this area (77.5%) than were officers with some college (69.7%) or those with a college degree or above (49.8%).

In Cincinnati, more than two-thirds of both male and female officers stated that COP was an important component of the police department. The difference in their responses was not significant. However, a significantly larger proportion of the African-American officers (89.6%) compared to the Caucasian officers (58.4%) stated that the program was important.

Contrary to what was found for the Cleveland officers, Cincinnati African-American officers were more likely to consider the program somewhat or very successful in reducing or solving drug problems, reducing school problems, providing police visibility, getting rid of street trash and junk cars, involving residents in crime prevention activities, securing abandoned buildings, keeping drunks and dangerous people off the streets, working with youth street gangs, and developing recreational activities in the community than were the Caucasian officers.

Male and female officers in Cincinnati did not differ significantly on their responses to the questions pertaining to the effectiveness of COP in reducing or solving community problems. This also proved to be the case when the responses to these questions were considered on the basis of age and education.

CONCLUSIONS AND DISCUSSION

The research described here focused on police officers' response to a community oriented policing program. In Cleveland and Cincinnati, it appears that the COP programs are not understood by many of the rank-and-file police officers. Some of their responses to the questionnaire tended to be guarded, noncommittal, or negative. The higher level administration has done a good job of *publicizing* the program and, based on past research, it was found that the people in the neighborhoods are becoming involved because they recognize the value of the program, but many officers need to be convinced that COP benefits their department as well as the city.

From their responses, it is apparent that many officers equate community policing with public relations. Some do not even consider it "real police work" and others believe the personnel and resources allocated to community policing should be used for more important activities.

Regardless of the reservations expressed, there was a consistent response pattern for both cities which considered community policing in a positive light. The patrol officers who had contact with the community policing officers tended to be more knowledgeable of that program and more likely to perceive it as being important to their department. A larger proportion of the Cincinnati officers stated that they had some form of interaction with the COP officers. This probably is the result of the way the program is structured, with the COP officers working out of the districts and being present for the role calls which are conducted before they go out to their duty stations.

On the other hand, the officers of the mini-station program are in a better position to establish a distinct identity and to identify with the community, learn its culture, and develop the types of cooperative relationships with the residents of the community that are so important to the goals of community policing. The mini-station officers have more autonomy and are likely to be less confused about their mission than community policing officers who are attached to the district commands within the police department. The contributions made by the mini-station officers are not as readily recognized as those made by other officers. Their work may be considered of a police community relations nature, and the importance of what they do may be minimized. Some perceive their position as a "cushy job," and the district officers and some administrators may fail to understand how community policing contributes to the overall mission of the department.

Community-oriented policing programs similar to the one discussed here may play a large role in defining the nature of police work in the future. Police are generally characterized as reactors rather than innovators, but, with COP they are put in the position of being the ones who introduce change. The political community and service agencies are turning toward the police for solutions to not only crime problems but also other community problems. In Cleveland and Cincinnati, the community policing officers, along with the citizenry, representatives of the Mayor and City Council, business organizations and community welfare organizations, have worked to develop crime watch programs, implement school programs in which community officers collaborate with school officials to prevent crimes from occurring in the schools and surrounding area, gather intelligence on gang activity, speak with students on the ill effects of alcohol and drugs, and be available for general counseling.

While the structuring and administration of the programs in the two cities differ, they both have incorporated the underlying premises and philosophies of community policing, and both cities have achieved considerable success in attaining community policing objectives and in gaining acceptance of the program from the rank-and-file officers in their departments. Perhaps the structuring and administration of community policing is not as crucial to its success as are such factors as the manner in which the program is implemented, the support given to the program by administrators, the information given to other members of the department, and the training given to the other officers on community policing.

This whole effort could be seriously compromised, however, if the rank-and-file police officers, particularly those out on patrol, do not understand and accept the concept. Training in community policing should be part of the academy program for all new officers, and advanced training for other officers should also be designed. When all of the officers are made aware that the activities of the community policing officers are compatible with those of other members of the department, and that they are just achieving these goals through different means, much of the skepticism and doubt about community policing which exists among the rank-and-file patrol officers may dissipate. We must recognize the fact that a change to community policing will be a gradual, long-term process.

During the course of the research, we had numerous opportunities to interview administrators, middle level supervisors, and patrol officers. It was apparent that some of them were skeptical of anything positive coming out of changes in police work. They have seen and heard it all before. However, as old administrators and officers are gradually replaced, there is likely to be more acceptance of the values of community policing, and the sought-after goals will eventually be embraced by more members of the departments.

Section V

COMMUNITY RESPONSES TO COMMUNITY POLICING

Part V comprises three readings that show empirically the positive effect that community policing has on community residents. The three articles are very different in their methodological approaches and describe three very different programs.

Cordner and Jones (Chapter 12) describe the focused efforts of a foot patrol program that has been developed specifically to address the crime problems associated with a public housing facility. Kratcoski, Dukes, and Gustavson (Chapter 13) have assessed citywide the impressions residents have of a special unit of the police department that is dedicated to community policing. DeLong (Chapter 14) describes the success of a collaborative effort between residents and police in recovering a neighborhood from crime.

The three articles also approach their topics somewhat differently. Kratcoski, Dukes, and Gustavson have employed traditional survey techniques to assess citizen impressions of and satisfaction with community policing. Cordner and Jones have used a similar technique and to this have added data on crime reduction in the area. From her unique position in the neighborhood, DeLong has been able to supply a more qualitative and theoretical discussion of the social and political process.

These three studies show that community policing is successful. More importantly, when taken together, they begin to show an important capability of community policing: it is able to be transformed into a successful working form in a variety of communities. In fact, the evolution of community policing programs in communities around the country is occurring so rapidly and producing such a wide variety of programs that it is confusing to many, even those who are experienced in policing and police administration.

12

The Effects of Supplementary Foot Patrol on Fear of Crime and Attitudes Toward the Police

Gary W. Cordner
Eastern Kentucky University

Michael A. Jones
Eastern Kentucky University

INTRODUCTION

This chapter presents information from an evaluation of a one-year supplementary foot patrol program in a public housing project in a mid-sized southern city. The program deployed two-officer pairs of foot patrol officers each day during afternoon and evening hours. The officers worked the foot patrols on an overtime basis. Consequently, different officers worked the foot patrols each day. A total of almost 150 officers participated in the program at least once, although eventually it was limited to a group of about 30 officers.

The housing project included 668 townhouse-style units that were built in the 1930s, 1940s, and 1950s. The number of units in the project had been reduced substantially over the previous several years through demolition of units, for the purpose of reducing population and housing density. At the same time, street re-routing and renovation of remaining units was begun; these physical changes are still under way.

As of early 1990, the housing project was identified by community members, housing authority staff, and police as having disproportionate levels of crime, drug offenses, fear, and public disorder. The site had become an open-air drug market, replete with dealers, runners, and signalmen. People from throughout the city and surrounding area came to the site to purchase drugs; traffic cruised slowly up and down the streets, drivers periodically pulling to the curb to make purchases. Many residents were intimidated by the individuals involved in this drug trade, who would block the sidewalks and offer menacing looks and gestures.

In 1990 a new police chief promised area residents that the police department would attend to their problems. In May a special task force was assigned to the area to carry out a crackdown. The supplementary foot patrol program that is the focus of this paper was then initiated in January 1991 (with federal grant funding) to maintain and augment police services in the area as the special task force was gradually withdrawn.

The "treatment" utilized in this program should be understood as supplementary part-time foot patrol. Because of a lack of permanent assignment to the foot beats, there is no presumption that the foot patrols amounted to full-fledged community policing. Similarly, due to the lack of assignment continuity and the absence of any special training or instructions, there is no presumption that the program amounted to problem-oriented policing. The program simply consisted of extra police presence in the form of foot patrol. The police and housing officials who designed the program primarily wanted to increase police visibility and enforcement in an area that had previously been largely neglected by the police department.

Any attempt to identify the effects of this supplementary foot patrol is inevitably affected by the earlier deployment of the task force to the area. In particular, it is suspected by many officials that fear of crime was reduced and attitudes toward the police were substantially improved after the task force was implemented in May 1990. Thus, the foot patrol program may have been initiated in an already-improved situation, perhaps reducing its chances of demonstrating any further dramatic effects.

LITERATURE

Current interest in community policing (Kelling & Moore, 1988) was largely sparked by foot patrol studies reported in the early 1980s. Following on the heels of the first wave of effectiveness-oriented police research, which tended to show that "nothing worked" (Cordner & Trojanowicz, 1992), the Newark and Flint studies (Police Foundation, 1981; Trojanowicz, 1982) fueled new hope that something police did had some effect—even if only on fear of crime. Interpretation of the findings of these foot patrol studies further widened interest by speculating that police attention to fear, disorder, and minor forms of crime could actually forestall neighborhood decline (Wilson & Kelling, 1982; Skogan, 1990). The popularization of this "broken windows" thesis, coinciding as it did with the war on drugs, led to a substantial reliance on foot patrol and other community-oriented tactics throughout the 1980s and early 1990s (Moore & Kleiman, 1989; Hayeslip & Weisel,

1992). Community policing became a major part of the federal Weed and Seed anti-drug strategy as well as a key plank in Bill Clinton's campaign platform.

The evidence on the effects of foot patrol is actually somewhat mixed. Some early studies of saturation foot patrol (doubling or tripling staffing levels) found indications of crime reductions while others did not (Wilson, 1975). The Newark study (Police Foundation, 1981), using an experimental design, found that foot patrol reduced fear of crime and increased citizen satisfaction with police, but did not significantly affect reported crime or victimization. The Flint study (Trojanowicz, 1982) reported crime and fear reductions due to the presence of foot patrol. A massive reintroduction of foot patrol in Boston failed to have discernible crime control or order maintenance effects (Bowers & Hirsch, 1987). Deployment of downtown foot patrols in a southeastern city reduced levels of disorder but did not affect overall crime rates or citizen support for the police (Esbensen, 1987).

In the face of these rather confusing findings, the prevailing view seems to be that foot patrol is an effective technique for reducing fear of crime, controlling street disorder, and enhancing police-community relations (Moore & Trojanowicz, 1988; Kelling, 1988). Many proponents also expect long-term reductions in crime and calls for service (Trojanowicz & Bucqueroux, 1990), but others are more skeptical (Greene & Taylor, 1988; see also Greene & Mastrofski, 1988 generally).

METHODS

The analysis reported here draws primarily upon pre- and post-surveys of community residents in the targeted public housing site, as well as researcher observations. Data gathering in comparison public housing sites and of official records information (arrests, calls for service, etc.) was also undertaken and is fully reported elsewhere (Cordner, 1993).

The community surveys were administered in January 1991, before the implementation of the foot patrol program, and one year later, in January 1992. In each case a systematic sample of one-third of the households in the site was drawn. Site residents were employed to distribute and collect the surveys. At sample addresses, all residents aged 14 and older were requested to complete the survey.

The number of survey respondents dropped from 184 in Phase 1 to 104 in Phase 2. This decrease in respondents occurred primarily for two reasons. One was that, due to substantial renumbering and renaming of streets between Phase 1 and Phase 2, the surveyors had considerable difficulty locating some sample addresses in Phase 2. Second, due to the renovation program underway at the site, more sample units were unoccupied during Phase 2 than had been during Phase 1.

Characteristics of survey respondents are presented in Table 12.1. Based on these criteria, Phase 1 and Phase 2 respondents seem quite similar except for gender—the percent female dropped from 83.9 percent in Phase 1 to 69.9 percent in Phase 2. (The high proportion of female respondents closely matches the site's population, which includes many single-parent households headed by young women.) Because of this rather substantial difference, which raises the possibility that the two samples are not truly comparable, the pre-post analyses that follow are done separately for male and female respondents.

The survey itself consisted of demographic items, several questions about recent experiences (e.g., within the last year, have you been the victim of a property crime), and items pertaining to attitudes toward the police, fear of crime, causes of crime, and quality of life. Responses to these items were made on a 7-point Likert scale ranging from very strongly disagree to very strongly agree.

RESULTS

In the first section below, changes in crime, calls for service, contacts with police, and neighborhood conditions in the project area are briefly discussed. Then information is presented on fear of crime and citizen attitudes toward the police department, the primary foci of this chapter.

Table 12.1 Respondent Characteristics

Characteristic	Phase 1 1/91	Phase 2 1/92
Number of Survey Respondents	184	104
Percent Female	83.9%	69.9%
Mean Age	35.4	37.1
Mean Years Lived in City	25.4	28.2
Mean Years Lived at Site	9.5	11.5
Mean Number of Residents Per Household	3.1	3.1

Crime, Calls for Service, and Contacts With Police

Observations made by the authors clearly revealed that the project area had ceased to be an open air drug market as of mid-1991. Based on interviews with police and housing officials, it seems likely that the police crackdown in 1990 displaced most of the street-level drug selling to other locations in the city. Almost three years after the crackdown, the street-level dealing had not returned; officials strongly believe that the foot patrols implemented in 1991 (and subsequently continued) deserve much of the credit for "maintaining" the area after the crackdown.

Other neighborhood conditions have also visibly changed. Cars no longer slowly cruise the area, and young men no longer cluster on the sidewalk and along the curb. More children can be seen playing in common areas and more elderly citizens sit on their porches and walk about. Because of physical renovations the site's buildings now look nicer, landscaping is more attractive, and cars are parked on off-street lots instead of on the street.

In keeping with these apparent improvements in neighborhood conditions, survey respondents generally agreed, at Phase 1 and at Phase 2, that the site had become a better place to live and that physical changes had made the area safer. At Phase 2, however, respondents were somewhat less likely than at Phase 1 to agree that drug problems had decreased during the past year. They also continued to agree that most of their crime problems were caused by drugs, gangs, outsiders, and unsupervised kids.

Recent crime victimization experiences (during the past year) of Phase 1 and Phase 2 survey respondents are presented in Table 12.2. Although some of the changes from Phase 1 to Phase 2 seem rather substantial, they should be viewed with considerable caution for two reasons. In the case of male respondents, the sample sizes are quite small (30 in Phase 1 and 31 in Phase 2), so that the experiences of just a few individuals could result in large percentage changes. Second, the base rates of personal crime victimization for both males and females were low to begin with, so that, again, experiences of just a few respondents could cause sizeable percentage changes.

Table 12.2 Crime Victimization During the Past Year

	Males		Females	
	Phase 1*	Phase 2**	Phase 1*	Phase 2**
Victim of a property crime	21.4%	11.1%	21.9%	20.3%
Victim of a personal crime	0.0%	3.7%	6.2%	3.2%

*Phase 1, 1990
**Phase 2, 1991

With these cautions in mind, it can be noted that property crime victimization among both male and female survey respondents decreased, as did female personal crime victimization. (The increase in male personal crime victimization, from 0.0 percent to 3.7 percent, represents the experience of just one respondent.) These victimization decreases are consistent with extensive analysis of rates of calls for police service in the housing site, which showed an overall decrease of 5.5 percent from 1989 to 1991, and a 35.8 percent decrease in domestic violence calls.

Changes in the nature of citizen contacts with police in the project area are presented in Table 12.3. Among both groups, males and females, the likelihood of having had positive contacts with police increased substantially from Phase 1 to Phase 2, while smaller increases in negative contacts also occurred. Apparently the increased police presence in the area, in the form of foot patrol, produced more citizen contacts of various kinds.

Table 12.3 Contacts With Police During the Last Year

	Males		Females	
	Phase 1	Phase 2	Phase 1	Phase 2
Had a positive contact with police	21.4%	29.6%	28.4%	34.4%
Had a negative contact with police	17.9%	18.5%	15.1%	17.5%

Fear of Crime

Responses to seven fear of crime items are presented in Table 12.4. On four of the items the changes from Phase 1 to Phase 2 for males and females are consistent, and in each case indicate increased fear. On the other three items males reported fear reductions while females reported increased fear.

Table 12.4 Mean Responses on Fear of Crime Items (response range 1 = very strongly disagree to 7 = very strongly agree)

	Males		Females	
	Phase 1	Phase 2	Phase 1	Phase 2
I often avoid going out during the daytime because I am afraid of crime.	2.64	2.96	3.18	3.40
I often avoid going out after dark because I am afraid of crime.	3.92	3.82	4.54	4.77
My fear of crime is very high.	4.04	4.54	4.40	4.56
I am more afraid of crime than I ever have been.	3.52	4.41	4.28	4.66
Fear of crime is very high in this neighborhood.	4.85	4.79	4.71	4.83
There is a good chance that I will be the victim of a property crime (theft, burglary) this year.	4.08	3.32	3.81	4.31
There is a good chance that I will be the victim of a personal crime (rape, assault) this year.	3.16	3.63	3.51	3.78

The items in Table 12.4 represent several different dimensions of fear of crime. The first two items pertain to the effects of fear on personal behavior. Not surprisingly, males report less staying home behavior because of fear than females, and both groups are more likely to stay in at night than during the day. During the project year, though, daytime staying-in reportedly increased while there was little change in staying home after dark.

The next two items in the table reflect personal feelings of fear. Females report more fear than males, but the gap narrowed substantially during the project year, mainly because of increased fear among males. Interestingly, though, there was little difference between males and females, and little change from Phase 1 to Phase 2, on the fifth item in Table 12.4, which asked about the level of fear in the neighborhood. It is also interesting that both males and females rated their own fear of crime lower than the level of fear in the neighborhood.

The final two items in the table explore perceived likelihood of crime victimization. Males' perceived likelihood of property crime victimization declined from Phase 1 to Phase 2, consistent with their actual experiences as reported earlier, but females scored higher in Phase 2, despite their slight decrease in actual victimization. Both groups reported increased likelihood of personal crime victimization at Phase 2. Males and females assessed their risks from personal crime at close to the same levels at Phase 2, which matches their actual experiences during 1991, as reported earlier.

Table 12.5 Mean Responses on Attitudes Toward Police Items (response range 1 = very strongly disagree to 7 = very strongly agree)

	Males		Females	
	Phase 1	Phase 2	Phase 1	Phase 2
The police department does the best job it can against crime in this neighborhood.	4.23	3.82	4.05	4.39
The police department is doing a better job in this neighborhood than it was a year ago.	4.81	4.56	4.83	4.81
I regularly see policeofficers on patrol in this neighborhood.	4.50	5.29	4.64	4.89
The police department hassles people too much in this neighborhood.	3.27	4.41	3.21	3.32
The police department should work closely with kids by organizing sports programs.	5.30	6.00 5	.54 5	.73

Attitudes Toward Police

Responses to items measuring attitudes toward the police department are presented in Table 12.5. The first two items, which are indicators of overall perceptions and support, provide a mixed picture. Males and females generally agreed that the police department was doing a better job than previously, but not any more strongly at Phase 2 than at Phase 1. However, at Phase 2 females thought the police department was doing a better job against crime than at Phase 1, while males disagreed. Female ratings of police on both of these global items were higher than males at Phase 2.

As indicated by the third item in Table 12.5, both males and females became more likely at Phase 2 to agree that they regularly saw police on patrol in their neighborhood. Males agreed even more strongly than females with this item. Males also agreed more strongly than females, especially at Phase 2, that the police department hassled people too much in the neighborhood. This is consistent with information presented earlier that males experienced fewer positive contacts with police than did females, and more negative contacts.

The final item in the table investigated support for the idea of police working closely with youth by organizing sports programs. The city police department did in fact have an ongoing Police Activities League (PAL) program in the area and was expanding its programs. Survey respondent support for this kind of police activity was high among both males and females at Phase 1 and got even stronger at Phase 2.

DISCUSSION

Overall, the supplementary foot patrol program seems to have succeeded in achieving greater police visibility in the public housing site, increased positive police contacts, and maintenance of the more orderly conditions initially accomplished by the special task force crackdown. In addition, calls for service in the area declined during the project year, and crime victimization, as measured by global survey items, decreased. However, fear of crime seemed to have increased at Phase 2 over Phase 1, while changes in attitudes toward the police were mixed. Male respondents, in particular, gave the police department lower marks at Phase 2 and became much more likely to agree that the police hassle people too much in the area.

The differences by gender in attitudes toward the police are quite interesting. Male and female attitudes were similar at Phase 1 but diverged at Phase 2. It is tempting to cite the fact that males had fewer positive police contacts than females and more negative contacts. However, at Phase 2 males had a greater preponderance of positive over negative contacts with police than at Phase 1, so that male attitudes could have been expected to become more positive rather than more negative.

Although the explanation for changes in male attitudes toward the police may not be directly connected to the number and nature of police contacts, it may be tied at least in part to the nature of the supplementary foot patrol program. The focus of the strategy was on visibility and enforcement, not community relations or problem solving. Inevitably, such a strategy concentrates largely on controlling the behavior of young males, whether through surveillance or intervention. The cumulative effect of the special task force crackdown and a year of concentrated enforcement-oriented foot patrol may have begun to wear on Phase 2 male respondents.

The failure of the supplementary foot patrol program to achieve beneficial effects on fear of crime is surprising in light of previous studies, but perhaps understandable given the history and nature of the program. Most importantly, it is quite likely that fear reductions were achieved by the special task force crackdown begun seven months before the foot patrols, and before the first community survey. If this was the case, then the Phase 1 survey measured fear of crime at an already-reduced level, thus compromising the chances of the foot patrols demonstrating their own fear reductions.

Another explanation for the equivocal fear results may be tied to lagged effects and rising expectations. The reassuring effects of increased police presence in the area may be delayed, especially if residents are skeptical about the police department's long-term commitment to their needs and problems. In addition, as of the Phase 2 survey residents of the area had been enduring physical renovations and downsizing for over two years and greatly increased police attention for over a year and a half. They may have been experiencing some degree of frustration that the renovations were not yet completed and that their lives were not yet completely tranquil. On the latter point, it can be noted that although calls for police service in the area had substantially decreased by Phase 2, the demand for police service in the area was still at a much higher level than in the jurisdiction as a whole.

The limited effects of the foot patrol on fear of crime and police-community relations are consistent with the design of the program and with our observations of the foot patrols. Few of the officers working the overtime foot patrol details exhibited any strong sense of identification with the area or any detailed knowledge of the residents. Some were clearly in it only for the overtime pay. In addition, some of the officers were obviously uncomfortable in the minority-dominated public housing site and not anxious to meet residents or deal with their problems. So, in fact, the main treatment was additional police presence (on foot), period.

Conversations with residents tended to confirm this view of the overtime foot patrol program. Residents seemed to be aware of the foot patrols, although some reported that they rarely saw them. Any lack of awareness of the foot patrols was probably due as much to the fact that a substantial amount of the patrolling was implemented after dark (especially in the winter) as to anything else, especially since the police department established reasonably strict controls to assure that the officers did, in fact, walk the area. However, the department did little to direct the foot patrol officers' actual activities, or to immerse them deeply in the community.

Many residents expressed skepticism about the officers' real effectiveness in the area. One item used only on the Phase 2 survey stated "the police officers who patrol around here really know what's going on." The overall mean response of 3.82 was slightly below the mid-point of the scale; while 42.4 percent of respondents agreed with the statement, 17.2 percent were uncertain and 40.4 percent disagreed. Male respondents were even more skeptical, with 55.5 percent disagreeing that police really knew what was going on in the area.

In sum, the supplementary overtime foot patrol program seems to have accomplished its objectives related to crime and disorder, but not to have had any substantial effects on fear of crime or attitudes toward the police department. Residents would generally agree that the supplementary foot patrols are better than nothing, but something less than a dramatic improvement in the delivery of police services.

13

An Analysis of Citizens' Responses to Community Policing in a Large Midwestern City*

Peter C. Kratcoski
Kent State University

Duane Dukes
John Carroll University

Sandra Gustavson
Radio Communications System Coordinator–City of Cleveland

INTRODUCTION

While attitudes toward police performance are quite positive among the general population, researchers, policy-makers and police practitioners have recognized that certain groups, youths, and minorities in particular, tend to be dissatisfied with the performance of the police. In response to their dissatisfaction, there have been various attempts to provide different types of policing that are more sensitive to the needs and cultures of special groups. Many of these have evolved under the label of community policing. This paper reports the effects of a particular community policing program, the Cleveland Police Mini-Station Program, on the attitudes toward the police, police service, and police performance for specific groups of minorities and women.

* Presented at the Annual Meeting of the Society for Applied Sociology, Annapolis, November, 1991. Portions of this research were supported by a grant (90-DG-D01-7098) from the Ohio Governors' Office of Criminal Justice Services.

199

VARIABLES AFFECTING ATTITUDES
TOWARD THE POLICE

The results of numerous surveys would seem to indicate that citizens generally respect most police officers and are satisfied with the services police provide. In addition, research shows that citizens generally accept the limited capacity of the police to prevent and solve crimes. However, citizens tend to be dissatisfied with the policies and methods of police work that distance them from the police (Kelling, 1988).

Rosenberg and Crane (1994) have recently completed a study of 200 households in Racine, Wisconsin, in an attempt to evaluate the effectiveness of community policing in that community. The community policing program was started in Racine in an attempt to control or eliminate the gangs and drug trafficking that had become entrenched in two racially mixed areas of the city. Residents of these neighborhoods who were interviewed expressed a desire to work with the community police officers to reduce crime and increase the quality of life in the surrounding area. The overall perception of police in this regard was positive. African-Americans and Latinos tended to mistrust police more than Caucasians and were less likely to give police a high rating; however, respondents from all ethnics groups agreed that they could work with the police to eliminate the common enemies: drugs and gangs.

Public attitudes toward the police are important because citizens, as victims, witnesses, and perpetrators, are major actors in the incidents police are called on to resolve. Studies show that at least 76 percent of all police activity is citizen-initiated (Decker, 1981).

Decker describes two types of variables affecting citizen attitudes toward he police: *individual* variables: age, sex, race, socioeconomic status, and personal experience with the police, and *contextual* variables: crime rates, community beliefs regarding the police, likelihood of victimization, and programmatic innovations designed to improve citizen attitudes. Race, sex, socioeconomic status, and age have been the most important predictors of attitudes (Decker, 1981). Research on race and satisfaction with police reveal that black ghetto residents tend to interpret the inequalities in the delivery of police services as racially biased (Hahn, 1971). The inequities of the criminal justice system are greater in black neighborhoods and further the dissatisfaction of blacks with police services. The likelihood of reporting a crime decreases with increased perceptions of inequality (Decker, 1981).

Skogan (1978) found that the manner in which the equality of service is perceived significantly impacts the formation of racial attitudes toward the police. He determined that race had an important effect on attitudes toward the police but that the quality of service explained the "polarization of racial attitudes" toward the police (Decker, 1981:81). While people in general are moderately positive toward the police, blacks are generally more likely than whites to rate police negatively.

Age also affects perceptions of police performance. In general, younger people tend to show greater dissatisfaction with the police. This is most pronounced for those under 30 (Decker, 1981).

Some researchers suggest a negative relationship between income and satisfaction with police and perceptions of police behavior. These hypothesized relationships should exist because of the differing types of contact with the police by citizens of different income levels. Overall, however, there does not appear to be a strong relationship between police performance ratings and social class. In addition, there is little difference in performance ratings of police by men and women (Decker, 1981).

Contextual variables appear to have greater influence on ratings of police than do individual variables. Neighborhood culture is of particular importance. Defined as "the contextual effect, generating and reinforcing negative attitudes toward the police," neighborhood culture accounted for within-race variation in one finding (Decker, 1981:83). The interaction between race and neighborhood was seen as explaining attitudes toward the police (Decker, 1981).

The emergence of neighborhood culture as a determinate of attitudes toward the police supports the importance of community policing, that is, directing police services at the neighborhood level as a means of improving relationships between police and citizens.

DEFINITIONS OF COMMUNITY POLICING

Various definitions of community policing have been developed. Some distinguish neighborhood-oriented policing from problem-solving policing, while others accept the terms as interchangeable. Some definitions are narrow, only recognizing specific problem-oriented strategies; others accept a wide range of community-related programs, special units or tactics aimed at improving levels of citizen satisfaction or reducing neighborhood crime.

The most encompassing view is to define community policing as a "strategy of policing that pervades all aspects of a police department" (Michaelson, Kelly & Wasserman, 1988:1). In this definition, the goals of community policing are: (a) controlling crime, (b) reducing fear of crime, (c) maintaining order and (d) improving the quality of life. Five elements are included in this definition: (1) accountability to the community and the organization, (2) management based on stated values, (3) decentralized structure, (4) shared decisionmaking with the community, and (5) empowering officers to solve problems (Michaelson, Kelly & Wasserman, 1988).

Although community policing is now in vogue, there is much confusion among police administrators and academics alike regarding an operational definition of both the process and the characteristics that community policing encompasses.

From the various research projects that have been completed on this topic, several conclusions regarding community policing are:

1. Programs labeled "Community Policing" are often started after the department had been extensively criticized by the community for its failure to solve a crime-related problem.

2. "Community Policing" programs are often geared more toward improving the image of the police rather than improving the community.

3. "Community Policing" programs are generally instituted without a great deal of planning. The programs tend to operate on a trial and error format with a number of changes and revisions being incorporated into the programs when it is realized that the original operations do not produce the desired results.

4. Since police administrators generally do not have clear conceptions of community policing, they are often confused about what new policies and organizational changes must be made, as what type of training is appropriate for the officers who will be assigned to the community policing project (Kratcoski & Albert, 1991).

CLEVELAND'S MINI-STATION PROGRAM

A grant was received from the Ohio Governors' Council on Criminal Justice Services for the specific purpose of assessing the Cleveland Police Mini-Station Program. The mini-station program in Cleveland, the subject of this research, is administered as a separate unit within the Cleveland Police Department. Officers in the unit operate independently of the basic patrol assigned through district command.

Cleveland's mini-station program was created through Community Development Block Grants and began operation in December, 1984. The purpose of the program was to provide more personal police protection to the neighborhoods. The mini-stations expanded police capacity to: (1) respond to complaints, (2) conduct preventative patrol in low and moderate income areas and (3) interact more directly with citizens through community organizations and crime watch meetings. The program emphasized crime prevention.

Mini-stations were established in 36 neighborhoods located throughout Cleveland. At the time of a survey completed in 1988, the mini-station staff included one captain who was responsible for the overall operation of the unit, a lieutenant to oversee daily operations, six sergeants responsible for direct supervision, and 54 patrol officers assigned to the 36 neighborhood bases. Many mini-stations shared facilities with auxiliary police headquartered in churches, storefronts, apartment complexes, and office buildings.

The officers' fundamental duties, as specified in the Block Grant contract, included: (a) handling walk-in complaints; (b) making reports; (c) performing foot or car patrol in their assigned areas; (d) maintaining contact with neighborhood and business organizations; (e) attending community meetings to encourage participation in the crime watch programs; (f) conducting crime watch training to assist the community in crime prevention; (g) maintaining an active presence in the schools, with an eye on youth gangs, delinquency, and drug abuse problems; (h) conducting safety programs for the elderly to enhance their street and home safety; (i) identifying and correcting hazardous conditions in the neighborhood such as poor sanitation, abandoned cars or trucks, poor street lighting or housing code violations in that such conditions could cause disorder or contribute to neighborhood crime; and (j) following up on incidents after the district police have filed a complaint.

Providing crime prevention training to neighborhood residents is also a major program component. Mini-station officers train residents in neighborhood or "block watch" home security, auto theft deterrence, and child protection.

In 1987, most stations were staffed by two officers. The stations operated from 8:00 a.m. to 8:00 p.m., Tuesday through Saturday. A telephone answering machine recorded messages when the officers were away from the station.

Presently, the mini-stations are staffed by one officer who rotates his/her schedule between two "shifts." One shift covers the days from 8:00 a.m. to 5:00 p.m. on Tuesday, Thursday, and Saturday. The other shift covers the afternoon/evenings from 12:00 noon to 8:00 p.m. on Monday and Wednesday.

Cleveland mini-station officers do not respond to calls for service dispatched from radio. However, citizens can request service for neighborhood problems by calling the mini-station directly.

RESEARCH DESIGN

The data for this paper was taken from several sources. Raw data from an earlier study focusing on the impact of the Cleveland Crime Watch program (Dukes, 1988) also contained information on the mini-station police, and was available to the authors. The data contained the responses of 573 men and women who completed one of the 2,500 questionnaires mailed to city residents. The questionnaire contained items specific to crime watch meetings, crime in the neighborhoods, attitudes toward police services, and victimization.

A stratified sampling procedure was utilized to assure that the survey would include both crime watch participants as well as those who had not been exposed to crime watch programs. This procedure assured that sampling represented all neighborhoods of the city, with their attendant variations in ethnicity and social class.

The participant sample was stratified to control for level of exposure to the program, based on the number of meetings attended. Participants were chosen for the sample from lists of persons attending one, two, or three crime watch meetings.

Potential participants who were not involved in Crime Watch were systematically sampled by selecting every 500th name from the census tracts in the City of Cleveland. The *Haines Directory* was used to obtain the information needed to secure the names and addresses of the people randomly selected for participation. The Cleveland Safety Department provided the information from which the crime watch participants were selected.

The following tabulation describes the sample stratification and response rate (Dukes, 1989).

Categories	Surveys Sent	Surveys Returned	Return Rate
No Crime Watch Training	500	71	14.2%
Attend 1 Session	850	140	16.4%
Attend 2 Sessions	750	197	26.3%
Attend 3 Sessions or more	400	165	41.3%
Total	2,500	573	22.9%

The items selected from the Dukes questionnaire were chosen in order to explore factors influencing citizen ratings of police service and the impact of neighborhood-style policing on the levels of community satisfaction with police performance and service.

In order to assess specific attitudes toward the mini-station program and the Cleveland District Police, the authors selected and examined specific attitudinal variables relating to police service and performance within the various neighborhoods in which the mini-station program operates. The effect demographic factors such as race, gender, income, education and age may have on the respondents' ratings of police performance and satisfaction with police service was also explored. In addition, the study examines the effect of having been victimized as well as the effect of being active in a crime watch program.

Since mini-station police often assist in the development of crime watch programs and participate in the meetings, it was assumed by the research team that contact with a crime watch program can be equated to contact with a mini-station officer.

Original research conducted within the Cleveland Police Department provided a second source of data on community policing. Captain Edward Herman, Commander of the Cleveland Police Neighborhood Response Unit developed a questionnaire based on earlier research conducted by the Seattle Police Department. This revised survey instrument was administered in Cleveland to a variety of citizens living in the mini-station areas (Gustavson & Kratcoski, 1991). This study attempted to tap the perceptions that community leaders, school administrators, church leaders, business owners and regular district police officers had of the performance of the mini-station program. Approximately 600 questionnaires were mailed to those whose names appeared on a list of Cleveland citizens identified as being involved in community affairs and residing in the mini-station areas. The questionnaire addressed specific problems the residents of neighborhoods must deal with and the effectiveness of the mini-station officers in solving these problems. Approximately 250 of those surveyed (50%) have returned a completed questionnaire.

A third source of information came from interviews of community residents, who were directly or indirectly involved with the mini-station program. These interviews were completed at the mini-station locations. The interviewees included members of the auxiliary police, participants in the Community School Resource Program, and members of various neighborhood community improvement groups.

FINDINGS

A major complaint of the residents in many inner city neighborhoods is that the police do not provide the services expected of them. In order to investigate citizens' perceptions of police efforts to provide services, several cross-tabs were constructed using citizens satisfaction with police attempts to provide the services that people in the neighborhood want with gender, race, income, education and age. As shown in Table 13.1, only race proved to be statistically significant in the response pattern to the question "Do you think the police department tries to provide the services that people tn your neighborhood need?"

A majority of the respondents in all of the categories for all of the variables answered yes to the question of police providing the desired services to the community with the exception of those who listed their race as Hispanic, Asian, American Indian, and other (N=15). Fifty-nine percent of the black respondents responded yes to this question compared to 76 percent of the white respondents. Although race is the only variable in which the response distribution is statistically significant, minorities, women, those with less than a high school education and those under 35 years of age were the least likely to agree that police are providing the services people want. The Cleveland mini-stations operate in the same neighborhoods in which the district police operate. While the specific functions of each unit are often not clearly defined, the charge of the mini-station units is closely aligned to community service functions whereas the charge of the district police is closely aligned to the standard functions of patrol: maintaining order and arresting law violators.

Several of the items on the questionnaire were used to tap citizens' satisfaction with the performance of the district police officers and the performance of the mini-station police officers. Respondents were asked to rate the performance of the district police and the mini-station police on performance scales ranging from very poor to very good. In this paper, for purposes of analysis, the categories were collapsed into poor, fair, and good. As shown in Table 13.2, 13 percent of the

Table 13.1 Police Provide the Services People Need

| | (Percentages) | | |
	Yes	No	N Significance
Gender			
Male	73	30	167 N/S = .05
Female	66	34	309
			476
Race			
Black	59	41	161 Sig. = .0001
White	76	24	297
Other	33	67	15
			473
Age			
< 35	61	39	82 N/S = −.05
36-50	70	30	108
51-65	68	14	145
66-80	76	24	116
> 80	70	30	10 461
Education			
< high school	65	35	52 N/S = −.05
high school	70	30	239
college/tech school	68	32	135
graduate school	76	24	
			461
Income			
< $ 5,000	69	31	23 N/S = −.05
$ 5,001-10,000	68	32	46
$10,001-15,000	69	31	30
$15,001-20,000	64	36	35
$20,001-25,000	69	31	36
$25,001-30,000	73	27	32
> $30,000	69	31	60
			251

respondents rated the district police as being poor in performance, 28 percent rated them fair, and 45 percent rated them good in performance. In comparison, only 3 percent of the respondents rated the mini-station police as being poor in performance, 12 percent rated them fair, and 58 percent rated the mini-station as being good in performance. Thus, while a majority of the respondents rated the district police and mini-station police as good, the proportion of good ratings was much higher for the mini-station police.

It should be noted that 22 percent of the respondents indicated that they didn't know how to rate the performance of the mini-station police compared to 8 percent of the respondents who answered "Don't Know" for the district police. This difference might be explained as resulting from the newness of the program or that these respondents just were not involved with the police, had no interest in police matters, were not in close proximity to the location of the mini-station or the service target area.

Table 13.2 Rating of Police Performance By Organizational Structure

| | Organizational Structure | |
Performance Rating	District	Police Mini-Station
Poor	72 (13%)	19 (3%)
Fair	163 (28%)	72 (12%)
Good	259 (45%)	334 (58%)
Don't Know	48 (8%)	123 (22%)
No Response	31 (5%)	25 (4%)
	573	573

*Percentages are rounded to the appropriate whole number.

The ratings of the performance of the district police were compared with the rating of the performance of the mini-station police controlling for the variables of gender, race, education, income and age. As shown in Table 13.3, the performance of the mini-station police was consistently rated higher than the performance of the district police in all categories of gender, race, income, education and age. Most dramatic was the difference in performance ratings by race. Only 33 percent of the black respondents rated the district police performance as good in comparison to the 71 percent of the black respondents who rated the mini-station police performance as good. Only 11 percent of the Hispanic, Oriental, and other race respondents rated the district police performance as good compared to the 73 percent of this category who rated the mini-station performance as good. A substantially larger proportion of both men and women respondents rated the mini-station police performance as being good than did those who rated the district police performance as being good. Although the rating of the mini-station police performance is substantially greater than that of the district police in all categories of education, the proportion of respondents in each education category who rated the performance of the mini-station police as being good is almost identical. It should also be noted that a larger proportion of the low and medium income groups rated the mini-station performance as being good than did the high income group.

Table 13.3. Police Performance Rating by Type of Organization

| | District Police | | | | Mini-Station Police | | | |
| | poor | fair | good | N | poor | fair | good | N |
		(percentages)				(percentages)		
Gender								
Male	13	30	57	167	3	17	80	142
Female	66	34	51	309	5	17	78	284
				476				426
Race								
Black	22	39	39	161	8	21	71	144
White	10	28	61	297	3	14	83	247
Other	33	67	67	15	0	27	73	15
				473				406
Age								
< 35	17	39	44	82	12	27	62	60
36-50	16	27	57	108	6	12	82	91
51-65	13	35	52	145	2	38	78	129
66-80	11	29	60	116	1	14	85	110
> 80		30	30	40	10	40	60	5
				461				395
Education								
< high school	21	29	50	52	8	16	76	50
high school	14	35	51	239	4	16	80	206
college/tech	15	31	54	135	4	16	78	111
graduate school	9	27	63	35	3	21	76	29
				461				396
Income								
< $10,000	15	34	51	132	5	14	81	111
$10,001 to $25,000	18	23	59	139	1	12	86	125
> $25,001	13	38	49	133	6	18	77	108
				404				344

No doubt much of the positive sentiment toward the mini-station police developed as a result of the citizens participation in Crime Watch programs. One of the primary duties of the mini-station police is to help the citizens of the neighborhood establish and maintain a crime prevention program. Table 13.4 shows the statistically significant difference in the rating of the mini-station police between those who participated in crime watch and those who did not. In fact, 84 percent of the active respondents rated the mini-station police performance as being good compared to 57 percent of the respondents who were active in a crime watch program who rated the district police performance as being good.

Table 13.4 Rating of Mini-Station Police Performance by Participation in a Neighborhood Watch Program

Active in Crime Watch

Performance Rating	No		Yes		Total
	N	%	N	%	
Poor	6	11	10	3	16
Fair	18	34	44	13	62
Good	29	55	278	84	307
	53		332		385

Significance –.00000

It would be logical to expect victims of crime to rate police performance lower than non-victims and this turned out to be the case. However, it is worth noting that the ratings given by crime victims for mini-station police performance was much better than the performance ratings given to district police by crime victims. While 52 percent of the crime victims rated the district police performance as being good, 72 percent of the crime victims rated the mini-station performance as being good.

A study of community leaders' perceptions of the importance of the mini-station program in Cleveland (Gustavson & Kratcoski, 1991) revealed that they were quite positive in their ratings of the program. This research concentrated on community leaders such as politicians, teachers and administrators, owners of businesses, and ministers who were known to be active in community affairs.

When asked what they perceived as the most important problems plaguing their neighborhoods more than 50 percent of the respondents mentioned drugs, robbery, residential burglary and fear for personal safety as the most important problems facing the neighborhoods in which they reside or work. Other problems such as getting the trash cleaned up, clearing out junk cars and enforcing housing violations were mentioned, but were given much less importance than the serious crime problems.

Ninety percent of the respondents stated that the neighborhood benefited from the mini-station program just by having an officer assigned to that specific neighborhood. By patrolling the neighborhood, getting to know the people, and by taking an active interest in crime prevention activities, the residents were benefiting. More than 80 percent of the respondents offered positive comments on the program. The larger majority of the respondents believed that the intensive patrolling of the neighborhoods by the mini-station officers and their involvement in crime watch activities conducted in the neighborhoods benefited the community a great deal and that these activities of the mini-station police should be expanded and intensified if the crime problems of the neighborhoods' were to be solved. A majority of the respondents believed that the number of officers assigned to the program should be increased and the times during the week that the mini-stations are staffed should be lengthened.

There was a strong belief that the mere visibility of the officer in the neighborhood prevented crime and reduced the fear of crime. Some of the respondents believed district or zone car officers should become more involved in community meetings and activities. In fact, there were some suggestions that the entire Cleveland Police Department could be restructured along a mini-station model.

In conclusion, while exploratory in nature, the results of the community leader survey and interviews suggest a great deal of support for the program, considerable satisfaction with the performance of the officers and a desire to have the program expanded. The crime control and prevention functions for the program seem to be the reasons why community leaders perceive it as beneficial.

DISCUSSION AND IMPLICATIONS

Although the findings of this research must be interpreted with caution, they do appear to support the notion that community policing programs such as the Mini-Station Police Program in Cleveland can be vehicles for improving the citizens' satisfaction with police performance, especially in those inner city neighborhoods that are predominately minority and poor. Research focusing on citizens' attitudes toward police reveals that the larger majority are generally quite satisfied with police performance and service with the exception of black and other minorities, the young and the poor. Our findings, which show blacks, Hispanics, and other minorities to be rather positive in their feelings about the performance and service of the police, especially mini-station police, is important because they illustrate that perceptions and opinions of job performance can change if the appropriate message is conveyed. As noted in the paper, even a large percentage of those who were victims of crime maintained that the mini-station police were doing a good job.

The Dukes data demonstrate that the citizens of Cleveland generally are more positive in attitudes toward the mini-station police than to the other officers who patrol their neighborhood, and the Gustavson interview data suggest that the very presence of the mini-station officers in the neighborhood and their activity in a neighborhood Crime Watch Program is a major factor affecting the attitudes of citizens toward the police and their satisfaction with the police. If the police gain the respect of the citizenry, it is likely that the citizenry will willingly give information to the police about various law-breakers in the community, and in fact may even assist in various types of police work such as is found in the Cleveland Police Mini-Station Program in which citizens volunteer to man the station in the absence of the assigned officer and also patrol in the role of auxiliary officers. This research also suggests policing programs in inner city neighborhoods can lead to a reduction of the fear of crime in those neighborhoods, which can result in an increase in activity outside the home by the residents. While it is difficult to prove conclusively, it is believed that street activity in the neighborhood is an effective deterrent to crime.

Some of the research on community policing has shown that with the police and the citizenry working together, not only are the services that the police provide likely to improve, but the services provided by other organizations such as schools and social work agencies likely to improve. When citizens start asking for more services, they often obtain more and better services because of the image of a "united front" that they are able to convey.

14

Police-Community Partnerships: Neighborhood Watch and the Neighborhood Liaison Officer Program in Kalamazoo, Michigan

Rhonda K. DeLong
Western Michigan University

INTRODUCTION

Community-based crime prevention programs are being utilized in many communities throughout the United States. Many of these programs seek to increase social networks among residents. As Elliott Currie has concluded, "there is considerable evidence that strong social networks play a large part in preventing crime" (Currie, 1985:254).

Neighborhood Watch is such a program, used as an approach to crime prevention. Not only do Neighborhood Watch programs seek to reduce and prevent crime, but they strive toward reducing the "fear of crime" among residents. Reducing the "fear of crime" is not only important to neighborhood watch and similar programs, but it is an important objective of any police foot patrol program (Currie, 1985:254). Setting priorities to reduce the "fear of crime" and by developing a working relationship between citizens and police officers, the creation of an environment where criminal activity is no longer tolerated becomes a possibility.

Due to the complexity of crime and the diversity of communities, one program alone cannot address the needs and concerns of citizens and the police. Programs that seek to develop a working relationship between citizen and police may help to increase overall satisfaction with quality of life in a neighborhood, assist in reducing the "fear of crime," and help to reduce crime activity within a given location. Resident satisfaction with the local environment, and respect and trust of police officers are integral components of the community-based crime prevention effort.

In the city of Kalamazoo, Michigan, neighborhoods and police officers have joined together in a working partnership to address the issue of crime and its prevention. The public safety department's "Neighborhood Liaison Officers" work closely with volunteers from neighborhood watch to effect change in the community. The Neighborhood Liaison Officers are practicing the philosophy of "community policing" by becoming partners with the residents. The officers have shed the traditional approach to policing requiring strict enforcement and have replaced it with a "proactive" method of serving the residents of the community.

This paper describes the Neighborhood Watch and Neighborhood Liaison Officer (NLO) partnership now operating in the Vine Neighborhood of Kalamazoo. Their joint effort has aided in the unification of many residents in the common goal of neighborhood revitalization. My experience in this effort has convinced me that reducing the "fear of crime," rebuilding neighborhoods, and renewing the relationships among the police and community through a working partnership can serve as the basis to bring about lasting change.

In May of 1990, I was hired as part of a State Grant funded program titled, "Crackdown on Crack." The grant provided for my position as Crime Prevention Organizer. The goals of the project included establishing block watches and fortifying the Neighborhood Watch network already established. Canvassing the neighborhood, setting up and participating in Neighborhood Watch meetings, and interacting with the residents and NLO were all part of my job description. This gave me a firsthand account of what the needs and concerns were of the neighborhood. The overall goal of the grant was to reduce the frequency of crack cocaine trafficking on the streets of the Vine Neighborhood, which was to be accomplished through the combined efforts of the Department of Public Safety and neighborhood residents.

My position as Crime Prevention Organizer put me in direct contact with the residents and the NLO. From May 1990 through January 1991 I talked with residents during Neighborhood Watch meetings, home visits, and telephone contacts. Our discussions centered around their perceptions regarding the effectiveness of Neighborhood Watch and the Neighborhood Liaison Officer programs as well as the issue of their "fear of crime." The majority of those I spoke with held a positive opinion of both programs. The presence of the NLO walking their streets provided them with a sense of security and assisted in reducing their "fear of crime." The participation of the Neighborhood Watch volunteers helped to reduce the level of suspicion directed toward their neighbors, and the NLO provided a feeling of safety both in their homes and on the street.

I also had the opportunity to accompany the NLO as he made his contacts and conducted crime prevention training throughout the neighborhood. For some residents, this was the first time they had seen an officer in the role of service provider and partner rather than enforcer. The NLO was invited into homes for coffee and to sit and discuss concerns one-on-one. For some, this was also the first time they had actually talked to an officer in a positive encounter. I observed a bond of trust develop as a result of this one-on-one interaction. Step by step, contact by contact, changes in the perceptions of residents toward their community and the police took place.

Free security lights were offered as part of the grant. The NLO provided instruction as to where to place the lights as well as other home security measures. Free paint was offered to residents to assist in neighborhood beautification. Residents began planting more flowers, playgrounds were kept clean and children once again began to play in these areas.

Through field observation, I received insight into the needs and concerns of the people of the Vine Neighborhood. Walking down the sidewalks, observing neighbors in their yard rather than behind closed doors, watching the NLO play basketball with the kids at the playground provided a renewed understanding that people and police working together toward a common goal can bring about positive changes.

THE CITY OF KALAMAZOO

The City of Kalamazoo, Michigan, is moderately sized city with a culturally diverse population of 80,277. Located approximately midway between Detroit and Chicago and near a major interstate that connects these two major cities, Kalamazoo faces social problems similar to those confronting Detroit and Chicago. Most importantly in recent years the city has experienced an increase in illegal drug sales, drug use, and drug-related crime. It would seem that the prevalence of this type of crime is due in part to its convenient proximity to both Detroit and Chicago. The seven neighborhoods that make up the core city appear especially vulnerable to criminal activity.

Because of its concern for the citizens of Kalamazoo, the Department of Public Safety examined its traditional approaches to policing, evaluating the way in which police services were being delivered to the public. It considered new and different approaches that might better address the apparently unstoppable problem. As a result of this policy and procedure analysis, the department turned to a "community policing philosophy" to better serve the citizens of Kalamazoo. The Department of Public Safety was not alone in seeking a "proactive" impact upon the crime problem. Residents formed Neighborhood Watch groups and joined with the Department of Public Safety to work on innovative ways to prevent crime.

THE KALAMAZOO DEPARTMENT OF PUBLIC SAFETY

The Kalamazoo Department of Public Safety (KDPS) employs approximately 265 sworn personnel, and is organized into the following six divisions:

> Office of the Chief/Administration
> Operations
> Criminal Investigation
> Kalamazoo Valley Enforcement Team
> Training
> Service

Each division has specific responsibilities and operates under the philosophy of "Community Public Safety." In 1992, the Department implemented its "Community Public Safety program for the purpose of improving the coordination of all departmental resources in support of the City neighborhoods" (Kalamazoo Department of Public Safety 1992 Annual Report).

THE VINE NEIGHBORHOOD

The City of Kalamazoo has seven predominant neighborhoods: Stuart, West Douglas, Northside, Eastside, Edison, Oakwood, and Vine. The Vine Neighborhood is home to approximately 8,500 residents from diverse racial, economic, and educational backgrounds. Eighty percent of the properties within the neighborhood are rentals. Because of this high percentage of rental properties relative to owner-occupied properties and a relatively large college student population, the neighborhood is not stable; every year a significant proportion of residents move in and out of the neighborhood.

Significant economic diversity between the southern and northern portions of the neighborhood is also apparent. The southwest area is economically affluent, with owner-occupied single family dwellings. The northern portion is much less affluent with multiple family dwellings located in aged housing stock.

Overall, the area is a mix of residential, small business, and commercial properties. Recreational opportunities are not readily available, and some residents turn to the street for their activities. Trafficking in crack cocaine has become a popular activity in the northwest and southeast sectors of the neighborhood. In some areas of the neighborhood, individual residents have witnessed open and repeated drug transactions taking place in front of their own homes; they have felt unsafe with such crime on their doorsteps but have also felt real fear in directly addressing the crime.

Neighborhood Watch was begun in hopes of reversing this trend through collective action. Neighborhood Watch has sought to involve residents in the task of eliminating this and other criminal activity not only through vigilance but through empowering local residents through "strength in numbers." Prior to the Neighborhood Watch program, neighbor-to-neighbor interaction was severely restricted when criminal activity took place in the streets of the neighborhood. Neighborhood Watch was intended to reclaim the strength that community residents provide each other through normal, healthy community interaction.

NEIGHBORHOOD WATCH

In 1984, a small group of Vine Neighborhood residents came together in an effort to reclaim their neighborhood from a variety of social problems, and Neighborhood Watch was created. Their goal was to reduce the amount of criminal activity in the neighborhood and begin to rebuild a "sense of community" among the residents.

Each year since the creation of Neighborhood Watch, the months of June, July, August, and September have been dedicated to neighborhood "canvassing." Members of Neighborhood Watch attempt to visit each household in the Vine Neighborhood and invite residents (both old and new) to attend an outdoor meeting that is scheduled nearby. The meetings have offered crime prevention tips, refreshments, and the opportunity to interact with each other as well as the "Neighborhood Liaison Officer." These face-to-face contacts are a vital component of the Neighborhood Watch program in Vine, and an important step in building strong social networks.

Elliot Currie elaborates on Neighborhood Watch programs in his book, *Confronting Crime*. He lists the two important objectives of the program as: (1) reducing the fear of crime and (2) bringing residents together (Currie, 1985:254-55). The Neighborhood Watch program in Vine seeks to meet these objectives through facilitating interaction among residents and emphasizing proactive responses to the crime problem.

Currie also cites several studies that indicate that the apparent successes of these programs may be due to the fact that criminal activity is being displaced from one neighborhood to another; namely to those less organized (Currie, 1985:255).

It is this very problem that the seven neighborhoods of Kalamazoo are addressing, for each has an organized Neighborhood Watch program in place. Each neighborhood is assigned one or two Neighborhood Liaison Officers to assist the residents. The hope is that by having Neighborhood Watch and the NLO programs operating throughout the city, criminal activity will be eliminated rather than displaced.

THE NEIGHBORHOOD LIAISON OFFICER PROGRAM

In 1980, the Kalamazoo Police Department initiated a change in their approach to policing. The "Neighborhood Police Officer" program was launched across the seven neighborhoods. The "NPO" program provided the groundwork from which to build a partnership between the police and community. It provided the officer with a unique opportunity to become involved on a more personal level with neighborhood residents. Officers integrated a service-based approach with their traditional enforcement duties.

Thus, the image of the officer began to change from an "enforcer" to "public servant" and partner. Enforcement of the law was still considered a vital part of the police officer's duty, but the officer's role now combined traditional law enforcement with a public service emphasis.

In 1984, the department replaced its police-only agency to one of public safety, and the "NPO" program became the "Neighborhood Liaison Officer" project. Since 1984, the personnel involved in the program has increased from four to 10 officers.

According to the department's 1992 Annual Report:

> a fundamental purpose of the NLO program is to resolve chronic crime problems which detract from the quality of life within selected neighborhoods. Throughout the year crime prevention activities included organizing and promoting Neighborhood Watch groups, conducting residential and commercial building security surveys, and giving public presentations on prevention related topics. The NLO works in direct cooperation with the public to preserve the peace, deter crime, reduce citizen fear, and provide for a safe environment. The major emphasis of the NLO activity is concentrated on problem solving at the local level, neighborhood development, prevention and education, liaison activities, and traditional public safety enforcement duties. Working in the neighborhood, the NLO concentrates on problems that cannot be resolved by routine police response methods (KDPS Annual Report, 1992:7-8).

Many police/public safety and community planning personnel are diligently searching for ways to revitalize urban communities. The Neighborhood Watch and NLO programs in partnership seek to promote revitalization and restoration of a "sense of community" among residents. It is the opinion of this author that restoration and revitalization can begin when people take pride in their community.

In order to create an atmosphere of trust between police and residents, the Neighborhood Liaison Officer has become a part of the neighborhood. In the early days of policing, when patrol vehicles were nonexistent and "walking the beat" was the norm, the officer was a part of the neighborhood. This relationship with the community and its residents may not only lend itself to effective crime prevention, but may also contribute to greater job satisfaction (Trojanowicz, 1990:178).

The emphasis of Neighborhood Watch and the NLO program is on "grassroots" organization and face-to-face interaction. The NLO becomes the neighborhood's link to the Department of Public Safety. Residents have the opportunity to interact with an officer on a daily basis, possibly helping to reduce their frustration and apathy over the conditions in their community.

LITERATURE REVIEW

The literature related to community-crime prevention and community policing is abundant. James Garofalo and Maureen McLeod (1989) have studied Neighborhood Watch extensively. Robert Trojanowicz (1990) has examined several programs operating under the philosophy of community policing in the United States and throughout the rest of the world. In evaluating the effectiveness of such programs researchers have often focused on the reduction of "fear of crime" and strengthening of social networks rather than a decrease in the overall crime rate (Currie, 1985:254).

Nationwide, Neighborhood Watch is one of the most popular and widely-used community crime prevention programs. Through the 1980s it had become a centerpiece of both local crime prevention efforts and federal funding for crime prevention (Garofalo & McLeod, 1989). The ease by which the program can be implemented, and its cost effectiveness are two of reasons for its popularity among federal and local officials.

But the fact that Crime Watch is in the hands of neighborhood residents and empowers them to help protect themselves is the most important feature in its acceptance by the residents themselves. Elliot Currie (1985), closely examined community-based crime prevention programs such as Neighborhood Watch. He has found considerable evidence to support the claim that "strong social networks play a large part in preventing crime and, for that matter, provide the context for administering effective "informal" social sanctions. He also states, "It seems clear, that in some cases Neighborhood Watch programs can bring otherwise atomized community residents together and, like police foot patrols, help reduce the *fear* of crime. These are not insignificant results, and they are surely worth encouraging (Currie, 1985:254).

According to Currie, "one key limitation of these programs is that they are oriented much more to "stranger" crime—and especially to property crimes like burglary—than to non-stranger violence. Indeed, some of the research on community crime prevention has a disturbing tendency to describe the world as divided into the community on the one hand, and strangers on the other; as the National Institute of Justice states, "Residents get to know their neighbors and so learn to distinguish strangers and recognize when the activity in the next yard or down the corridor may not be legitimate" (Currie, 1985:255).

Curries accepts the fact that traditional programs have their limitations. "Community crime prevention is not a mistaken concept, it only needs to encompass a much broader range of potential community activities." (1985:256) Neighborhood Watch in the Vine Neighborhood is attempting to broaden its range of community activities by providing social events to promote positive relationships among neighbors and strive toward the goal of neighborhood revitalization. Vital to both the Neighborhood Watch and NLO programs is the support offered to residents coupled with a broad range of community activities. The Annual National Night Out is one such event that serves to bring neighbors together. The Department of Public Safety closes off several streets within the neighborhood for this event, giving residents the opportunity to hold block parties into the night. The Chief of Public Safety, along with other city leaders, takes part in the event by attending the many block parties in the community. This enables the residents to meet with the leaders of their community informally. This environment is conducive to open discussion and the citizenry share their concerns as well as praise for the work of the Department of Public Safety.

THEORIES

In order to better understand the role of Neighborhood Watch and NLO programs upon a community, application and integration of two very different theories are needed. "Ecological Theory" and "Social Bond Theory" have very different roots in sociological and criminological analysis and direct us toward some different conclusions about policy and practice in this area. Together, however, they are very useful in understanding the ways in which the Crime Watch and Neighborhood Liaison Officer program have succeeded in meeting the needs of the community.

ECOLOGICAL THEORY

Clifford Shaw and Henry McKay's research in Chicago during the early 1920s helped produce the "Ecological Theory" of the Chicago School. Shaw and McKay observed transitions within the central city of Chicago and made several assumptions regarding crime causation and neighborhood conditions (Siegel, 1986:193).

Population growth in the city had brought with it a diverse cross-section of people. "The newcomers occupied the oldest housing and therefore faced numerous health and environmental hazards. Physically deteriorating sections of the city soon developed" (Siegel, 1986:193). Shaw and McKay saw this changing urban environment as one factor in the causation of crime. Their research showed that

Chicago had developed into "distinct neighborhoods, some marked by wealth and luxury, others by overcrowding, poor health, sanitary conditions and extreme poverty" (Siegel, 1986:194).

Shaw and McKay viewed crime as a product of ". . . the decaying transitional neighborhood which manifested social disorganization and maintained conflicting values and social problems." Clifford Shaw describes the concept of social disorganization in the following paragraph:

> The successive changes in the composition of population, the disintegration of the alien cultures, the diffusion of divergent cultural standards, and the gradual industrialization of the area have resulted in dissolution of the neighborhood culture and organization. The continuity of conventional neighborhood traditions and institutions is broken. Thus, the effectiveness of the neighborhood as a unit of control and as a medium for the transmission of the moral standards of society is greatly diminished. (Siegel, 1988:194)

The basis for Shaw and Mckay's theory was that neighborhood disintegration and slum conditions are primary causes of criminal behavior (Siegel, 1986:194).

CONTROL THEORY

Control theory maintains that all people have the potential to commit criminal acts and that current societal conditions provide the opportunity to do so. The focus of control theory is not upon why people commit crime but rather on "why don't people commit crime?" Control theorists answer this question by contending that "people refrain from committing crime because they have a stake in conformity—a real, present and logical reason to obey the rules of society" (Siegel, 1986:233).

One of the most widely recognized and criticized control theories is Travis Hirschi's Social Bond theory. Hirschi contends that criminogenic behaviors occur during a person's youth when the ties that bound him/her to society were weakened. The ties to family, friends, neighbors, school and job serve to prevent the individual from engaging in criminal acts. The individual fears that these criminal acts would endanger his/her important relationships. "Without social bonds, and in the absence of sensitivity to and interest in others, a person is free to commit criminal acts" (Siegel, 1986:233).

Four elements of Hirschi's social bond theory relevant to this discussion are: attachment, commitment, involvement, and belief. Attachment refers to a "person's sensitivity to and interest in others. Commitment involves the time, energy and effort expended in conventional lines of action. Involvement in community, school and family leaves little time for illegal behavior. Somehow, this involvement serves to insulate a person from the lure of criminal activity. Finally, the sharing of common moral beliefs by those who live in the same social setting helps to strengthen the bonds of attachment, commitment and involvement" (Siegel, 1986:233).

Neighborhood Watch and the NLO program each attempt to influence the degree of attachment one has to the neighborhood. The close interaction of officer and citizen is one method used by the Vine Neighborhood and Department of public Safety to increase this feeling of attachment. Neighborhood Watch programs emphasize the importance of knowing your neighbor and taking pride in your neighborhood. The NLO program emphasizes the importance of police/community interaction. It is possible that a person who develops a sense of attachment and ownership will be more likely to become actively involved in community projects and activities. Neighborhood Watch and the Neighborhood Liaison Officer programs seek to create feelings of attachment through motivational neighborhood meetings, crime prevention training sessions, and neighborhood-wide social events.

A vital component of Neighborhood Watch and the NLO program is the participation of dedicated and enthusiastic individuals in leadership positions. My interaction with the people of the Vine Neighborhood has shown that those who have ownership in the neighborhood appear more likely to exhibit attachment and commitment. This is especially true in the case of the Neighborhood Liaison Officer.

The position of NLO should be filled by officers who share a genuine concern for the community in which they serve. Those officers who seek power and strive for heavy enforcement are not the type of individual best suited for the position of NLO. Veteran officers who have become cynical from years of dealing with the negative side of humanity should not be considered. The ideal NLO must be vested in the job of fulfilling a role as public servant if the program is to be effective.

Placing an emphasis on communication and "people skills" will assist in promoting positive police/community relations. Too often police agencies place their emphasis upon physical skills, firearms, and enforcement tactics. In order for the program to be effective, the officer's primary focus should be on the service aspects of the job rather than strict enforcement. This focus may assist in developing the bonds of attachment, commitment, involvement, and belief, not only for the residents, but for the officer as well.

Neighborhood Watch encourages involvement in neighborhood affairs. The NLO enhances this by developing innovative programs that help to increase resident satisfaction by directly involving them in the decision-making process. Once involved in this process the residents may begin to feel an attachment to their environment and to the officer. This in turn may lead to a commitment to the goal of neighborhood revitalization through crime prevention measures.

Encouraging adoption of a belief system is an important goal of Neighborhood watch and the NLO. Even with the diversity found in urban communities, common beliefs can be identified. Values such as "sharing, sensitivity to the rights of others, and admiration of the criminal code" are common beliefs supported by Neighborhood Watch and the NLO (Siegel, 1986:234).

Each element of Hirschi's Social Bond Theory is important to the success of Neighborhood Watch and the NLO program. The purpose of these programs extends beyond the basic goal of crime prevention. In partnership, the neighborhood watch and NLO programs seek to restore a "sense of community" among the residents. Through neighbor and police interaction, attachment, commitment, involvement, and belief within the community is strengthened.

METHODS OF OBSERVATION

The primary method used to look at the neighborhood watch and NLO programs was field observation. The majority of the conclusions are a direct result of my interaction with the people of the Vine Neighborhood and the Neighborhood Liaison Officer assigned there. Approximately 330 individuals out of the 8,500 residents were asked to share their perceptions of the programs. Seventy-five percent of these were contacted during Neighborhood Watch meetings. The remaining twenty-five percent were contacted by phone, during visits to the Vine Neighborhood Office, or while walking through the neighborhood.

Field observations provided important information regarding both programs. During the weekly outdoor meetings, residents from various ethnic and racial groups came together and discussed common concerns. Children played together and the fear of being out after dark was not apparent. The meetings provided residents with a forum from which to voice their concerns about the neighborhood and gave the NLO an opportunity to offer suggestions and possible solutions to their concerns.

As a result of these meetings neighbors became acquainted and organized their "block" into a neighborhood watch. I observed an attitudinal shift from general suspicion to genuine concern for their neighbor. In some cases, stereotypes were broken as neighbor interacted with neighbor.

The following questions assisted in structuring my field observations and personal contacts with the people of the Vine Neighborhood.

1. Is there a relationship between the presence of Neighborhood Watch/Neighborhood Liaison Officer program and the fear of crime in the Vine Neighborhood?

2. Does the Neighborhood Watch and NLO program impact positively or negatively upon the neighborhood in terms of resident satisfaction?

3. Is there a relationship between the presence of the NLO and the level of reported crime in the area?

4. Is there a decrease in the number of police/community relations complaints when an NLO is present in the neighborhood?

5. Has the NLO program assisted in the development of positive relationships among officer and resident?

In determining the success of a program one should first define what success is in terms of the surroundings. A lower incidence of reported criminal activity may define success for some, while others may define it as an increased sense of security. Reliance on data from departmental reports can be deceiving in this regard. These data show only reported crime and do not address the "fear of crime" issue which is important when examining community-based crime prevention efforts.

It is probable that Neighborhood Watch programs may produce an increase in reported crime. A strong emphasis is placed on crime reporting techniques by both Neighborhood Watch and the NLO. The residents may be more likely to report criminal activity when they have a relationship with the NLO. If researchers rely too much on official departmental data, accurate evaluations of community-based crime prevention programs may not be possible.

How can these programs be accurately evaluated? Utilization of several methods may provide insight into why they work, not just how they work. Columns of numerical data do not always give an accurate picture of what is taking place. Official statistics cannot effectively measure a resident's level of anxiety concerning crime in the neighborhood, nor can they accurately evaluate the level of pride and attachment one has to the neighborhood.

In evaluating social intervention programs such as Neighborhood Watch and the NLO program, the researcher should not reduce the research process down to a simple experimental design. Methods that alienate the researcher from the people may not furnish an accurate portrayal of what actually is taking place as a result of these programs.

My findings relative to these questions are very clear. Residents stated that they felt less afraid and more secure in their neighborhood with the presence of these programs. They also indicated that they were generally more satisfied with their neighborhood environment because of the neighborhood watch and the NLO. Police-community relations has improved so much since the establishment of the NLO program that there has not been one formal complaint lodged against an NLO. In fact, although I have yet to determine if the NLO program has substantially affected the relationahip between other public safety officers and citizens, initial findings indicate an overall decrease in the number of police/community complaints in relation to the total number of calls for service. It is difficult to determine the overall effect of this program on crime, though; reported crime, especially Part II offenses actually rose in the neighborhood. This is probably a measure of the success of the NLO, who has instructed residents in the proper reporting procedures.

CONCLUSIONS

Community-based crime prevention strategies are an essential component of an effective public safety department. Implementation of an NLO program enhances the probability for success in the prevention of crime and the building of positive police-community relations. Further studies are necessary in order to better determine "what works" in community-based crime prevention. Each community must assess itself and determine what programs would best be suited to their particular needs. When a community needs face-to-face interaction among people and the establishment of a long term commitment, programs such as Neighborhood Watch and the Neighborhood Liaison Officer have the capability to be successful in the fight against crime. The restoration of a "sense of community" and pride in one's neighborhood that they help provide can begin the process of neighborhood revitalization and crime reduction.

Section VI

POLICY ISSUES AND THE FUTURE OF COMMUNITY POLICING

The literature on community policing has grown rapidly in the past five years but most of this literature addresses the topic from either of two directions: (1) a general discussion of the philosophy of community policing, or (2) a detailed description of a specific program that is currently operating in a police department in a major American city.

A much smaller literature however, addresses the crucial operational issues of community policing. This book has attempted to contribute to this literature in a number of ways, not the least of which is to approach the crucial evaluation of community police programs. In general, the literature on this topic is positive.

The selections in Part VI reflect this. But just how these evaluations are done, and what measures are used becomes the real issue in operating a community policing program. We have found that three sources of relevant evaluative data are available: (1) officer daily conduct related to community policing, including amount of community contact and problem resolution; (2) reduction of crime and/or increase in crime reporting in the neighborhood; and (3) reported satisfaction and/or reduction of fear of citizens.

The effects of community policing are difficult to measure because community policing takes place in an active world; other police and justice efforts take place simultaneously with it. Community policing operates side-by-side with traditional policing. Thus, it is difficult to separate the effects of the two. In fact, a myriad of social, political, and economic forces both promote and discourage crime while we are trying to measure the effects of one program. Furthermore, community policing is, by definition, a dynamic and prevention-oriented approach to policing. It is defined and redefined in its application by officers and supervisors every day. How do we measure the effect of something when that "thing" is really a concept that takes on different operational form even as we watch it? And it is difficult to measure crimes that *did not* take place. Remember, the success of a community policing program from an impact evaluation standpoint is, essentially, that nothing happened. More than a methodological issue, this political and policy issue can threaten a program when its success is taken for granted.

Finally, very little specific information has been collected that bears directly on the actual daily duties of community police officers, including the number of offenses processed by them. For these reasons, evaluation has been uneven, controversial and difficult to complete. Cardarelli and McDevitt provide a very thorough examination of these issues.

When asked to give their opinions on community policing, many veteran police officers remarked that they have seen many fads in police work come and go and no doubt they will eventually see community policing replaced with some new policing fad. These officers as well as many administrators believe that there is only one method of policing and it is the traditional way. Thus some police administrators have resisted introducing community policing into their organization until it became clear that it would be politically expedient to embrace it. The fact that community policing is currently being strongly endorsed by politicians on all levels has already been alluded to in several chapters of this book. Police administrators who oppose this pet project of the politicians may find themselves under considerable disfavor and even out of a job.

Some administrators have been known to use the "community policing mania" which appears to be in place as an avenue to pursue their own goals or to enhance the image of the department. Ross addresses the issue of using community policing rhetoric as a way to improve police-community relations. Since most community policing programs have not been systematically evaluated, it has yet to be determined what effect they have had on prevention and controlling crime and improving the quality of life. The public relations facet of community policing is the promise of improved communications between the police and the citizens a decrease in crime and fear of crime and more citizens becoming involved in the fight against crime. He argues that the evidence that these things are actually accomplished is not evident.

Turner and Wiatrowski conclude that the introduction of community policing into communities throughout the country has led to a situation in which the police are becoming innovators in these communities. They are taking the lead in soliciting assistance from various governmental institutions and agencies to assure that the health and fire codes are enforced, residents receive the social service which are available to them and obtain other benefits that are within their realm to grant. Many agency administrators may be uncomfortable with the proactive approach to solving community problems being employed by the police and some situations that can be asked to reduce the resistance of these administrators are given.

15

Toward a Conceptual Framework for Evaluating Community Policing

Albert P. Cardarelli
University of Massachussetts—Boston

Jack McDevitt
Northeastern University

INTRODUCTION

As the present volume makes clear, police departments across the United States are at a critical juncture in the formulation of a law enforcement philosophy able to meet the challenges associated with an ever-changing and diverse society. In most large cities, and increasingly in many smaller municipalities, police officials are being asked to do more with less resources at their disposal. Severe budget constraints coupled with a range of social and economic problems that show little or no sign of diminishing make this task a formidable one.

To meet this challenge many departments are currently experimenting with a wide range of policing strategies loosely defined as "community policing" programs (Goldstein, 1990; Skogan, 1990; Trojanowicz & Bucqueroux, 1990; Brown, 1989; Kelling et al., 1988). Stressing quality police services and greater accountability to the community, these programs emphasize the need for a cooperative relationship between police and community to deal with the variety of problems associated with crime, fear, and urban decay (Brown, 1989).

While community policing is still in its formative stage, the potential participation of community residents in policing efforts signifies a fundamental break with traditional policing where a more reactive style of policing prevails (Goldstein, 1987). The move toward a style of policing embracing a philosophy of participatory democracy is not without significant obstacles. Given the history of tension and distrust between police and some communities, especially communities of color, there is likely to be considerable reluctance on the part of both parties to any suggestion of partnership in solving neighborhood problems. An additional barrier to community policing involves serious revenue shortfalls facing most large municipal governments. In the current economic climate, public officials are likely to give serious scrutiny to proposed programs calling for added resource allocations. Absent adequate and appropriate evidence to overcome these challenges, community policing programs may fall victim to the vagaries of budget reductions and the growing demands by municipal governments for cost-effective policies and procedures.

Convinced that community policing offers a viable alternative to traditional policing, the present chapter endeavors to establish a model for evaluating the diverse programs being implemented under the rubric of "community policing." The need for evaluation cannot be overstated. The evaluation materials that do exist are of limited use due to the paucity of information on the effectiveness of intervention strategies associated with community policing (National Institute of Justice, 1992). In addressing this scarcity of evaluative data, emphasis is directed to two areas of need, each viewed as critical to efforts aimed at improving the art and science of community policing. The first involves the need to establish clear and shared documentation of the elements around which community policing programs are constructed; a second involves the need to determine the interrelationships between and among the elements of community policing programs (Skolnick & Bayley, 1988).

To meet these admittedly difficult objectives, a conceptual framework addressing several variables likely to effect the conceptualization, design, implementation, and evaluation of community policing is presented. The framework builds upon the existing literature on community policing as well as data solicited from police chiefs throughout the United States. In our attempt to understand the current state of community policing in large city police departments, questionnaires were mailed during 1992 to police departments of the 40 largest cities in the United States. Returns were received from 34 departments. The questionnaire was concerned with determining factors police executives view as important in establishing community policing programs; the criteria departments utilize in establishing these programs; and whether the programs are implemented on a citywide basis, or restricted to certain neighborhoods. Data from more than 250 police departments in Massachusetts were also considered in our approach to establishing a framework for understanding community policing. In both surveys, police chiefs described what they considered to be both the major elements, and barriers to community policing. Selected findings from the large-city survey are included to illustrate current thinking by police executives as to the direction of community policing in the United States.

TOWARD A CONCEPTUAL FRAMEWORK
OF COMMUNITY POLICING

In view of the persistent levels of crime and unrest in many of the large urban areas of the United States, the move toward community policing is understandable. Unable to significantly impact the persistently high levels of crime and delinquency through traditional policing policies, an increasing number of police departments are exploring new ways in which to involve community residents along a proactive continuum of activities. In our national review of large city police departments, for example, 29 of the 34 departments reported they either have a community policing program in place or one planned for the future. Yet, as we noted above, an examination of the literature on community policing indicates a decided lack of comprehensive information regarding the effectiveness of these programs. Part of the reason for this lack of data rests with the fact that community policing is a relatively new development. Few of the cities surveyed have long-established city-wide community policing programs. Of the 25 large city departments with some form of community policing in place, 24 began their programs within the past three to five years. The "newness " of these programs is reflected in the confusion among law enforcement officials as to the meaning of community policing. Some police chiefs view it as involving neighborhood foot patrols and periodic meetings with community residents; others, as some form of community relations and outreach; only a small number of police officials envision community residents sharing in the decision-making processes related to community policing. The data from the national survey also indicate that for a small number of departments, early reform strategies (team policing, foot patrols, community relations) have simply been reclassified as "community policing." For the vast number of large departments, however, much more fundamental changes in the delivery of services are currently under way.

Given these conditions, it becomes essential for police chiefs to direct appropriate concern to those issues likely to have a decided impact on the outcome of community policing programs. In the pages below, a conceptual framework for understanding some of the dynamics associated with community policing is suggested. Additionally, we include an evaluation model bound by neither the specific interventions nor the character of the community where such strategies are targeted. The framework builds upon the existing literature on community policing as well as data from the surveys noted above. In establishing this framework, we were guided by Goldstein's view that community policing should include programs that demonstrate ". . . a [police] presence in the community; that they [police] are easily accessible, frequently visible, and caring in their relationships with citizens" (Goldstein, 1987).

The External Environment

Figure 15.1 presents a framework for understanding the conceptualization, design, and implementation of community policing. Additional emphasis is placed on several program elements around which most community policing programs are structured. Taken together, these elements provide a paradigm for the collection and analyses of data essential to the evaluation of community policing. By placing the evaluation model within a broader framework emphasis is directed to the importance of the interactive effects of the external and internal environments on community policing. The implementation of community policing, for example, may be effected more by structural factors of a state or national character over which police administrators and program managers have little control, than by those of a local nature. The continued transition of large cities from manufacturing to service economies; the outflow of manufacturing and retail jobs to suburban malls and industrial parks; the higher than average rates of unemployment, especially among minority youth; the growing populations of homeless and those in the underclass have changed the character and milieu of many American cities and have made modern policing more difficult (Wilson, 1987; Skogan, 1990). Police policies to deal with the homeless, for example, have been largely unsuccessful and in most cases result in a no-win situation for police officials. Legislative authority, demographic shifts and court-ordered procedures are just a few of the other factors effecting police departments throughout the country. In addition to these agents of change, annual budgetary struggles provide significant challenges to the operationalization of community policing.

When the demands of community residents are added to these factors, it is all the more important for police departments to address pre-existing socioeconomic conditions in the planning and implementation of community policing. A brief discussion of several of the above conditions in terms of their potential consequences for community policing is provided below.

Figure 15.1 Community Policing: A Conceptual Model

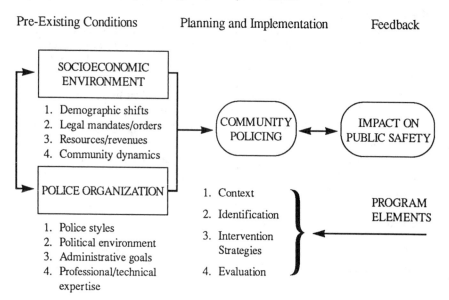

Demographic Shifts

Throughout the country, large cities have undergone significant changes in the racial and ethnic make-up of their populations. Additionally, many of the larger cities have witnessed both the gentrification and diversity of older neighborhoods. These changes have not only resulted in the displacement of low-income families, but in some cities they have led to significant power struggles over the appropriate use of existing housing and commercial facilities (Taylor & Covington, 1988). While police departments are certainly in no position to control demographic shifts, they can only ignore the consequences at their own peril. Increased demands for more minority representation on police forces in cities undergoing rapid racial and ethnic changes, as well as challenges to existing police affirmative action programs, have not been uncommon (Bopp & Whisenand, 1980).

These changes directly impact the management of large city administrations, including police departments. When racial and ethnic conflicts erupt into manifest violence, police departments are expected to achieve equilibrium as swiftly as possible. When they are unable to do so, they are usually held accountable and severely criticized (e.g., the Los Angeles riots in 1992). Implementing community policing without appropriate consideration of the racial and ethnic demographics in the community will likely lead to failure, or at best an unwillingness on the part of minority residents to participate.

Legislative Mandates and Court Orders

During the last two decades, major reforms associated with victims of violence (e.g., domestic violence and hate crimes) have been mandated by legislative bodies across the United States. Throughout the country, police departments are now required to deal with behavior once viewed as private, and for which a "hands-off" policy was commonplace. The growing political power of women has resulted in legislative initiatives affecting the rights of victims, especially those of domestic violence. Today any reluctance on the part of police to arrest domestic violators is likely to result in public criticism by advocacy groups demanding more stringent arrest policies. Even where a determined commitment on the part of the police to carry out these policies exists, police efforts may be constrained by the absence of resources or training needed for successful implementation.

Besides legislative mandates, police departments must constantly be prepared to respond to court orders beyond those directly tied to arrest and interrogation policies. In some states, for example, legal rulings on prison overcrowding have resulted in the early release of large numbers of inmates. Faced with the likelihood of limited holding space for arrestees, police officers may be hesitant to book misdemeanant offenders with little likelihood of confinement. From this perspective, changes in the criminal justice environment are likely to affect police departments and the success of community policing.

Budgetary Constraints

In recent years, police departments throughout the country have had to contend with major budgetary limits and reductions. While most police chiefs adhere to the position that community policing should be implemented citywide, our survey found that some departments were forced to target their programs to a select number of neighborhoods because of limited resources. These targeted programs may, however, lead to unintended consequences if police departments are not sensitive to the needs of the entire community. Neighborhoods most in need of services may lose out to those whose residents are more skilled in the give-and-take politics common to most large city governments.

Inadequate resources also affect the ability of police departments to involve other municipal agencies or departments in developing community policing strategies. Thus, in the event that a police department and community reach agreement that gang activities are serious disruptions to social cohesion, the need for youth activities programs to accompany police intervention will likely be suggested. In the absence of strong linkages to service agencies, the ability of community policing to effectively contain instances of public disorder may be seriously hindered.

The Importance of Community

As community policing programs have grown in number, there has been renewed interest in research concerned with the relationship between community cohesion and the nature and extent of crime and delinquency associated with the community (Reiss & Tonry, 1986; Skogan, 1990; Jencks & Peterson, 1991; Bursik & Grasmick, 1993). Building upon a rich tradition of ecological studies in sociology and criminology, researchers have begun to focus more closely on how community dynamics affect the ability of residents to achieve or maintain some sense of social control within the public realm of their neighborhoods (Sampson, 1987; Fischer, 1981; Dunham & Alpert, 1988). Since it is the neighborhood where community policing functions, the degree of social cohesion is a critical element to consider in the plan and design of community policing strategies. Sampson, for example, in analyzing the effects of formal and informal social control in 171 American cities found official sanctions (i.e., formal social control) had significant deterrent effects on criminal offending, while family disruption (i.e., informal social control) had strong effects on robbery and homicide offending (Sampson, 1986). In terms of family disruption Sampson also noted that communities with high divorce rates have many more isolated persons, thereby providing more vulnerable targets of victimization (Sampson, 1986). In communities of this kind, attempts by police to establish positive relationships with community residents will take considerable time and effort. Further, the promise of positive results is likely to be long in being realized. Under these conditions, the ability of police and residents to maintain a level of commitment to the program may be seriously tested.

In calling upon police organizations to account for neighborhood social cohesion in planning for community policing, we are not unaware of the need to establish objective standards for classifying neighborhoods along some dimension of social cohesion. This task, however, is beyond the scope of this paper. Rather, our purpose is to highlight the vital role of community cohesion in establishing effective crime control policies. Research has shown, for example, that local residents provide the best source of information about neighborhood problems of concern to the community (Pate et al., 1986). While police bring a level of expertise to the task of crime analyses, neighborhood residents are usually far more proficient in identifying potentially disruptive behaviors. Like other researchers, we believe there is a clear need for police organizations to construct strategies in terms of the views of neighborhood residents as to which behaviors are appropriate to the normative standards of the community. This observation in no way means all neighborhood residents have shared values or beliefs. Rather, our position is that there is likely to be general consensus on appropriate public behavior, and that this behavior symbolizes a level of social cohesion within the respective community or neighborhood. Finally, because socially cohesive neighborhoods may be more alike than not, it should be possible to establish strategies that lend themselves to evaluation over time, even while it will be difficult to establish a policing model applicable to all neighborhoods.

The Internal Environment

In addition to the pre-existing conditions associated with the external environment, advocates of community policing must factor into the community-policing equation those internal elements around which pre-existing law enforcement activities are generated. Figure 15.1 includes several elements (police styles, political environment, administrative goals, technical expertise) associated with police departments, and for which a rich array of research exists (Wilson, 1968; Sherman, 1986, 1992; Langworthy, 1986; Slovak, 1986). These elements are briefly described below.

Styles of Policing

Ever since the publication of James Q. Wilson's *Varieties of Police Behaviors,* researchers have documented the important roles that organization and style of policing play in law enforcement activities (Wilson, 1968; Langworthy, 1986; Lundman, 1979; Walsh, 1985; Crank, 1990; Reiss, 1992). Because individual police officers have wide discretion in their dealings with the public, the style of policing endorsed by the organizational norms of the department will affect the range of police actions and rates of arrest in the community (Swanson, 1978; Crank, 1990). Since community policing envisions the active cooperation of residents to prevent and control crime and disorder within the community, we are likely to witness major changes toward a service-oriented style of policing in urban departments over the next decade. Whether the kinds of policing associated with the "watchman" and "legalistic" styles of policing discussed by Wilson and others will be part of this change remains to be seen (Wilson, 1968; Slovak, 1986; Goldstein, 1987; Hartmann, 1988; Brown, 1989; Tonry & Morris, 1992).

Political Environment

In understanding police organizations, there is little doubt that police behavior is affected in some fashion by the political culture of which the department is part (Langworthy, 1986). Although today's police departments are recognized as being more professional than at any time in the past, they are not immune to the political environment in which they function. In those instances where political interference or favoritism is shown toward particular neighborhoods, we are likely to witness widespread cynicism on the part of the participating officers, and an attitude of "politics as usual" among community residents. Under these conditions, the formation of a working partnership between police and community will be all the more difficult (Rosenbaum, 1986). Further, in the absence of any partnership, neither party is likely to hold itself responsible for any unresolved public safety issues.

Administrative Structure and Police Expertise

Other elements associated with police organizations include departmental specialization and expertise (Swanson, 1978; Brown, 1989; Langworthy, 1986), and the centralization of decision-making processes (Bayley, 1992; Kelling & Bratton, 1993). If community policing is to be successful it seems clear that the delivery and selection of police services must involve individual officers assigned to specific areas within the community or designated neighborhood. The permanent assignment to neighborhoods or police sectors will enable individual officers to become familiar with the social and physical settings that characterize the neighborhoods they are assigned to patrol (Sparrow, 1988; National Institute of Justice, 1992).

Since community policing programs are by their very nature proactive in their response to criminal activities and incivilities disruptive to public order, these policing efforts require a whole new range of skills. The need for new job skills for community policing was voiced by virtually all departments responding to the surveys described above. Of the 25 large-city police departments with some community policing programs under way, all but two voiced the opinion that the skills needed for community policing are sufficiently different from those associated with traditional policing and, therefore, require changes in the ways in which officers are trained and supported in their day-to-day activities with community residents.

Because community policing involves the establishment of a collective response to identified problems within defined geographic areas, intervention strategies must be based, in part, on what residents in partnership with police can accomplish. Where neighborhood resources are insufficient to effectively impact the existing problems, community policing programs must look beyond the individual officers assigned to the areas for appropriate solutions. In these instances, it may be more appropriate for community police officers to take on the role of facilitator or triage officer by bringing together the kinds of experts or agencies experienced in dealing with similar problems and behavior. Because traditional police and city administrations have not supported police as facilitators this will not be an easy task. Further, if the facilitative role is to be successful, community police officers will have to establish follow-up procedures for assuring community residents that these problems are being addressed in an appropriate fashion, and that some resolution will be forthcoming. The trend toward cooperation between police, the community, public, and private agencies signifies an important shift away from traditional police strategies that have been largely reactive in their content (Trojanowicz, 1972; Brown, 1989; Hartmann, 1988). In moving beyond traditional law enforcement, it is our view that interagency cooperation will be a major key to the success of community policing.

Although each of the above mentioned elements is critical to understanding the future direction of policing in the United States, other significant difficulties must also be overcome if community policing is to be part of the American law enforcement landscape. Confusion over the meaning of community policing, resistance by either police or community residents to establishing some form of partnership to deal with crime and the fear associated with its effects, restricted and/or reduced revenues for municipalities, as well as conditions beyond the control of police all figure to make community policing more difficult to operationalize. It is in response to these challenges that the above described framework is being proposed as a guidepost to the kinds of research needed for understanding those factors associated with the success and failure of community policing.

MEASURING THE IMPACT OF COMMUNITY POLICING: AN EVALUATION MODEL

Because community policing is best envisioned as a fluid strategy capable of adjusting to the unique needs and problems of vastly different communities, the development of an evaluation model to account for these differences is much more difficult to accomplish. Given the everyday contingencies associated with law enforcement, the implementation of an evaluation model approximating the classical experimental design seems most doubtful. These obstacles do not, however, lessen the need for police departments to establish objective assessments of their operational programs; much the opposite is demanded if we are to advance beyond the current rhetoric associated with community policing.

The observation that police organizations and communities are constantly evolving in response to changing conditions in both the external and internal environments argues, we believe, for a process model of evaluation as being best suited for assessing community policing programs (Sylvia et al., 1991). Process evaluations employ both quantitative and qualitative methods of data collection to assess the quality and purpose of program activities relative to desired program outcome.

Since community policing programs must continually adjust to changes having little to do with the programs themselves, the selection of evaluation strategies flexible yet rigorous enough to produce data understandable and useful to police administrators and program staff is critical. The development of a process model within the conceptual framework discussed above does not preclude the introduction of impact measures when more stringent data analyses are desired or demanded. In fact, it should facilitate this process. At the present stage of community policing, however, the conditions necessary to yield meaningful impact evaluations are difficult to establish, and few community policing programs have been developed sufficiently to expect quantifiable impact data.

The model, as described below, was originally developed for evaluating delinquency prevention programs (Walker, Cardarelli & Billingsley, 1976), and with some modifications utilized by the National Council on Crime and Delinquency to evaluate prevention programs nationwide (N.C.C.D., 1981). The process data demanded by the model are organized around a paradigm consisting of four major elements associated with the design and implementation of community policing programs. Each of these elements and their sub-elements are briefly described below.

Figure 15.2 Community Policing: Program Elements

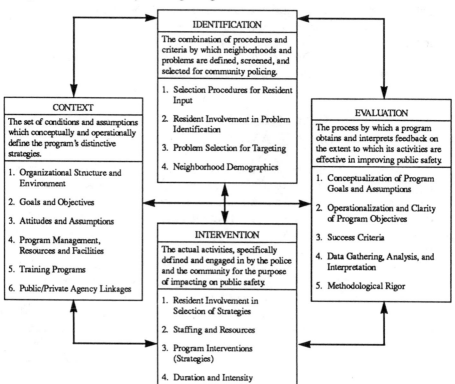

IDENTIFICATION

The combination of procedures and criteria by which neighborhoods and problems are defined, screened, and selected for community policing.

1. Selection Procedures for Resident Input
2. Resident Involvement in Problem Identification
3. Problem Selection for Targeting
4. Neighborhood Demographics

CONTEXT

The set of conditions and assumptions which conceptually and operationally define the program's distinctive strategies.

1. Organizational Structure and Environment
2. Goals and Objectives
3. Attitudes and Assumptions
4. Program Management, Resources and Facilities
5. Training Programs
6. Public/Private Agency Linkages

EVALUATION

The process by which a program obtains and interprets feedback on the extent to which its activities are effective in improving public safety.

1. Conceptualization of Program Goals and Assumptions
2. Operationalization and Clarity of Program Objectives
3. Success Criteria
4. Data Gathering, Analysis, and Interpretation
5. Methodological Rigor

INTERVENTION

The actual activities, specifically defined and engaged in by the police and the community for the purpose of impacting on public safety.

1. Resident Involvement in Selection of Strategies
2. Staffing and Resources
3. Program Interventions (Strategies)
4. Duration and Intensity

Context refers to the set of conditions and assumptions that conceptually and operationally define the program's distinctive strategies. Related sub-elements include the organizational, financial, physical and theoretical perspectives underlying the community policing programs. Equally important are the program's linkages with public and private agencies, as well as several antecedent characteristics such as length of time in existence; changes in philosophy since program commencement; and the existence of training programs for both police and community residents. Within "context," the matter of fundamental assumptions represents an area requiring special attention and documentation. Under ideal conditions, the fundamental assumptions of a program should define the bases upon which the targeted audiences are identified, the intervention strategies selected and implemented by program managers, and the logic and procedures which are to be employed in the evaluation itself. Because no single program will be able to articulate and document the fundamental assumptions underlying the full selection of community policing strategies, the focus on "context" must be flexible but cognizant of the internal linkages with the elements of identification, intervention, and evaluation.

Identification describes the combination of procedures and criteria by which neighborhoods and problems are defined, screened, and selected for community policing. Key among the sub-elements are the procedures police departments use to both select and involve residents in identifying the particular kinds of problem areas that should be targeted. Absent the involvement of community residents, police officials are more likely to target behaviors and problems associated with official crime statistics, rather than those viewed as disruptive by residents. Evidence of this policy is present in the responses by police chiefs to our national survey. For the large-city police chiefs, crime rates were listed as the most important data in targeting community policing programs. The existence of drugs, gangs, and availability of firearms were also considered to be important determinants. Quite unexpected was the finding that only one-third of the police chiefs listed the stability and economic conditions of the neighborhoods as important variables in the design and implementation of community policing.

In contrast to this perspective, the present model argues that the pre-existing socioeconomic conditions (e.g., unemployment rates, neighborhood racial composition, business and commercial density, housing stock, etc.) not only be considered, but that they be analyzed in terms of their relationship to the problems being addressed by the community policing. In today's large cities, racial conflicts, neighborhood deterioration and high rates of mobility may have more far-reaching implications for community policing than "criminal" activities per se.

Intervention refers to the actual activities specifically defined and engaged in by the police and community residents. Of critical importance is the process by which residents are included in the decisions associated with the selection of program strategies. Programs that are entirely relevant to cohesive communities may be inappropriate to communities or neighborhoods that are highly disorganized or in the process of transition or decline. During the last two decades, most large cities have been subjected to important economic and cultural changes that raise serious doubts about the existence of any "uniformity of interests" among residents. In acknowledging the diversity of community interests, community policing officials must be especially careful to include residents that are not only knowledgeable about the problems disruptive to the community or neighborhood but as important, able to provide insightful suggestions as to the kinds of strategies that have some chance of being successfully implemented.

Additional areas of concern for evaluators include the duration and intensity of program strategies, whether any changes have been incorporated since the program's inception, as well as the stated reasons for these changes. In documenting the conditions under which program events occur over time, process evaluation permits systematic interpretation of how changes in program content are related to observed attainment of program goals. Significant factors and changes not anticipated when program strategies are designed and implemented can be identified and accounted for in the evaluation process.

Evaluation refers to the process by which a program obtains and interprets any information regarding the effectiveness of intervention strategies. An ideal program will attempt to explain both its successes and failures in terms of the implications for program improvement. With this as a goal, program evaluators and managers must give serious consideration to establishing thorough and precise documentation of the fundamental assumptions of the community policing program. Consideration should also be given to those factors beyond the control of program staff, but which may positively or negatively influence the effects of the intervention strategies. Other areas of concern involve the formulation and documentation of quantifiable success criteria and objectives, unbiased interpretations, and reporting of findings. Finally, special consideration should also be given to those factors which limit the generalization of program effects to other communities and neighborhoods. The ready acceptance of program strategies, without due consideration of their applicability, may lead to results that could jeopardize the future of community policing as the central core of the police agency.

Although each of the above elements can be individually addressed, the relationships that exist among the elements are critical to determining the ways in which particular variables will influence program outcomes. Theoretically, at least, community policing programs should have high levels of internal consistency between the program elements. The types of strategies that are developed (intervention) should not only be logically related to the program's key assumptions and objectives (context) but to the neighborhoods and problems (identification) to which the services are directed. Questions that address these linkages include, but are not limited to, the following: Are the fundamental assumptions about the existence of community problems consistent with the selection of neighborhoods and/or target groups (CONTEXT-IDENTIFICATION)? Do the assumptions about these problems suggest intervention strategies (CONTEXT-INTERVENTION)? Are the actual intervention strategies suggestive of criteria for selecting residents for program inclusion (IDENTIFICATION-INTERVENTION)? Are the evaluation measures directly relevant to the goals and objectives of the intervention strategies (INTERVENTION-EVALUATION)?

Focusing on the degree of congruity between program elements not only allows for a dynamic analysis of the internal and external forces impacting on the program, but just as important, it maintains the focus of program administrators on the overall program objectives, and provides a framework for examining the reasons for any apparent incongruities that manifest themselves over the life of the program. In recording the conditions under which program events occur over time, the model allows for systematic analysis of observed program goals and objectives.

Because social action programs like community policing are not static, the ability to measure progress is much more difficult. The content and methods of community policing are likely to be dynamic and complex and the goals and objectives may need to be transformed in the course of efforts to attain them. Even some of the basic premises underlying the program's operations may change or evolve over time. To overcome the problems associated with the measurement of community policing, we believe the above model provides a realistic approach for police organizations that, by definition, are continuously subject to change and demands from both internal and external sources.

SUMMARY

In large cities across America, and increasingly in smaller municipalities, major efforts aimed at police reform are currently taking place under the broad umbrella of community policing. Yet it is increasingly clear, if community policing is to become the dominant philosophy of America's law enforcement community, programs established under its rubric must be subjected to continuous evaluation and assessment. Absent systematic data on the effects community policing programs have on the levels of crime and fear, police administrators will likely encounter increased resistance to requests for new and expanded programs of a similar nature. Just as important, neighborhood residents may become less active in community policing programs if evidence that their efforts are being met with some level of success is lacking.

The above model provides one method for amassing the kinds of data needed to make community policing a reality. As presented, the model emphasizes the need for police administrators and researchers to give serious consideration to the pre-existing conditions within the external and internal environments of police organizations before community policing is implemented.

In terms of this model, police departments who ignore, or fail to consider both the agents of change and community dynamics in which they operate are likely to establish programs resembling traditional policing models, rather than those called for under community policing (Trojanowicz & Bucqueroux, 1990). Further, the model demands major consideration be directed to the processes associated with the conceptualization, planning, and implementation of the programs themselves. Additional concerns must also include changes made in program strategies and why they occurred. The systematic gathering and assessment of data within the above framework will provide police administrators with an understanding of the complex interaction of variables associated with the social and behavioral problems they are being asked to prevent, reduce, or resolve.

Because police and public administrators must continually respond to the political environments in which they function, the demand that evaluation be a high priority is likely to be resisted. To overcome this potential resistance, police administrators must be convinced that the allocation of resources for evaluation will improve the quality of the administrative decision-making process. The above model provides the first step toward accomplishing this.

16

Confronting Community Policing: Minimizing Community Policing as Public Relations*

Jeffrey Ian Ross
Kent State University

INTRODUCTION

Municipal policing in many advanced industrialized democracies is in a state of crisis. This government institution is increasingly loosing legitimacy due to public and governmental concerns over the lingering memories of police corruption, as well as perceptions concerning inadequate response to crime, and excessive police violence. The way police choose to define, react, deflect, and/or resolve the resultant negative publicity, strongly influences present and future police behavior and police, community/public, and government relations. Like so many other public relations techniques,[1] community policing is the latest tool in police-community public relations. Even though community policing has a series of laudable goals, and in some cases has ameliorated a number of social and community problems, many police, academics, politicians, and community organizations have overstated the success of community policing. Moreover, there has been a disproportionate emphasis on public relations programs in support of community policing initiatives in lieu of implementing community policing as its originators intended it to be (Manning, 1988; Klockars, 1988).

The process of community policing as public relations has a series of causes and effects that are detrimental both to the police and constituencies they serve

* This chapter has benefited from the comments of my wife, Natasha J. Cabrera, and the research assistance of Paul Bond and Sam Matheson.

243

and protect. This process subsumes three interrelated interpretations: more energy is expended on public relations efforts promoting community policing than in the implementation of actual community policing programs; public relations methods to promote community policing are used instead of implementing community policing initiatives; and the practice of community policing is simply a public relations exercise.

In this chapter, the author reviews the literature and evidence that support the position that community policing is a manifestation of all three interpretations of the relationship between community policing and public relations; explains how community policing is implemented as a public relations tactic; posits some of the effects of community policing as public relations; and, suggests a number of strategies to minimize community policing as public relations, in order to maximize what the framers of community policing conceived that it would achieve.

LITERATURE REVIEW

Despite definitional vagaries, community policing is conceptualized as a policing program that consists of a set of actors, behaviors, and orientations whose purpose is to improve police-community relations, increase citizens participation in crime control by helping them to police themselves, and reduce crime as well as citizen's fear of crime. This group of actors, behaviors, and orientations includes such practices as "Policing by Objectives;" "Problem-Oriented Policing;" using bike cops to patrol a community; setting up mini police stations; establishing or increasing the use of neighborhood meetings with the police; increasing the frequency and visibility of crime prevention programs, patrol by beat cops; and police getting more involved in community activities.

Without question, several academics (e.g., Alderson, 1979; Goldstein, 1987; Skolnick & Bayley, 1986; 1988), and police professionals have advocated community policing. Most of them stress the prosocial goals and achievements of community policing. By the same token, there have been a number of individuals and organizations who have difficulties with community policing as it currently exists and question both the assumptions for its implementation and the evidence marshaled for the success of these types of initiatives (e.g., Manning, 1988:24).

In general, there are several general critiques (e.g., Manning, 1984:212-213; Manning, 1988:29-30; Smith, 1987; Weatheritt, 1988:116-118) and analyses of obstacles to (Skolnick & Bayley, 1988:Chapter Four) community policing. More common are specific difficulties with respect to particular assumptions underlying the concept of community policing. Conceptually, community policing has been criticized for being built upon fallacious assumptions about crime, criminals, and communities; definitional problems (Manning, 1984); and the variety of methods which it entails (Ekblom & Heal, 1982). Other problems with community policing include its inability to reduce crime and fear (Weatheritt, 1983; 1987); poorly conceptualized evaluation studies (Trojanowicz, Steele & Trojanowicz, 1986:1); lack of transferability of community policing models from one setting to another; insensitivity to cultural differences among and inside advanced industrialized states; failure to build the partnership between the police and the community (Morgan, 1987); poor response time to citizens and crime (Trojanowicz, Steele & Trojanowicz, 1986:12-13); police officers' negative view of community policing (Trojanowicz, Steele & Trojanowicz, 1986:12); emphasis on intelligence gathering rather than attempts to reach out to the community; increased politicization of the police; increased potential for police corruption (Trojanowicz, Steele & Trojanowicz, 1986:1); and, the use of community policing as public relations (Bayley, 1988; Klockars, 1988; Manning, 1988).

Although the literature makes a good case that community policing is a public relations technique, it does not provide strategies whereby academics, community activists, or well informed and intentioned police officers and administrators can either stop or minimize community policing efforts as a public relations tool and redirect it into what it is supposed to accomplish. Departing from the position that community policing is mainly an exercise in public relations, the author goes beyond diagnosis of community policing as public relations to offer some recommendations to control and hence change how community policing is currently implemented.

The discussion of community policing as public relations can be broken down into three categories: (1) the characterization of community policing as public relations, (2) its causes, and (3) its effects. This chapter is structured around these three processes and concludes with a series of recommendations for change.

CHARACTERIZATIONS OF COMMUNITY POLICING AS PUBLIC RELATIONS

In the main, public relations actions employ symbols and myths to counter, manipulate, or convince others of a position that is favorable to the initiator of the communication. In the context of police organizations, public relations actions are introduced to manipulate public and governmental reactions and external control initiatives.[2] There are five basic characterizations of community policing as public relations. First, community policing is another reform movement in the history of policing and as such is another circumlocution (e.g., Klockars, 1988). This evasive practice "worked by wrapping police in aspirations and values that are extremely powerful and unquestionably good" (Klockars, 1988:257).

Second, community policing is characterized as a new ideological position in the continuum of existing ideologies. Manning (1988) argues that community policing is "a new ideological theme . . . emerging in police rhetoric just as . . . community identification and the symbolic authority of the police and other U.S. institutions is declining" (1988:28). He adds,

> Clearly, as in the past, the symbols created, organized, and displayed by police are ways of shaping thinking, focusing attention, and defining the meaning of situations. The community policing strategy, which is both a rhetoric and an operational strategy taking many tactical forms, is a new tool in the drama of control. (1988:28)

Third, community policing as public relations is merely a rhetorical device to pacify the public (Bayley, 1988:226). And as another rhetorical strategy, police use it to manage impressions about their power, efficacy, impact, as well as to maintain control over their operations (Manning, 1988:40).

Fourth, community policing is simply "a trendy phrase spread thinly over customary reality" (Bayley, 1988:226). Given the number of "efforts to improve the police over the past several decades," we may cynically or skeptically "dismiss the programs labeled `community policing' as simply another fad in long series of proposals for improving policing that have been enthusiastically advanced, and shortly thereafter abandoned" (Goldstein, 1987:7).

Finally, community policing has been described, in whole or in part, and depending on the jurisdiction (Skolnick & Bayley, 1988:33), as the repackaging of pre-existing police programs or police missions (Bayley, 1988:226; Manning, 1988:28). For instance, many crime prevention initiatives, such as neighborhood watch, are now amalgamated with, or presented to the public as community policing programs, or given a higher profile in a police department's public relations efforts.

In sum, community policing as public relations is the promise of better relations between police and citizens, a decrease in crime, a reduction in fear of crime, and improved community participation. This promise has not been kept by implementing programs that can meet these goals. In the absence of "real concrete" change in the incidence and perception of crime, community policing remains a public relations effort to convince the public, government, and members of the police force that something is being done.

REASONS POLICE USE COMMUNITY POLICING AS PUBLIC RELATIONS

In general, there are at least seven interrelated reasons police departments use public relations efforts in the implementation of community relations. These factors, from least to most important, are discussed below.

A Highly Partisan Context

Initially, community policing decisions are often made in a *partisan political context* where expedience is more important than ameliorative and long term effects. Many times a new mayor, police chief, or municipal administration is sworn into office and they need a new program to sell to the public. Alternatively, immediately following a major act of police deviance, the administration realizes that it must implement something new or keep the heat off the police department. Community policing is conceptually used to fend off criticism. According to Skolnick and Bayley (1988:33) ". . . three of the most ambitious experiments in community policing have taken place where there was a sense of strategic need." At other times, a community's or police department's prestige is challenged when a neighboring community introduces community policing. Hence they feel compelled to implement their own version of community policing. In Skolnick and Bayley's (1988:33) words,

> Some senior managers jump on the community police band-
> wagon simply because to do so is progressive . . . Such leaders
> talk a good game, but they rarely follow through. They are
> more concerned with appearances than reality. Others recog-
> nize that community policing has tremendous emotional
> appeal to the public. It provides a rationale for urging the public
> to support the police. Without necessarily being consciously
> cynical, such leaders tend to develop one directional outreach
> programs. They form specialized media relations units.
> (1988:33)

Crises of Legitimacy

The emphasis of community policing as public relations represents a natural response to *crises of legitimacy*. Crises of legitimacy are created after acts of police deviance (regardless of the criminal or noncriminal nature) become public. In general, there are four principle outcomes to crises of legitimacy: (1) external control initiatives, (2) internal resistance, (3) public relations, and (4) internal control initiatives. These processes may operate independently or in concert. Police department responses to crises of legitimacy can be ordered along a continuum of "tangible" (e.g., firing an officer/s) versus "symbolic" actions (e.g., press conferences) (e.g., Schumaker, 1975; Gusfield, 1963; Edelman, 1964; 1971). The distinction between tangible and symbolic actions is difficult because tangible actions carry with them symbolic benefits as well (e.g., Wilson, 1973). The use of community policing as a public relations technique in crises of legitimacy fulfills both symbolic and, when implemented properly, tangible goals.

Cost Effectiveness

Using public relations approaches that draw attention to community policing techniques is more *cost effective* than actually implementing a community policing program. Public relations efforts costs less than retraining officers, leasing, or purchasing space for mini or storefront police stations, redesigning job classifications, and other costs incurred in dealing with related problems of reorganization that a community policing program can create. Skolnick and Bayley (1988:89) write that "Despite the benefits claimed for community policing, programmatic implementation of it has been very uneven." The results of such sporadic implementation range from real change to repackaging of old programs (Skolnick & Bayley, 1987:1).

Alternative or Additional Tool of Public Relations

Community policing is used as an *additional or a different tool* in a wide arsenal of public relations techniques that after a while get worn out, become dull, or stale. Police public relations methods have traditionally been initiated through the Police Chief's office, Community Relations, Public Affairs, Public Relations, or police conduits such as the Police Athletic League, police or community crime prevention division/department. These units may issue a series of press releases sent to the media, and/or the chief or head of a particular division, or a public affairs spokesperson appearing on radio or television delivering their message through press conferences. The police spokesperson may also write articles or guest editorials for the local newspapers, or try to enlist the support of local opinion leaders such as the mayor, city councilors, and heads of chambers of commerce (Beare, 1987).

In general, police use most of the same public relations techniques that large corporations use. These methods, however, lose their novelty and must be periodically changed or replaced. Consequently, community policing becomes a new and innovative passive technique and as such it represents another example of the iron fist and the velvet glove approach to policing that was utilized and documented by observers of the police during the 1960s (CRCJ:1977). Even when changes are implemented, they are often symbolic.

Availability of Police Resources

Police organizations, like most governmental departments, have at their disposal an enormous number of resources both material, physical, and ideological. To mount a community policing campaign these *resources can be marshaled and* utilized. It is much easier to manipulate public opinion than it is to implement changes in the structure and practices of police organizations. Most of the initiatives that would bring some sort of long-term resolution to the problems that community policing is supposed to ameliorate are not introduced because they are seen as a threat to the ability of the police to accomplish its mission.

Media Propagation and/or Co-Optation

Promotion of community policing depends, in part, on a series of factors related to the operation of mass media organizations.[3] In general, *media propaga-*

tion and/or co-optation are important in the use of community policing as public relations. Of paramount importance is the role of the local media, especially the working relationship between police and crime/police reporters. The structure of reporters' jobs and editorial decisions precludes in-depth coverage of particular issues (e.g., Fishman, 1978).

The police are a major source of information for the media. Since criminals and citizens rarely contact the media to report on sensational crimes, the media depend on the police for this sort of information. Media stories on the police tend to reflect this dependence. For example, the majority of articles and editorials on community policing in newspapers are favorable and are almost always accompanied by photos that portray community policing in a positive fashion. On the other hand, there is little critical analysis, investigative reporting, or editorial pieces on community policing.

According to Herman and Chomsky (1988):

> The mass media are drawn into a symbiotic relationship with powerful sources of information by economic necessity and reciprocity of interest. The media need a steady, reliable flow of the raw material of news. They have daily news demands and imperative news schedules that they must meet. They cannot afford to have reporters and cameras at all places where important stories may break. Economics dictates that they concentrate their resources where significant news often occurs, where important rumors and leaks about, and where regular press conferences are held. . . . On a local basis, city hall and the police department are the subject of regular news 'beats' for reporters. . . . Businesss corporations and trade groups are also regular and credible purveyors of stories deemed newsworthy (1988:18-19).

Inevitably then, alternative versions of reality are marginalized when the media serves a propaganda function.

An Apathetic, Deferent, Alienated, and/or Uneducated Public

An *apathetic, deferent, alienated, and/or uneducated public* share culpability in this process.[4] Regardless of the reasons for its causes, the general public is relatively content to have the police take responsibility for the implementation of new policies. The assumption that communities that are affected by police and crime will participate to democratically alter political, economic, or social conditions is unfounded. Most citizens in advanced industrialized democracies are apathetic with respect to political participation. Apathy may stem from a degree of conformity, a learned belief in the infallibility of authority, ignorance about how to effect change in democratic systems, inequality, or a feeling that "if it does not affect me personally, why get involved" (e.g., Lamb, 1975). On the other hand, participation in any democratic process involves a series of cost-benefit calculations made by individuals of affected communities.

One of the outcomes of such process is the rationalization that there is more to lose (i.e., absenteeism from work and lost wages) than to gain in criticizing the police, for example. Alternatively, apathy may also be disguising a more real and potentially damaging factor, that is, people may not be aware of police activities. Whatever the source, people's activities in ameliorating their situation regarding police activities are short-lived or nonexistent.

Although affected communities may not react to police activities, they may respond to other issues that are also politically salient but have more immediate impact such as rent hikes, transit strikes, rezoning proposals etc. In this context, apathy is a function of urban rather than rural life (e.g., Higgens, 1977:193) or municipal versus state/provincial or federal politics. In other words, citizens participate in political issues more at the state/provincial, and more so at the federal level than at the local level (Hanson & Slade, 1977).

Closely related to apathy is acceptance, obedience, or deference to authority. According to Piven and Cloward (1977):

> people usually remain acquiescent, conforming to the accustomed patterns of daily life in their community and believing those patterns to be both inevitable and just. . . . most of the time people conform to the institutional arrangements which enmesh them, which regulate the rewards and penalties of daily life, and which appear to be the only possible reality. Those for whom the rewards are most meager, who are the most oppressed by inequality, are also acquiescent. Sometimes they are the most acquiescent . . . (1977:6).

One of the reasons that people are deferent or obedient to authority structures such as the police is that citizens "have little defense against the penalties that can be imposed for defiance" (Piven & Cloward, 1977:6). As with apathetic responses, obedience to authority may be the result of cost-benefit calculations that lead citizens to conclude that they have more to lose than to gain from protesting against police practices.

Cities in advanced industrialized democracies attract large numbers of minorities. Newly arrived immigrants, in particular, those from developing nations, often have illegal status, language problems, and are less knowledgeable about their constitutional rights, than their naturalized counterparts. These conditions make new arrivals shy away from political participation and, by default, defer to authority. Even those members of minority groups who have citizenship can be relatively silent. Coterminously, there is also a deep feeling of distrust against the police, which varies with the ethnic, class, and racial composition of each neighborhood and community.

EFFECTS OF COMMUNITY POLICING AS PUBLIC RELATIONS

Building on the previous analysis, there are at least 10 major interrelated problems with community policing implemented as public relations, many of which are subsumed under the larger criticism of police use of public relations. These effects, from least to most important, in the severity of disturbance, are discussed below.

Utilizing Scarce Resources

The public relations efforts of community policing *consumes valuable resources* that could be invested in other more profitable policy initiatives and programs either inside the police department or administered by other agencies (Turque et al., 1990:37). Many of these resources have been obtained Leighton (1991) suggests, by police chiefs who have used community policing initiatives "to solicit additional funds" from other sources. He argues that:

> During the 1960s and 1970s, when crime rates were increasing rapidly, chiefs could argue for more officers and resources on the grounds of a crime wave. With overall crime rates settling down, chiefs have had to shift their argument form 'quantity policing' to 'quality policing'. . . That is, in order to deliver high quality policing services, as represented by community policing, then they require additional officers and resources (1991:508).

In short, police, academics, and captured community organizations have invested a great deal of resources to promote rather than implement community policing.

Implementing a Defense Strategy

Both the promise and the actual implementation of community policing are often *defensive strategies* used by law enforcement agencies. In general, Manning (1988) argues that police "seek to reduce information that will damage this [police] sense of order and control and to amplify information that enhances this sense of order and control" (1988:40). Bayley (1988) adds that:

> Community policing is a superb defensive strategy for the police. Whatever happens to public safety, they cannot lose. If

> community policing fails to protect, police can argue that it was a bad idea and more resources are needed for customary strategies. If community policing succeeds, police can argue that they are on the right track and additional funds for it are required. Either way, the result is that the police remain at the center of society's strategy for crime reduction (1988:228).

In the same vein, Klockars (1988) suggests that community policing is used "to conceal, mystify, and legitimate police distribution of nonnegotiably coercive force" (1988:240). At the same time it is used to "increase the autonomy and independence of police, making them not only less receptive to demands from indigenous neighborhood action and interest groups, but also less tractable to control by elected political leaders" (1988:250). He writes, that movements like community policing "Progressively, . . . left a void in municipal government."

"For awhile [these movements] increased the autonomy of police, they robbed them [police] of both their popular and political support" (1988:250). In turn community policing as public relations helps the police maintain their monopoly in self-control power. If public relations efforts to appease the citizens were minimized, then there would be a reduction of police ability (i.e., power) to exercise independent control over their organization (either legally or symbolically). Thus, any public relations efforts, particularly the promotion of community policing, constitute attempts by police to minimize community and governmental criticism and control over their operation. This, then helps the police maintain their position as the primary mediators of community conflict.

Fostering an Unrealistic Expectation of Police and Citizen Capabilities

In promising that community policing will cure most social ills, the police are *fostering unrealistic expectations in the community* at large. Klockars (1988) "oppose[s] . . . the creation of immodest and romantic aspirations that cannot, in fact, be realized in anything but ersatz terms." He argues that:

> Police can no more create communities or solve the problems of urban anomie than they can be legalized into agents of the courts or depoliticized into pure professionals. There is no more reason to expect that they can prevent crime than to expect that they can fight or win a war against it (1988:257).

Legitimating State Rather than Community Forms of Social Control

Community policing programs as public relations exercises *legitimize state forms of social control* (Bayley, 1988:230). According to Bayley (1988), "The whole purpose of community policing is to bridge the gap between the populace and the law's enforcers" (1988:230). Community policing still places the onus of social control on mechanisms beyond the family, peers, and schools.

Temporarily Diverting Attention from Non-Police Processes that Could Reduce Crime and Fear of Crime

Public relations tactics connected to community policing *temporarily divert attention* from alternative strategies that would achieve the same types of objectives that community policing is supposed to. Other forms of social control (e.g., the family; "big brothers;" "big sisters") that are perhaps less coercive might provide the same mechanism as community policing. Techniques which might solve community problems are either not introduced, or for all intents and purposes community problems may in fact be unresolveable.

Increasing Public Disaffection

An emphasis on selling community policing programs to the public rather than carrying these promised projects through can *increase citizen disaffection* and cynicism for the police and those agencies responsible for monitoring them, and, consequently diminish the police force's legitimacy as keepers of public order. Citizens who realize that community policing is simply or disproportionately a public relations exercise may continue or begin to withdraw support from the police in a variety of ways. For example, they may fail to report crime, or come to the assistance of a police officer, etc.

Increasing Public Complacency

Community policing as public relations may lead to *external complacency* about crime, police, and community values, because the nonpolice community may perceive that the police idea of community policing is mainly rhetorical and has none or minimal effect on the level and type of problems that community policing was supposed to have solved. This external apathy accompanied by feelings of alienation, helps maintain and advance the power of the police organization.

Temporarily Satisfying the Public

Community policing as public relations may *temporarily satisfy* the public. When community policing programs are blatantly reactive and implemented quickly with minimal or no analysis, public relations efforts in the service of community policing gives the public the impression that something is being done. However, when community policing is evaluated by critical observers, and it often falls short of its stated or inferred objectives, community dissatisfaction is the typical reaction.

Increasing Officer Dissatisfaction

Many police officers resist changes in departmental policies as well as programs such as community policing (e.g., Cohn, 1990). Forced to engage in public relations exercises in support of community policing, *officers may become cynical,* thus minimizing the proper implementation of community policing (e.g., Turque, et al., 1990). This cynicism may lead to increased number of job actions and deviance such as the "blue flu" or "cooping."

Leaving the Day-to-Day Activities of the Average Police Officer Untouched

Finally, a well-organized public relations campaign to promote community policing generally *leaves the day-to-day activities* of the average police officer untouched. When community policing efforts are implemented they often are not done force-wide thus leaving the responsibility to a limited number of officers to perform these types of duties. Typically a handful of officers are delegated to becoming community policing officers. Alternatively, crime prevention officers are euphemistically called community policing officers thus serving as easy referent when the police administration is questioned about their efforts to implement community policing.

OVERCOMING COMMUNITY POLICING AS PUBLIC RELATIONS

A number of authors have offered suggestions to improve the implementation of community policing programs. Bayley (1988), for example, outlines four improvements including, systematically monitoring the effectiveness "of community policing as a crime-control strategy . . . by government if necessary, out of police budgets" (1988:236); giving "an institution outside the police . . . the authority and capacity to determine whether community police operations conform to the rule of law" (1988:236-237); improving the "selection" and "training" of police officers who will engage in community policing (1988:237); and, "develop[ing] the capacity to formulate and implement general policies of policing, calling on all resources both public and private so as to provide effective and equal protection to all segments of the population" (1988:237).

According to Manning (1984), "If a community police scheme is to be successful it will require: structural and legal change, changes in habits of dispute settlement and definition, in organizational structure, performance evaluation and in reward structures within the police" (1984:224). These suggestions are necessary to help community policing become a concrete reality, but are not in and of themselves sufficient. As formulated, these proposed changes do not minimize the public relations processes and its unflattering effects connected to community policing.

Opinion leaders, academics, observers of the police, the media, community activists, and well-informed police officers and administrators should oppose the use of community policing for public relations purposes. This constituency can accomplish this worthwhile task by persistently exposing the causes for and the negative effects of using public relations techniques in lieu of implementing community policing projects, and suggesting alternative methods for improving implementation of this latest development in modern policing. Six basic interrelated strategies should be employed by those so-called "devil's advocates" of community policing to minimize the public relations component of community policing. These interrelated methods, from least to most important, are discussed below.

Refusing to be Co-Opted into Public Relations Legitimizing Exercises

When contacted by police departments, the media, and politicians who ride the community policing public relations bandwagon searching for support, devil's advocates of community policing should politely withdraw (or refuse to be *co-opted*) from these types of efforts to prevent turning community policing into public relations gestures. They should expose poor or misguided policies, practices, research and media accounts which are conducted on community policing, refuse to participate in public relations legitimating exercises, and suggest better methods of implementation or amelioration of community problems.

Educating Others

Educating others, such as the police, the public, the government and other political actors can minimize the use of community policing as public relations. This strategy can be achieved by speaking out at public/community forums, lecturing to students in the academic courses devil's advocates teach, and informing the media about the causes and effects of public relations and community policing. Prudence, however, must be exercised. The various forms public relations may take, as well as the hidden agenda behind its use, may not be apparent to the average citizen. Moreover, a high profile member of the community may have more clout and hence be a better choice than devil's advocates at convincing the police, public, and government to change the method by which they implement community policing. According to Trojanowicz and Bucqueroux (1990):

> Business owners, corporate executives, community leaders, and the affluent can often make their wishes known through formal and informal contacts. A busy police chief cannot make time for every private citizen who might call for an appointment, but most will try to make time to meet with the president of a major corporation or the elected leader of a powerful community group (1990:343).

These authors suggest that seeking out "power brokers" in the community is an effective strategy to lobby the police. This elite "often interact informally or socialize with police officials at meetings at luncheons, or as friends" (1990:343). Power brokers can be identified by looking for those individuals, organizations, and businesses who advertise in the local newspaper, and pro-police publications, which are sometimes published by the police or local newspapers. Failing this strategy, the elite are often members of the Bar Association, Chamber of Commerce, and Real Estate Board.

Many academics can see no further than the next class, conference paper, publication, or departmental meeting. This type of schedule may prevent them from attending public forums that are occasionally developed when the police sensitize the public to community policing and lobby for the unconditional support of the media. Devil's advocates must, however, make time in their busy schedules to publicly address the logic, methods, and evaluation of community policing.

Many community policing programs are introduced with the help of the local media. But, reporters are often generalists and lack contextual understanding of issues and institutions. Devil's advocates should write letters to the editor of local newspapers, articles on the topic for local newspapers and magazines, and contact police or crime reporters, particularly those that are overly sympathetic or uncritical with respect to the police and/or community policing. Devil's advocates' lobbying should not be relegated only to the print media; public access television stations depend on local activists for participation in their programming.

Instructors (particularly those who teach criminal justice, criminology, and urban studies) should include in their syllabi, sections on community policing. This will allow their students to better appreciate the intricacies of community policing; and, perhaps learn to critically determine which community policing programs are nothing more than public relations propaganda, and what roles political actors play in this process. In addition to their own classes, devil's advocates can volunteer their services (in the forms of lectures, workshops, and seminars) to their local police department.

This teaching activity can include the development of bibliographies of literature, films, and videos on community policing in order to increase public awareness about the potential pitfalls of community policing. Additionally, one might develop a list of persons who are good speakers on the issue, capable of making a informed opinion on the subject of community policing, and distribute it among interest groups and organizations who might have an interest in community policing in their jurisdiction. Alternatively, a packet of articles can be assembled and made available for the local chief of police, the individual who heads up community policing, and the local crime/police reporters.

Organizing Concerned Community Actors to Influence the Process on Community Policing

Devil's advocates must use and expand their contacts and links with politicians, bureaucrats, and leaders at all levels of government, religious, ethnic, and race-related organizations, and social service, service, social justice agencies. Devil's advocates can also speak to their local precinct or division commander, and chief of police about community policing. They can invite police officers and administrators to speak to devil's advocates classes about community policing programs. Such intervention, education, and *organizational activities,* especially around election time, may help to design better and implement well thought out plans for community policing or put pressure on police for modifications of existing projects. Devil's advocates can encourage letter-writing campaigns, radio and television talk show hosts to hold shows that focus on this issue and start and sign petitions.

Educating Yourself

In addition to educating others, you must *educate yourself* about community policing. By now a burgeoning literature has developed on community policing. Familiarizing oneself with this literature increases legitimacy and offers a more informed dialogue between community and academics on what works or does not work. Acquainting oneself not only with pro community policing research but also with that which is critical from a variety of sources is important if community policing is to succeed.

Conducting Research on Community Policing Programs

Researchers should *conduct independent research* on community policing. Small research projects on community policing can be conducted with a minimum of resources. A simple content analysis of articles which mention community policing published in the local paper is a good starting point. Alternatively, sitting down with the local chief of police or officer in charge of community policing with a set of prepared questions is an excellent way to understand hands on how community policing is conceptually implemented. Devil's advocates can also encourage their students to engage in research on community policing. Students taking courses in such subjects as "Deviance," "Social Control," "Urban Politics," "Social Problems," and "Policing" should be encouraged to conduct research and write papers on community policing. Outsiders to the police, who may not have the time, can also participate by donating other types of resources in order that researchers can investigate and evaluate community policing projects.

Assisting the Police in the Implementation and Evaluation of Community Policing

In particular, devil's advocates *should volunteer to assist the police in the implementation and evaluation of community policing programs.* This includes serving on community consultative committees, providing the chief with information, designing a survey of police and citizen attitudes, etc. Devil's advocates should work with officers to waylay misperceptions about community policing, for example, that it is more than just foot patrol or reified crime prevention.

The above-mentioned techniques are a handful of many possibilities that are only limited by our creativity and imagination. By becoming involved in community policing, devil's advocates will develop a repertoire of experience from which to draw the best way to approach the police, governmental officials, media, and general public in order to prevent uncritical acceptance of actual or postured community policing initiatives.

CONCLUSION

Challenging community policing is not welcomed by most police administrators, politicians, or citizens who have championed its implementation. Criticizing community policing is comparable to attacking a widely accepted and/or sacred institution, like majority rule or equal rights. Devil's advocates actions may very well be interpreted as counterproductive. Criticisms against the implementation, methods, and effectiveness of community policing as it is commonly perceived, will be interpreted as an attack against its goals, and the core values and assumptions of the processes (e.g., Klockars, 1988:256-257). However, the drawbacks of using community policing as public relations is far more damaging to a community and its police force than being branded as unsympathetic to this change in policing. In sum, I argue that it is preferable to be an informed realist than a naive idealist.

NOTES

[1]   These methods may include, but are not limited to: provision of space for reporters, allowing reporters access to two way police band communications, establishing of public relations/affairs departments, publishing of annual reports, participating in pro police television shows, lifting the suspension on an officer, terminating an investigation, dismissing a departmental charge, rejecting a complaint, submitting letters to the editor of a newspaper or magazine, publicizing the agency's ability to combat crime, refusing to answer reporters' questions, censoring reporters whom they normally would not, holding a press conferences, and soliciting the support of various pro-police community organizations, such as the police association or the police athletic league/organization.

2   Public relations should be distinguished from strategies that police use to manage their public appearance. The CFRCJ (1977:48) calls this the "Iron Fist and Velvet Glove" of the police. "One is a 'hard' side, based on new forms of community pacification and other attempts to 'sell' the police to the public. The 'hard' side was the first to be seriously developed, but today both sides are usually mixed together, and used interdependently, in the practice of any given police agency: the iron fist in the velvet glove." Some of the public relations measures that they classify include the "tokenistic hiring of Third World people and women, . . . bogus community relations programs such as team policing, and through such gimmicks as dressing the police in blazers or giving lectures to high school students on the dangers of drugs" (1977:180). This is also achieved by labeling units in palatable terms (e.g., anti-strike forces as labor relations units). See, for example, Gourley (1953); Harding (1972); Harring et al. (1977); Garner (1982); Garner (1987); and Manning (1971), for a review of public relations efforts by police.

3   While the media are often seen as the primary agenda setter (e.g., Gitlin, 1980), it does not mean that other institutions and vehicles of communication are not important.

4   Apathy is closely connected to alienation, but the work on alienation and political activity, or lack of, is contradictory (e.g., Kraus & Davis, 1976:181-183; Sniderman, 1981).

5   For additional techniques see, for example, Alinsky (1971).

17

Community Policing and Community Innovation: The 'New Institutionalism' in American Government

Robyne Turner
Florida Atlantic University

Michael D. Wiatrowski
Florida Atlantic University

INTRODUCTION

Police departments are examples of social institutions that governments establish to carry out specific functions as the need emerges. Governmental institutions also establish management and policy orientations of the organizations including police departments. Likewise, the police department conveys the norms of approaching problem solving to the various sub-entities within its organization. Institutions then, set parameters, that is, rules governing the approach to policy issues (DiMaggio, 1988; Wilson & McLaren, 1977). Yet, with the emergence of community policing, there are indications that the relationship of policing, as a social institution, to the community and to other elements of government is changing in a very fundamental way. It is important to assess the nature of this change in relation to both policing and to other changes that are taking place in American governmental institutions (Osborne, 1990).

Traditionally, the study of institutions has been centered on organizational behavior within the confines of that structure (Hall, 1987). This has also been extended to the study of the professional model of policing as an institution (Crank & Langworthy, 1992). Neoinstitutionalism rejects that research focus and contends that it is more important to give attention to the relationship between organizations and their environment (DiMaggio & Powell, 1991:12). This strong shift in the approach to the study of organizations suggests that researchers should examine the environmental changes as reflected by institutions rather than internal changes where the institution is the source of any reform. Though organizational change may be implemented internally, it represents cognitive recognition by the organization changes in the environment. Neoinstitutionalists recognize the environment as:

> . . . the level of industries, professions, and nation-states rather than in the local communities that the old institutionalists studied, and to view institutionalization as the diffusion of standard rules and structures rather than the adaptive custom-fitting of particular organizations to specific settings." (DiMaggio & Powell, 1991:27).

To understand the emergence of community policing from an institutional and administrative standpoint, neoinstitutionalism offers some insightful options. Institutional inertia as the reliance on standard operating procedures, is most likely to be broken when external influences gather momentum. Therefore, the community policing phenomenon cannot be explained solely as an innovation that is being shared, but should rather be understood as part of a larger structure of environmental change affecting governments in this country. The recent emphasis of public administration to incorporate external expertise within local government is a factor in explaining the advent of community policing. Simply stated, the various constituents that comprise the community are involved in community policing rather than simply only the police department defining how the community should be policed. Community policing has evolved beyond the experimental stage and now represents an attempt by a traditionally isolated police bureaucracy to restate and share its mission with the community as well as interact with other agencies within local government.

COMMUNITY POLICING

"A quiet revolution is reshaping American policing" (Kelling, 1974). Kelling describes a revolutionary change in the manner in which the police relate to the public. This revolution is not the violent overthrow of an established institutional order, but it is akin to a revolutionary paradigm shift as described in *The Structure of Scientific Revolutions* (Kuhn, 1970). Specifically, community policing is differentiated from the professional model of policing which preceded it by changes in strategy, authorization, function, organization, demand, environment, tactics, and outcomes.

Kelling and Moore (1987) summarize the strategy of the professional model as follows: Its *authorization* is based in the criminal law and its primary function is crime control. As a result, the *primary outcome* on which it is evaluated is the ability to control the crime problem in the community. *Organizationally* it is designed to be bureaucratic and centrally controlled to reduce discretionary decisionmaking. It is isolated from its political and social environment to reduce the opportunities for partisan politics. The result is that the demand for services is centrally controlled through a dispatch system that reduces the opportunity and in fact may punish individual initiatives which have not been approved by the chain of command. The *primary tactics* are controlled through the chain of command and include preventive patrol and rapid response to calls for service.

The community policing model is challenging the professional model. The community policing model derives its *authorization* and legitimacy from community support for its function of maintaining order in the community and responding to a broad range of demands for services. It recognizes that manifestation of the lack of cohesion or disorganization in the community. *Organizationally,* decision making is placed at the community police officer level. The officer is assumed to be a competent and cognitive individual who has the ability to make decisions within broad parameters. The officer may be teamed with other officers as well as community groups to respond to community-level problems. The result is that the officer develops a close relationship with the political and social environment for which he is responsible and correspondingly responds to demands from that environment. The tactics that are used include the traditional police power of arrest, but are expanded as community policing recognizes that underlying problems which actually may be causing crime problems can be confronted or solved. As a result, the model emphasizes involvement with the law-abiding citizens of the community and includes making contacts through a wide range of mobilizing methods including bicycles, walking, motorscooters, horses, cars, and golf carts.

	PROFESSIONAL MODEL	COMMUNITY POLICE MODEL
Authorization	Law and Professionalism	Community-based along with law and professionalism
Function	Crime Control	Order maintenance and services
Organizational Design	Central-Classical Model	Decentralized
Relationship to Environment	Professionally Remote	Involvement
Demand	Controlled Centrally	Community determined
Tactics and Technology	Preventative patrol and rapid response/arrest	Community involvement, foot patrol, problem solving
Outcomes	Crime Rates	Quality of life, citizen satisfaction

These become "normal" experiences and positively affect the social psychology of the community. The citizens have a reduced fear of crime. Officers now have the power to resolve recurring problems which in the past were stressful and frustrating. The *outcome* is more broadly defined than the professional model and includes improvements to the quality of community life, increased social cohesion in the community, solutions to the crime problem, reduced fear of crime, and increased citizen satisfaction.

Much of the discussion evaluating the changes in community policing have treated those changes as if they were a revolution taking place in isolation. In reality, however, community policing is part of a larger phenomenon of changes in American public institutions. That phenomenon has contributed to an environment that made the revolution in community policing possible.

Community policing can be understood as a development of at least two significant, interrelated factors. The first factor is the change in research on the tactics employed by the police, questioning the effectiveness of those methods. Research on preventive patrol questioned whether citizens felt more secure and crime rates could be reduced by preventive patrols. For example, a tripling of the police effort in Kansas City in an experimental research design revealed no differences in areas with intensive patrol and those with no police patrol at all (Kelling & Moore, 1987).

Additional challenges to methods revealed that in rapid responses to calls for service, after about two minutes, there is no payoff for decreased response times (Biecke, 1980). Finally, it was determined that in most cases detectives gather little additional information beyond that which is initially transcribed by the patrol officer. For instance, while specialized detective units are necessary such as for homicide and sex crimes, most of the time the general detective function in police departments has little impact on the crime problem in the community (Wilson, 1978). The second major factor fostering community policing was the perception that the police had become estranged from the communities they served. The police viewed the public with suspicion rather than as a source of support and the public viewed the police as anonymous figures in sunglasses cruising by in patrol cars (Trojanowicz & Bucqueroux, 1990). The public had no relationship to their police. The incidence of civil suits against police is an indication that tensions between public and police were rising. It is important to note that in light of the understanding of changes from the professional to the community policing model, that policing programs typically go through an evolution as the new model is implemented. Community policing efforts usually begin as small programs in specific geographic areas such as neighborhoods or communities to which officers are assigned. The larger police force continues to accomplish its function within the professional model. The community policing units gain knowledge of the community and become involved in the community through a wide variety of activities. These involvements include working with community organizations, identifying and working with community leaders and identifying and channeling community and governmental resources.

At some point, there are more demands for community policing, and as the size of those units grows they conflict with the professional model. The general police organization may then be forced to resolve the conflict by making a commitment to adopt the community model. This transformation is difficult because the professional model is deeply embedded in the training and socialization of the officers, and the investments that the higher ranking officers have made in the professional model.

To bring about this adoption, community policing officers may advocate their position to the community. This may involve approaching other governmental entities such as departments of parks and recreation, sanitation, and code enforcement, delinquency or drug prevention specialists, or community educators to convince them that community problems frequently extend across the boundaries of any one organization. Community policing then, can work in tandem with these other community-based institutions, without losing the identity of its own policing mission.

The community policing model also relies on the officer assuming a radically different role. In the professional model the discretion of the individual officer is highly controlled through extensive policies and procedures encoded in operational manuals which attempt to describe every conceivable situation as a means to provide appropriate guidance for the officer. Community policing recognizes that officers must be able to assess situations, determine if there are broader underlying problems contributing to the crime or disorder problem, and then develop a plan of action to attack the cause of that problem. While they continue to exercise their arrest authority it is acceptable to recognize it as a last, rather than first resort of action.

Community policing appears to take place in the context of a rediscovery of "community" sentiments. In that sense, community norms can be strengthened and used to create an environment that is not hospitable to disorderly elements in the community. Community norms can be brought to bear as a means to bring those who litter, are loud, or who do not maintain their property into compliance with those established community norms. Community policing stresses innovation and searching for new solutions as an alternative to past methods that have not been effective.

Bureaucratic Entrenchment

Bureaucracies as dynamic organizations go through a number of stages in their development (Downs, 1967). As young organizations they are populated by advocates and zealots who are eager to apply new concepts and try out new strategies and programs. As a new entity, the staff is flushed with victory upon garnering resources to establish its new base. As the organization ages, it becomes more entrenched. It gets comfortable in its position and seeks to maintain that position. This may result in behaviors that focus on protecting turf against any encroachment on resources or innovation in the approach to their mission and goals. As bureaucratic organizations age, they establish a base of clients that become political supporters. This creates a symbiotic relationship where any diminishment of the organization is seen as a mutual threat.

The development of constituencies and entrenchment may lead to stagnation or, at minimum, a routine approach to problem solving. The organization dynamic becomes more rigid and relies on rule-bound behavior to protect its assets (Simon, 1946). However, there is a limit to the control that can be exerted in a hierarchical organization such as a bureaucracy. Therefore, the lowest level of the bureaucracy, at the point of service delivery, becomes the entry point for change. At the "street level" the bureaucracy is likely to be flexible in dealing with its clients (Lipskey, 1980). Innovations are introduced as a necessity to cope with the changing needs of the people who are service recipients. This phenomenon can create a set of operational expectations at the street level that are not filtered up into the higher levels of the organization. Innovation then, is ad hoc and is not recognized by the organization as a whole.

The rational actor model portends that administration is self-interested and protective of its turf. Thus, the institution is not expected to be responsive to external changes. Change is expected to be slow, and implemented in small components of the organization, rather than as wholesale change throughout the organization. This complies with the model's basic premise that change will seep into the organization, rather than be a new process that is radical in nature and scope.

In order for the organization to innovate, the upper levels of management must be open to change. The development of an organization may become less rigid and rule bound, in the classic Weberian (Weber, 1947) sense, as its management becomes receptive to new ideas. Organizations can keep themselves young and dynamic, avoiding stagnation and entrenchment (which will lead to entropy), if they learn and adapt innovations to their organization (Walker, 1969). For example, moving from the professional the community policing model is innovation. As more departments make this change, the more acceptable the change becomes to other departments. A new norm is established in which the "innovation" becomes more acceptable as other departments perceive the success associated with the new community policing model. However, the willingness to accept change has less to do with the particularistic needs of any one organization and its locale, and more to do with the professional environment that provides a context for that organization. Its receptivity to embrace an innovation is heightened as the professional environment supports such change. Bureaucratic behavior, then, changes as institutional environments and expectations change.

Organizational management can adapt its style to be more flexible, change oriented, and responsive to its staff. The evolution of organizational dynamics suggests that alternative management styles that disperse autonomy and authority within the organization will produce a more energetic and dynamic bureaucracy (Perrow, 1979).

Organizations that are dominated by a rigid hierarchical structure are not adaptable. They may very well be successful as a rigid hierarchy, depending on how they define their goals and mission. Police departments that define their mission traditionally may approach crime from a rigid, military hierarchy style. If they define their mission as community crime prevention, then a different bureaucratic model may be more appropriate and emerge. How an organization changes its mission definition and subsequently alters the structure of its bureaucracy is *dependent* on the *environment* in which it operates.

The change in policing methods that incorporates community and foot patrols in the neighborhood is an example of changing the definition of the mission. An orientation toward preventing crimes and incidents is added to the role of police officers and the role is structurally changed by the location and format of their job.

We can begin to understand this bureaucratic change by examining the movement in the environment external to the police department. Changes in public administration affect how public services are delivered. This is the environment of public sector management. Changes in that environment affect the acceptability of changes in the bureaucratic perspective of police departments.

Public administration has been evolving in its definition since the 1960s (Guy, 1989). What has occurred over these years is a redefinition of what is acceptable in the field of public administration. For example, privatizing and contracting for service have become acceptable methods of service delivery since that time, yet these are in opposition to the traditional principles of bureaucratic operation (internal control and bounded by established rules). Other changes in public management include an emphasis on efficiency and cutback management that forced retrenchment during the 1970s (Levine, 1980), privatization as a rational response to changing fiscal situations (Savas, 1987), and the 1980's redefinition of service delivery as public/private partnerships (see for instance, Frieden & Sagalyn, 1989).

Most important to understanding changes in policing is the entrepreneurial approach to public management (see Eisenger, 1988). In the 1990s, this redefinition is further refined as "reinventing government," with the emphasis on consumer-oriented delivery systems and competitive approaches to bureaucracy, borrowing heavily from market-based models of the private sector (Osborne, 1990; Osborne & Gaebler, 1992). This emphasis since the 1960s on redefinition and new responses to old problems represents a change in the public bureaucratic environment. While innovation may begin as a unique adaptation to a problem in a specific service delivery area, its transference in an institutional setting is likely only if it is redefined as part of an institution's goal or mission.

These changes in the public management environment provide an explanation for the bureaucratic acceptance of changes in policing. Community development represents the entrepreneurial redefinition of the public sector (Friedland & Alford, 1991) and has created an opening to redefine constituency groups. Instead of clients being defined by class as sharing socioeconomic characteristics, clients are just as likely to be defined by the geographic location they occupy and share. The public/private partnership phenomenon has emphasized redevelopment of certain locations within the city such as downtown, waterfronts, industrial parks, and old factories as a new means to address the local economy. Advocates of neighborhood revitalization picked up on this territorial perspective and formed homeowner associations and neighborhood groups to advance the conditions of their space.

Such redefinition is the impetus for a behavioral change within local government institutions. Police departments incorporated this environmental change by orienting their new community policing programs toward the neighborhood and community, and by making the officer responsible for the areas to which he or she may be assigned. Incorporating territory at the individual level indicates a change from anonymous patrol zones to the establishment of accountability and a relationship at the community level. Thus the changing climate of public institutions that redefined bureaucratic service delivery methods and client groups contributed to a public sector environment that enabled the advent of community policing.

ASSESSING THE CHANGE TO COMMUNITY POLICING

The popularity and subsequent reliance on public/private partnerships represent an emphasis on including nonbureaucratic participants in the operations of government. Nongovernmental partners include businesses, neighborhood organizations, and citizen groups. The shift in emphasis represents an environmental change in public administration and has contributed to the acceptability of the community approach to policing and its emphasis on nonprofessional residents as an element of successful service delivery and problem solving. This breaks from the traditional rules of bureaucratic, hierarchical-based decisionmaking in local government agencies.

An important element of this "reinvention" and institutional change is the acceptability of approaching problem solving from an interdisciplinary standpoint, rather than from the perspective of one bureaucratic organization. For example, if trash removal in declining neighborhoods is a severe problem (as it frequently is) then community police officers and the public sanitation department can work together to achieve a solution to that problem. They would do this because the mission of both organizations is addressed by giving attention to the quality of life in the community.

The result is a change in administrative expectations, driven by changes in the institutional environment. The likely result is that institutions will alter their approaches to decision making and management. This represents an alternate approach to interpreting the changes in the institutional environment of the community. It has resulted in pressure on the police organization to shift from the professional policing model to the community policing model.

Bureaucratic Climate for Community Policing

Traditional bureaucratic behavior is rule-bound and routinized, resistant to exceptions and change, even if initiated within the organization (Weber, 1947). Indeed, one characteristic of the professional policing model is the proliferation of policies and procedures manuals designed to reduce the discretion of the officer in situations where a decision is required (Sparrow, Moore & Kennedy, 1990:118-124). Neoinstitutionalism suggests that changes in the environment will penetrate the organization, and the bureaucracy will adapt through a cognitive recognition of new expectations. This will affect the expectation of who should participate such as residents and business groups as partners, and how to solve problems such as with market styled competition, public choice, inter or intra-organizational approaches, and preventative treatment rather than punitive response. An example in community policing is the use of various consensus building techniques applied by community police officers at the community level (Wiatrowski & Campoverde, 1993).

Reinventing Police Work

The entrepreneurial approach to service delivery differs from traditional bureaucratic routine by relying on a pragmatic orientation and using the principles of market incentives (Osborne & Gaebler, 1992). It suggests that government ought to concentrate on facilitating solutions to problems rather than emphasizing the procedure of service delivery. In policing this might be reflected in the change from a response orientation to emergencies through 911 crime calls, to the variable approach through problem oriented policing, stressing the analysis and resolution of recurring problems (Goldstein, 1990), community organization (Wiatrowski & Campoverde, 1993) and community policing approaches (Trojanowicz & Bucqueroux, 1990).

The community orientation that has developed in policing represents the entrepreneurial styled approach to public service delivery that local governments are assuming as they change their expectations of traditional service functions. It also represents the important step of combining service delivery with the development of an external sense of community as well as an internal sense of organization. This support for the development of institutions that incorporate the residents and community enables investment in neighborhoods and supports residents taking charge of their surroundings. Thus, the concept of empowerment is connected to the orientation of the public institution government and its agencies (Zimmerman, 1990; Price, 1990).

The movement of police departments toward community policing reflects the larger movement toward what has been characterized as the community oriented phase of alternative governing. This also is manifested in the interorganizational response that government employs for community policing. For example, community police officers have worked with code enforcement officers to insure that unscrupulous landlords do not criminally victimize tenants in deteriorating neighborhoods. It breaks down the bureaucratic barriers and traditional rule bound behavior, allowing for flexibility in administrative response. The change over time in the approach to policing reflects this evolution in governing in cooperation with the community that is being policed. This is reflected in newly stated missions, goals, and approaches, illustrating administrative evolution.

The process through which community policing programs are implemented is not uniform. Typically community policing begins with a department defining a new mission statement and value structure to guide its future mission (Sparrow, Moore & Kennedy, 1990:129-149). The reason for this is that community policing is at least in part viewed as a repudiation of the old way of doing business. The purpose of this paper has been to argue that community policing can best be viewed in the context of larger changes that are taking place in government in the United States. This diversity in approaches to community policing is a recognition that there is probably not one "best" way to undertake community policing. Instead as these programs develop and evolve, they will be in the context of the rich and developing tradition of reinventing government and the creation of new institutions that are responsive to the needs of the community.

Bibliography

Albritton, J.S. (1991). "The Technique of Community-Oriented Policing: An Alternative Interpretation." Unpublished paper presented at Academy of Criminal Justice Sciences meeting, Pittsburgh, PA.

_____ (1992). "The French National Police System: Continuity, Ambiguity, and Change in the Recent Politics of Decentralization." Unpublished paper presented at the Academy of Criminal Justice Sciences, Kansas City, MO.

Alderson, J.C. (1979). *Policing Freedom.* Plymouth, MA: MacDonald and Evans.

Alinsky, S. (1971). *Rules for Radicals.* New York, NY: Random House.

Alpert, G.P. & R.G. Dunham (1992). *Policing Urban America.* Prospect Heights, IL: Waveland Press.

Alpert, G.P. & M.H. Moore (1993). "Measuring Police Performance in the New Paradigm of Policing." In J. DiLulio (ed.) *Performance Measures for the Criminal Justice System.* Washington, DC: U.S. Department of Justice, Office of Justice Programs, Bureau of Justice Statistics.

Argyris, C. (1982). *Reasoning, Learning, and Action: Individuals and Organizations.* San Francisco, CA: Jossey-Bass.

Argyris, C. & D.M. Schoen (1978). *Organizational Learning.* Reading, MA: Addison Wesley.

Austin, D.M. & Y. Baba (1990). "Social Determinants of Neighborhood Attachment." *Sociological Spectrum,* 18:59-78.

Babbie, E. (1989). *The Practice of Social Research* (5th ed.). Belmont, CA: Wadsworth Publishing Company.

Bandura, A. (1982). "Self-Efficacy Mechanisms in Human Agency." *American Psychologist,* 18:122-147.

Bayley, D.H. (1988). "Community Policing: A Report From the Devil's Advocate." In J.R. Greene & S. Mastrofski (eds.) *Community Policing: Rhetoric or Reality?* New York, NY: Praeger.

271

———— (1992). "Comparative Organization of the Police in English-Speaking Countries." In M. Tonry & N. Morris (eds.) *Modern Policing.*

Beare, M.E. (1987). "Selling Policing in Metropolitan Toronto: A Sociological Analysis of Police Rhetoric, 1957-1984." Unpublished doctoral dissertation. New York, NY: Columbia University.

Bell, D. (1968). *Toward the Year 2000: Work in Progress.* Boston, MA: Houghton Mifflin.

Bennett, S.F. & P.J. Lavrakas (1989). "Community-Based Crime Prevention: An Assessment of the Eisenhower Foundation's Neighborhood Program." *Crime and Delinquency,* 35:345-364.

Bennett, T. (1989). "Factors Related to Participation in Neighborhood Watch Schemes." *British Journal of Criminology,* 2:224-228.

Bennett, W.W. & K.H. Hess (1992). *Management & Supervision in Law Enforcement.* St. Paul, MN: West Publishing Company.

Bennis, W. & C. Cleveland (1980). "Ripping Off the Cops." *Chronicle of Higher Education,* 28:64.

Bercal, T. (1970). "Calls for Police Assistance." *American Behavioral Scientist,* 13:681-691.

Beutler, L.E., A. Storm, P. Kirkish, F. Scogin & J.A. Gaines (1985). "Parameters in the Prediction of Police Officer Performance." *Professional Psychology,* 16:324-335.

Bieck, W.H., W. Spelman & T.J. Sweeney (1991). "The Patrol Function." In W.A. Geller (ed.) *Local Government Police Management* (3rd ed.). Washington, DC: International City Management Association.

Biecke, W. (1980). "Response Time Analysis." Unpublished manuscript. Kansas City, MO: Kansas City Police Department.

Bittner, E. (1970). *The Functions of Police In Modern Society.* Chevy Chase, MD: National Institute of Mental Health.

Block, C.R. (1987). *Homicide in Chicago.* Chicago, IL: Center for Urban Policy, Urban Insights Series No. 14.

Bolman L.G. & T.E. Deal (1991). *Reframing Organizations: Artistry Choice and Leadership.* San Francisco, CA: Jossey-Bass.

Boostrom, R.L. & J.H. Henderson (1983). "Community Action and Crime Prevention: Some Unresolved Issues." *Crime and Social Justice,* Summer.

Bopp, W. & P. Whisenand (1980). *Policy Personnel Administration* (2nd ed.). Englewood Cliffs, NJ: Prentice-Hall.

Bouza, A.V. (1990). *The Police Mystique: An Insider's Look at Cops Crime and the Criminal Justice System*. New York, NY: Plenum Press.

Bowers, W.J. & J.H. Hirsch (1987). "The Impact of Foot Patrol Staffing on Crime and Disorder in Boston: An Unmet Promise." *American Journal of Police*, 6:17-44.

Bowman, G.W., S. Hakim & P. Seidenstat (1992). *Privatizing the U.S. Justice System: Police, Adjudication, and Corrections Services from the Private Sector*. Jefferson, NC: McFarland and Company, Inc.

Braiden, C. (1986). "Bank Robberies and Stolen Bikes: Thoughts of a Street Cop." *Canadian Police College Journal*, 10:1-29.

_____ (1992). "Community Policing: Nothing New Under the Sun." In *Community Oriented Policing and Problem Solving*, pp. 17-22. Sacramento, CA: Crime Prevention Center, Office of the Attorney General.

Broderick, J.J. (1990). "Community Policing, Community Organization and the Legacy of Saul Alinsky." Unpublished paper presented at the American Society of Criminology annual meeting, Baltimore, MD.

Brown, L.P. (1984). "A Police Department and Its Values." *Police Chief*, 11:24-25.

_____ (1989). *Community Policing: A Practical Guide for Police Officers*. Washington, DC: National Institute of Justice and Harvard University, Perspectives on Policing, No. 12.

_____ (1991). *Policing New York City in the 1990s: The Strategy for Community Policing*. New York, NY: New York City Police Department.

_____ (1992a). *Q and A with the Police Commissioner*. New York, NY: New York City Police Department.

_____ (1992b) "Policing in the 90s." In *Sourcebook: Community-Oriented Policing*, pp. 138-139. Washington, DC: IMHA.

_____ (n.d.) *The P.C.'s Post*. New York, NY: New York City Police Department.

Brown, L.P. & M.A. Wycoff (1988). "Policing Houston: Reducing Fear and Improving Service." *Crime and Delinquency*, 34:71-89.

Brown, M.K. (1981). *Working the Street: Police Discretion and the Dilemmas of Reform*. New York, NY: Russell Sage.

Bureau of Justice Statistics (1992). *National Update*. Washington, DC: U.S. Department of Justice.

Burke, J.G. (1972). *The New Technology and Human Values*. Belmont, CA: Wadsworth.

Burke, R.J. (1989). "Career Stages, Satisfaction, and Well-Being Among Police Officers." *Psychological Reports*, 65:3-13.

————— (1989). "Examining the Career Plateau: Some Preliminary Findings." *Psychological Reports*, 65:295-307.

Burkhart, B.R. (1980). "Conceptual Issues in the Development of Police Selection Procedures." *Professional Psychology*, 13:121-129.

Bursik, R.J. Jr. & H.G. Grasmick (1993). *Neighborhoods and Crime: The Dimensions of Effective Community Control*. New York, NY: McGraw-Hill.

Caldwell, D.S. (1991). "Preventing Burnout in Police Organizations." *The Police Chief*, 58:156-160.

Cardarelli, A.P. & J. McDevitt (1992). "Community Policing: Prospects and Challenges to Successful Implementation." Unpublished paper presented at the annual meeting of American Society of Criminology, New Orleans, LA.

Carpenter, B.N. & S.M. Raza (1987). "Personality Characteristics of Police Applicants: Comparisons across Subgroups and with Other Populations." *Journal of Police Science and Administration*, 15:10-17.

Carrot, G. (1992). *Histoire de la Police Française*. Paris, FR: Librairie Jules Tallandier.

Carte, G.E. (1976). "Technology Versus Personnel: Notes on the History of Police Professional Reform." *Journal of Police Science and Administration*, 43:285-297.

Carter, D.H. (1990). "Methods and Measures." In R. Trojanowicz & B. Bucqueroux, *Community Policing: A Contemporary Perspective*, Cincinnati, OH: Anderson Publishing Co.

Carter, D.L., A.D. Sapp & D.W. Stephens (1989). *The State of Police Education Policy Direction for the 21st Century*. Washington, DC: Police Executive Research Forum.

Center for the Research of Criminal Justice (1977). *The Iron Fist and the Velvet Glove: An Analysis of the United States Police*. Berkeley, CA: Center for the Research of Criminal Justice.

Chang, D.H.(1988). "Crime and Delinquency Control Strategy in Japan: A Comparative Note." *International Journal of Comparative and Applied Criminal Justice*, 12:14-32.

Check, J.V. & J.F. Klein (1977). "The Personality of American Police: A Review of the Literature." *Crime and Justice*, 5:33-46.

Cohen, R. & J. Chaiken (1972). *Police Background Characteristics and Performance: Summary Report R-999-DDJ*. New York, NY: Rand Institute.

Cohn, A. & E.C. Viano (1976). *Police-Community Relations: Images, Roles, and Realities*. Philadelphia, PA: Lippincott Company.

Cohn, B. (1990). "A 'People's Cop' Ruffles His Macho Men." *Newsweek*, August 27, 1990:38.

Coleman, M.J. (1992). *Police Assessment Testing.* Springfield, IL: Charles C Thomas, Inc.

Commission on Accreditation for Law Enforcement (1989). *Standards for Law Enforcement Agencies.* Fairfax, VA: CALEA.

Community Policing (1992). "Community Policing." *National Institute of Justice Journal,* 225:1-31.

Congressional Quarterly Research (1993). "Community Policing." Washington, DC: *Congressional Quarterly Research,* p. 35.

Cordner, G.W. (1978). "While on Routine Patrol . . .: A Study of Police Use of Uncommitted Patrol Time." Unpublished doctoral dissertation. East Lansing, MI: School of Criminal Justice, Michigan State University.

_____ (1979). "Police Patrol Workload Studies: A Review and Critique," *Police Studies,* 2 (summer):50-60.

_____ (1985). "The Baltimore County Citizen Oriented Police Enforcement COPE Project: Final Evaluation." Final Report to The Florence Barden Foundation." Baltimore, MD: Criminal Justice Department, University of Baltimore.

_____ (1986). "Fear of Crime and the Police: An Evaluation of a Fear Reduction Strategy." *Journal of Police Science and Administration,* 14:223-233.

_____ (1988). "Issues in a Problem-Oriented Approach to Community-Oriented Policing." In J. Greene & S. Mastrofski (eds.) *Community Policing: Rhetoric or Reality?* New York, NY: Praeger.

_____ (1993). "Public Housing Drug Elimination Program I: Evaluation Report." Unpublished paper. Richmond, KY: Eastern Kentucky University.

Cordner, G.W. & D.C. Hale (1992). *What Works in Policing? Operations and Administration Examined.* Cincinnati, OH: Anderson Publishing Co.

Cordner, G.W. & R.C. Trojanowicz (1992). "Patrol." In G.W. Cordner and D.C. Hale (eds.) *What Works in Policing? Operations and Administration Examined,* pp. 3-18. Cincinnati, OH: Anderson Publishing Co.

Cordner, G.W. & G.L. Williams (1993). "The Compatibility of Community Policing and Accreditation." Unpublished paper presented at annual meeting of the Academy of Criminal Justice Sciences, Kansas City, MO.

Crank, J.P. (1990). "The Influence of Environmental and Organizational Factors on Police Style in Urban and Rural Environments." *Research in Crime and Delinquency,* 27:166-189.

Crank, J.P. & R. Langworthy (1992). "An Institutional Perspective of Policing." *Journal of Criminal Law and Criminology,* 83:338-363.

CRESAP (1991). City of Houston Police Department. Washington, DC: CRESAP.

Critchley, T.A. (1972). A History of Police in England and Wales. Montclair, NJ: Patterson-Smith.

Cumming, E., I. Cumming & L. Edell (1965). "Police Man as Philosopher, Friend and Guide," Social Problems, 12.

Currie, E. (1985). Confronting Crime: An American Challenge. New York, NY: Pantheon Books.

Decker, S.H. (1981). "Citizen Attitudes Toward the Police: A Review of Past Findings and Suggestions for Future Policy." Journal of Police Science and Administration, 91:80-87.

del Carmen, R.V. (1991). Civil Liabilities in American Policing. Englewood Cliffs, NJ: Prentice-Hall.

DiMaggio, P. (1988). "Interest and Agency Institutional Theory." In G. Zucker (ed.) Institutional Patterns and Organizations: Culture and Environment. Cambridge, MA: Ballinger.

DiMaggio, P.J. & W.W. Powell (1991). "Introduction." In W. Powell & P. DiMaggio (eds.) The New Institutionalism in Organizational Analysis. Chicago, IL: University of Chicago Press.

Donahue, M.E. (1993). "A Comprehensive Program to Combat Violent Crime: The Savannah Experience." The Police Chief, 609:12, 14, 18, 21-22.

Downs, A. (1967). Inside Bureaucracy. Santa Monica, CA: RAND Corporation.

Dukes, D. (1992). "Characteristics of the Neighborhood Police Officer: What Are the Important Personal and Demographic Characteristics?" Unpublished paper presented a the annual meeting of the Academy of Criminal Justice Sciences, Denver, CO.

Dunham, R. & G.P. Alpert (1988). "Neighborhood Differences in Attitudes Toward Policing: Evidence for a Mixed Strategy Model for Policing in a Multi-Ethnic Setting." Journal of Criminal Law and Criminology, 79:504-523.

Dwyer, W.O., E.P. Prien & J.L. Bernard (1990). "Psychological Screening of Law Enforcement Officers: A Case for Job Relatedness." Journal of Police Science and Administration, 173:176-182.

Eck, J.E. & W. Spelman (1987a). Problem-Solving: Problem-Oriented Policing in Newport News. Washington, DC: Police Executive Research Forum.

———— (1987b). "Who Ya Gonna Call?" Crime and Delinquency, 34:1.

Edelman, M. (1964). The Symbolic Uses of Politics. Urbana, IL: University of Illinois Press.

_____ (1971). *Politics as Symbolic Action: Mass Arousal and Quiescence*. Chicago, IL: Markham Publishing Company.

Eisenger, P. (1988). *The Rise of the Entrepreneurial State*. Madison, WI: University of Wisconsin Press.

Ekblom, P. & K. Heal (1982). *The Police Response to Calls from the Public*. Research and Planning Unit Paper 9. London: Home Office.

Ellul, J. (1964). *The Technological Society*. New York, NY: Alfred A. Knopf.

_____ (1965). *Propaganda: The Formation of Men's Attitudes*. New York, NY: Alfred A. Knopf.

_____ (1980). *The Technological System*. New York, NY: Continuum.

Ericson, R. (1982). *Reproducing Order: A Study of Police Patrol Work*. Toronto, CN: University of Toronto Press.

Elbert, N.F. & R. Discenza (1983). *Contemporary Supervision*. New York, NY: Random House.

Esbensen, F. (1987). "Foot Patrol: Of What Value?" *American Journal of Police*, 61:45-65.

Farrell, M.J. (1988). "The Development of the Community Patrol Officer Program: Community-Oriented Policing in the New York City Police Department." In J.R. Greene & S.D. Mastrofski (eds.) *Community Policing: Rhetoric or Reality?* New York, NY: Praeger.

Fenster, C.A. & B. Locke (1973). "Neuroticism Among Policemen: An Examination of Police Personality." *Journal of Applied Psychology*, 57:358-359.

Figlio, R.M., S. Hakim & G. Rengert (eds.) (1986). *Metropolitan Crime Patterns*. Monsey, NY: Criminal Justice Press.

Fischer, C.S. (1981). "The Public and Private Worlds of City Life." *American Sociological Review*, 46:306-316.

Fishman, M. (1980). *Manufacturing the News in Austin, TX*. Austin, TX: University of Texas Press.

Forgas, J.P. (1983). "Episode Cognition and Personality: A Multidimensional Analysis." *Journal of Personality*, 51:34-48.

Friday, P.C. (1988). "The Scandinavian Efforts to Balance Societal Responses and Offenders: Crime Prevention and Social Control." *International Journal of Comparative and Applied Criminal Justice*, 12:46-59.

Frieden, B. & L. Sagalyn (1989). *Downtown, Inc.* Cambridge, MA: MIT Press.

Friedland, R. & R.R. Alford (1991). "Bringing Society Back In." In W. Powell & P. DiMaggio (eds.) *The New Institutionalism in Organizational Analysis.* Chicago, IL: University of Chicago Press.

Friedmann, R.R. (1992). "Community Policing: Comparative Perspectives and Prospects," pp. 79-80. New York, NY: St. Martin's Press.

Gaines, L.K., M.D. Southerland & J.E. Angell (1991). *Police Administration.* New York, NY: McGraw-Hill.

Garner, G.W. (1987). "Chief, the Reporters are Here!": *The Police Executive's Personal Guide to Press Relations.* Springfield, IL: Charles C Thomas.

Garner, J. (1982). "Meet the Press: Media Relations for Police." *Law and Order,* 302:28-32.

Garofalo, J. & M. McLeod (1989). "The Structure and Operation of Neighborhood Watch Programs in the United States." *Crime and Delinquency,* 35(3):326-344.

Gendron, B. (1977). *Technology and the Human Condition.* New York, NY: St. Martin's Press.

Gibbons, D.C. (1990). "From the Editor's Desk: A Call for Some Outrageous Proposals for Crime Control in the 1990s." *Crime and Delinquency,* 36:195-203.

Gitlin, T. (1980). *The Whole World Is Watching.* Berkeley, CA: The University of California Press.

Goldstein, H. (1977a). *Policing a Free Society.* Cambridge, MA: Ballinger.

———— (1977b). *The Urban Police Function.* Cambridge, MA: Ballinger.

———— (1979). "Improving Policing: A Problem-Oriented Approach." *Crime and Delinquency,* 25:236-258.

———— (1987). "Toward Community-Oriented Policing: Potential, Basic Requirements, and Threshold Questions." *Crime and Delinquency,* 31:6-30.

———— (1990). *Problem-Oriented Policing.* New York, NY: McGraw-Hill.

Gourley, G.D. (1953). *Public Relations and the Police.* Springfield, IL: Charles C Thomas.

Greene, H.T. (1993). "Community-Oriented Policing in Florida." Unpublished manuscript.

Greene, J.R. (1989a) "Police and Community Relations: Where Have We Been and Where Are We Going?" In R.G. Dunham & G.P. Alpert (eds) *Critical Issues in Policing,* pp. 349-368. Prospect Heights IL: Waveland Press.

———— (1989b). "Police Officer Job Satisfaction and Community Perceptions: Implications for Community-Oriented Policing." *Journal of Research in Crime and Delinquency,* 26:168-184.

Greene, J.R. & C.B. Klockars (1991). "What Police Do." In C.B. Klockars & S.D. Mastrofski (eds) *Thinking About Police: Contemporary Readings* (2nd ed.). New York, NY: McGraw-Hill.

Greene, J.R. & S.D. Mastrofski (1988). *Community Policing: Rhetoric or Reality?* New York, NY: Praeger.

Greene, J.R. & R.B. Taylor (1988). "Community-Based Policing and Foot Patrol: Issues of Theory and Evaluation." In J.R. Greene & S.D. Mastrofski (eds.) *Community Policing: Rhetoric or Reality?*, pp. 195-223. New York, NY: Praeger.

Gudjonsson, G.H. & K.R. Adlam (1989). "Personality Patterns of British Police Officers." *British Journal of Sociology,* 46:233-249.

Guido, D. (1993). *Presentation to Department of Law and Police Science.* New York, NY: John Jay College.

Gusfield, J.R. (1963). *Symbolic Crusade: Status Politics and the American Temperance Movement.* Urbana, IL: University of Illinois Press.

Gustavson, S. & P.C. Kratcoski (1991). "An Analysis of Citizens Responses to Neighborhood Policing in a Major Midwestern City." Unpublished paper presented at the Society for Applied Sociology, Annapolis, MD.

Guth, W.D. & I.C. Macmillan (1986). "Strategy Implementation Versus Middle Management Self-interest." *Strategic Management Journal,* 7:313-327.

Guy, M.E. (1989). "Minnowbrook II: Conclusions." *Public Administration Review,* 49:219-220.

Hadar, I. & J.R. Snortum (1975). "The Eye of the Beholder." *Criminal Justice and Behavior,* 2:37-54.

Hahn, H. (1971). "Ghetto Assessments of Police Protection and Authority." *Law and Society Review,* 6:183-194.

Hall, R.H. (1987). *Organizations: Structure, Process and Outcomes* (4th ed.). Englewood Cliffs, NJ: Prentice-Hall.

Hanewicz, W.B. (1978). "Police Personality: A Jungian Perspective." *Crime and Delinquency,* 24:152-172.

Hanson, R.O. & K.M. Slade (1977). "Altruism Toward a Deviant in City and Small Town." *Journal of Applied Social Psychology,* 73:272-279.

Harring, S., T. Platt, R. Speigelman & P. Takagil (1977). "The Management of Police Killings." *Crime and Social Justice,* 8:34-43.

Hartman, F., L. Brown & D. Stephens (1988). *Community Policing: Would You Know It If You Saw It?* East Lansing, MI: The Neighborhood Foot Patrol Center.

Hartmann, F.X. (1988). "Debating the Evolution of American Policing." *Perspectives on Policing.* Washington, DC: National Institute of Justice.

Hayeslip, D.W., Jr. & D.L. Weisel (1992). "Local Level Drug Enforcement." In G.W. Cordner & D.C. Hale (eds.) *What Works in Policing? Operations and Administration Examined,* pp. 35-48. Cincinnati, OH: Anderson Publishing Co.

Herman, E.S. & N. Chomsky (1988). *Manufacturing Consent.* New York, NY: Pantheon Books.

Hiatt, D. & G. Hargrave (1988). "MMPI Profiles of Problem Peace Officers." *Journal of Personality Assessment,* 524:722-731.

Higgens, D.J.H. (1977). *Urban Canada: Its Government and Politics.* Toronto, CN: Gage Publishing Ltd.

Hoover, L.T. (1992). "Police Mission: An Era of Debate." In *Police Management: Issues and Perspectives.* Washington, DC: Police Executive Research Forum.

Hornick, J.P., B.A. Burrows, I. Tjosvold & D.M. Phillips (1989). *An Evaluation of the Neighborhood Foot Patrol Program of the Edmonton, Canada Police Service—Report Prepared for Edmonton Police Department.* Edmonton, CAN: Edmonton, Canada Police Department.

Iadicola, P. (1985) "Community Crime Control Strategies." Washington, DC: *Crime and Social Justice* No. 25.

International City/County Management Association (1992). *Workbook: Community-Oriented Policing: An Alternative Strategy.* Washington, DC: International City/County Management Association.

Jencks, C. & P.E. Peterson (eds.) (1991). *The Urban Underclass.* Washington, DC: Public Affairs Press.

Jones, R. (1993). "Community Oriented Policing." *The Ohio Police Chief,* June:37-39.

Kalamazoo Department of Public Safety (1992). *1992 Annual Report* (Unpublished Report). Kalamazoo, MI: Kalamazoo City.

Kanter, R.M. (1983). *The Change Masters.* New York, NY: Simon and Schuster.

Kelling, G.L. (1974). *Kansas City Preventive Patrol Experiment.* Unpublished manuscript. Washington, DC: The Police Foundation.

_____ (1988). *Police and Communities: The Quiet Revolution—Perspectives on Policing.* Washington, DC: National Institute of Justice.

_____ (1990). "Community Policing." In R. Trojanowicz & B. Bucqueroux (eds) *Community Policing: A Contemporary Perspective.* Cincinnati, OH: Anderson Publishing Co.

_____ (1994). "It's Time To Let Beat Cops Do Their Job." *New York Daily News,* March 9, 1994:27.

Kelling, G.L. & W.J. Bratton (1993). *Implementing Community Policing: The Administrative Problem.* Washington, DC: National Institute of Justice.

Kelling, G.L. & M.H. Moore (1987). *From Political Reform to Community: The Evolving Strategy of Police.* Cambridge, MA: Harvard University John F. Kennedy School of Government.

_____ (1988). "The Evolving Strategy of Policing." *Perspectives on Policing.* Washington, DC: National Institute of Justice.

_____ (1988). "From Political to Reform to Community: The Evolving Strategy of Police." In R. Greene & S.D. Mastrofski (eds) *Community Policing: Rhetoric or Reality?* New York, NY: Praeger.

Kelling, G.L. & J.K. Stewart (1989). *Neighborhoods and Police: The Maintenance of Civil Authority.* Washington, DC: National Institute of Justice, and the John F. Kennedy School of Government, Harvard University, Perspectives on Policing #10.

Kelling, G.L., R. Wasserman & H. Williams (1988). "Police Accountability and Community Policing." Washington, DC: National Institute of Justice, Perspectives on Policing.

Kennedy, D.M. (1993). "The Strategic Management of Police Resources." Washington, DC: National Institute of Justice and the John F. Kennedy School of Government, Harvard University, Perspectives on Policing #14.

Klein, L., J. Luxenburg & M. King (1989). "Perceived Neighborhood Crime and the Impact of Private Security." *Crime and Delinquency,* 35:365-377.

Klockars, C.B. (1985a). *The Idea of Police.* Beverly Hills, CA: Sage.

_____ (1985b). "Order Maintenance, the Quality of Urban Life and Police: A Different Line of Argument." In W.A. Geller (ed.) *Police Leadership in America,* pp. 309-321. New York, NY: Praeger.

_____ (1988). "The Rhetoric of Community Policing." In J.R. Greene & S.D. Mastrofski (eds.) *Community Policing: Rhetoric or Reality?* New York, NY: Praeger.

Kratcoski, P. & L. Albert (1990). *Akron Community Police Proposal.* Unpublished manuscript.

Kratcoski, P.C. & S. Gustavson (1991). "Community Satisfaction with Police: An Exploration Analysis of the Effects of Neighborhood Policing," p. 7. Unpublished paper presented at the North Central Sociological Association. Dearborn, MI.

Kraus, S. & D. Davis (1980). "The Effects of Mass Communication on Political Behavior." Unpublished paper. University Park, PA: Pennsylvania State University.

Kuhn, T.S. (1970). *The Structure of Scientific Revolutions.* Chicago, IL: University of Chicago Press.

Kuhns, W. (1971). *The Post-Industrial Prophets: Interpretations of Technology.* New York, NY: Harper.

Kuykendall, J. & R.R. Roberg (1982). "Mapping Police Organizational Change." *Criminology,* 38:144-157.

Lamb, C. (1975). *Political Power in Poor Neighborhoods.* New York, NY: John Wiley & Sons.

Langworthy, R.H. (1986). *The Structure of Police Organizations.* Cincinnati, OH: Anderson Publishing Co.

Lasley, J.R. (1991). "LAPD Proves That Muscle Works." *Los Angeles Times,* March 31, 1991:M21.

——————— (1992). "Fulfilling the Mandates of the Law: The Consent Decrees and Compliance." In G. Felkenes & P.C. Unsinger (eds.) *Diversity, Affirmative Action, and Law Enforcement,* pp. 167-173. Springfield, IL: Charles C Thomas.

——————— (1993). "The Impact of the Rodney King Incident on Citizen Attitudes Toward Police." *Policing and Society,* 3:20-35.

——————— (Forthcoming). "Ethnicity, Gender and Police-Community Relations." *Social Science Quarterly.*

Lasley, J.R. & G. Felkenes (1993). "Implications of Hiring Women Police Officers: Police Administrator's Concerns May Not Be Justified." *Policing and Society,* 2:11-25.

Lasley, J.R. & R.L. Vernon (1992). "Police/Citizen Partnerships in the Inner-City." *FBI Law Enforcement Bulletin,* May: 18-22.

Ledot, D., M. Antoni, P. Calvet & H. Luccioni (1988). "The Offspring of North African Immigrants at an Army Selection Center in Tarascon, France: A Psychological Study Among 104 Recruits." *Psychologie Medicale,* 20:1485-1488.

Lefkowitz, J. (1975). "Psychological Attributes of Policemen: A Review of Research and Opinion." *Journal of Social Issues,* 31:3-26.

_____ (1977). "Industrial-Organizational Psychology and the Police." *American Psychologist*, 32:346-364.

Leighton, B.N. (1991). "Visions of Community Policing: Rhetoric and Reality in Canada." *Canadian Journal of Criminology*, 33:485-522.

Levine, C. (1980). *Managing Fiscal Stress*. Chatham, NJ: Chatham House.

Levy, R.J. (1967). "Predicting Police Failures." *Journal of Criminal Law, Criminology and Police Science*, 58:265-276.

Licata, R. (1991). "Community Outreach Program." *The FBI Law Enforcement Bulletin*, 60:18-20.

Lipskey, M. (1980). *Street-Level Bureaucracy*. New York, NY: Russell Sage Foundation.

Lundman, R.J. (1979). "Organizational Norms and Police Discretion." *Criminology*, 17:159-171.

Lynch, R.G. (1986). *The Police Manager* (3rd ed.). New York, NY: Random House.

Magenau, J.M. (1989). "Sociopolitical Networks for Police Role-Making." *Human Relations*, 42:547-560.

Manning, P.K. (1971). "The Police: Mandate, Strategies, and Appearances." In J.D. Douglas (ed.) *Crime and Justice in American Society*, pp. 149-194. New York, NY: The Bobbs-Merrill Company, Inc.

_____ (1977). *The Social Organization of Policing*. Cambridge, MA: MIT Press.

_____ (1984). "Community Policing." *American Journal of Police*, 32:205-227.

_____ (1988). "Community Policing as a Drama of Control." In J.D. Greene & S.D. Mastrofski (eds.) *Community Policing: Rhetoric or Reality?* New York, NY: Praeger.

_____ (1992). "Technological Dramas and the Police: Statement and Counterstatement in Organizational Analysis." *Criminology*, 30:303.

Marx, G.T. (1988). *Undercover: Police Surveillance in America*. Berkeley, CA: University of California Press.

_____ (1989). "Commentary: Some Trends and Issues in Citizen Involvement in the Law Enforcement Process." *Crime and Delinquency*, 35:500-519.

Marzulli, J. (1994a). "Beat Cops Are a Bust." *New York Daily News*, January 24, 1994:A2.

_____ (1994b). "Community Cops Mostly 9-to-5ers." *New York Daily News*, January 24, 1994:B3.

Mastrofski, S. (1992). "What Does Community Policing Mean for Daily Police Work?" *National Institute of Justice Journal,* 225:23-27.

McDowell, C.P. (1975). *Police in the Community.* Cincinnati, OH: Anderson Publishing Co.

————— (1993). *Criminal Justice in the Community.* Cincinnati, OH: Anderson Publishing Co.

McElroy, J., C.A. Cosgrove & S. Sadd (1990). *COP: The Research.* New York, NY: The Vera Institute of Justice.

————— (1993). *Community Policing: The CPOP in New York.* Newbury Park, CA: Sage.

McCaskey, M.B. (1982). *The Executive Challenge: Managing Change and Ambiguity.* Marshbell, MA: Pitman.

Meese, E. III (1993). "Community Policing and the Police Officer." *Perspectives on Policing,* Washington, DC: U.S. Department of Justice.

Mesthene, E.G. (1970). *Technological Change.* New York, NY: Mentor Books.

Michaelson, S., G. Kelling & R. Wasserman (1988). "Toward a Working Definition of Community Policing." Unpublished paper for program in *Criminal Justice Policy and Management.* Cambridge, MA: John F. Kennedy School of Government, Harvard University.

Michalowski, R.J. (1983). "Crime Control in the 1980s: A Progressive Agenda." *Crime and Social Justice,* Summer: 221-235.

Miller, S.M. (1987). "Monitoring and Blaming." *Journal of Personality and Social Psychology,* 52:345-353.

Miller, W.R. (1977). *Cops and Bobbies: Police Authority in New York and London, 1830-1870.* Chicago, IL: University of Chicago Press.

Mischel, W. (1990). "Personality Dispositions Revisited and Revised: A View After Three Decades." In L.A. Pervin (ed.) *Handbook of Personality: Theory and Research.* New York, NY: Guilford Press.

Moore, M.H. (1992). "Problem Solving and Community Policing." In M. Tonry & N. Morris (eds.) *Modern Policing.* Chicago, IL: The University of Chicago Press.

Moore, M.H. & M.A.R. Kleiman (1989). "The Police and Drugs." *Perspectives on Policing.* Washington, DC: National Institute of Justice.

Moore, M.H. & R.C. Trojanowicz (1988a) "Corporate Strategies for Policing." *Perspectives on Policing.* Washington, DC: National Institute of Justice.

————— (1988b) "Policing and the Fear of Crime." *Perspectives on Policing.* Washington, DC: National Institute of Justice and Harvard University.

Moran, T.K. & E.B. Silverman (1991). "Values in Police Education and Training: A Comparative Approach." Unpublished paper presented at the annual meeting of the American Society of Criminology, San Francisco, CA.

More, H. & P. Unsinger (eds.) (1987). *The Police Assessment Center.* Springfield, IL: Charles C Thomas, Inc.

Morgan, R. (1987). "The Local Determinants of Policing Policy." In P. Willmott (ed.) *Policing and the Community.* London: Policy Studies Institute.

Mumford, L. (1963). *Technics and Civilization.* New York, NY: Harcourt, Brace, Jovanovich.

_____ (1970). *The Myth of the Machine.* New York, NY: Harcourt, Brace, Jovanovich.

Munro, J.L. (1974). *Administrative Behavior and Police Organization.* Cincinnati, OH: Anderson Publishing Co.

Murphy, C. & G. Muir (1985). *Community-Based Policing: A Review of the Critical Issues.* Ottawa, CN: Office of the Solicitor General Canada.

Murrell, M.E., D. Lester & A.F. Arcuri (1978). "Is the 'Police Personality' Unique to Police Officers?" *Psychological Reports,* 43:298.

Naisbitt, J. (1984). *Megatrends.* New York, NY: Warner Books.

National Council on Crime and Delinquency (1981). *The Evaluation of Delinquency Prevention: Final Report.* Washington, DC: National Council on Crime and Delinquency.

National Crime Prevention Institute (1986). *Understanding Crime Prevention.* Louisville, KY.

National Institute of Justice (1984). *Using Research: A Primer for Law Enforcement Managers.* Washington, DC: The Police Executive Research Forum.

_____ (1992a). "Community Policing." *National Institute of Justice Journal,* 225.

_____ (1992b). "Community Policing in Seattle: A Model Partnership Between Citizens and Police." *National Institute of Justice Journal,* 226.

New Yorker (1993). "Comment." *New Yorker,* July 5, 1993:4.

Nisbet, R.A. (1969). *The Quest for Community.* New York, NY: Oxford University Press.

O'Block, R.L. (1981). *Security and Crime Prevention.* Stoneham, MA: Butterworth Publishers.

O'Brien, R.M. (1985). *Crime and Victimization Data.* Beverly Hills, CA: Sage Publications (Law and Criminal Justice Series No. 4).

O'Neill, M. & C.J. Bloom (1972). "The Field Officer: Is He Really Fighting Crime?" *Police Chief,* 39 (February):30-32.

Oettmeier, T.N. & L.P. Brown (1988). *Developing a Neighborhood-Oriented Police Style*. New York, NY: Praeger.

Osborne, D. (1990). *Laboratories of Democracy*. Cambridge, MA: Harvard Business School Press.

Osborne, D. & T. Gaebler (1992). *Reinventing Government*. New York, NY: Addison Wesley.

Pate, A.M., M.A. Wycoff, W.G. Skogan & L.W. Sherman (1986). *Reducing Fear of Crime in Houston and Newark: A Summer Project*. Washington, DC: The Police Foundation.

Payne, D.M. & R.C. Trojanowicz (1985). *Performance Profiles of Foot Versus Motor Officers*, East Lansing, MI: National Neighborhood Foot Patrol Center, Michigan State University.

Perrow, C. (1979). *Complex Organizations* (2nd ed.). New York, NY: Random House.

Peters, T. (1985). *A Passion for Excellence*. New York, NY: Warner Books.

Peters, T.J. & R.H. Waterman, Jr. (1982). *In Search of Excellence: Lessons From America's Best Run Companies*. New York, NY: Warner Books.

Piven, F. F. & R. Cloward (1977). *Poor People's Movements*. New York, NY: Pantheon.

Police Foundation (1981). *The Newark Foot Patrol Experiment*. Washington, DC: The Police Foundation.

Portland Police Bureau (1990). *Community Policing Transition Plan*. Portland, OR: Portland Police Bureau.

Postman, N. (1992). *Technopoly: The Surrender of Culture to Technology*. New York, NY: Alfred A. Knopf.

Price, H.R. (1990). "Wither Participation and Empowerment?" *American Journal of Community Psychology*, 18:163-167.

Putti, J. (1988). "Personal Values of Recruits and Officers in a Law Enforcement Agency: An Explanatory Study." *Journal of Police Science and Administration*, 16:249-254.

Pynes, J. & H.J. Bernardin (1989). "Predictive Validity of an Entry-Level Police Officer Assessment Center." *Journal of Applied Psychology*, 4:831-833.

———— (1992). "Entry-Level Police Selection: The Assessment Center is an Alternative." *Journal of Criminal Justice*, 20:41-52.

Radelet, L.A. (1977). *The Police and the Community* (2nd ed.). Toronto, CN: Collier Macmillan.

Reiss, A. (1971). *The Police and the Public*. New Haven, CT: Yale University Press.

Reiss, A. & D. Bordua (1967). "Environment and Organization: A Perspective on the Police." In *The Police: Six Sociological Essays*, D. Bordua (ed.). New York, NY: John Wiley & Sons.

Reiss, A.J., Jr. (1992). "Police Organization in the Twentieth Century." In *Modern Policing*, M. Tonry & N. Morris (eds). Chicago, IL: University of Chicago Press.

Reiss, A.J. Jr. & J.A. Roth (eds). (1993). *Understanding and Preventing Violence*. Washington, DC: The National Research Council on Violence, Panel on the Understanding and Control of Violent Behavior, National Academy Press.

Reiss, A.J. Jr. & M. Tonry (eds.) (1986). *Communities and Crime*. New York, NY: John Wiley & Sons.

Reith, C. (1952). *The Blind Eye of History*. London, UK: Faber and Faber Ltd.

Renner, K.E. & C.T. Barnett (1984). "A Conceptual Framework for Police Functions & Services." *Journal of Criminal Justice*, 15:303-312.

Reuss-Ianni, E. (1983). *Two Culture of Policing: Street Cops and Management Cops*. New Brunswick, NJ: Transaction Books.

Riechers, L. & R. Roberg (1990). "Community Policing: A Critical Review of Underlying Assumptions." *Journal of Police Science and Administration*, 18:172.

Roberg, R.R. & J. Kuykendall (1990). *Police Organization and Management*. Pacific Grove, CA: Brooks/Cole.

Rogers, E.M. & F.F. Shoemaker (1971). *Communications of Innovations: A Cultural Approach*. New York, NY: The Free Press.

Rosen, M.S. (1992). "An Interview with Commissioner Lee P. Brown of New York." *Law Enforcement News*, 18(358):10, 11, 14.

Rosenbaum, D.P. (1986). *Community Crime Prevention: Does It Work?* Beverly Hills, CA: Sage.

_____ (1988). "Community Crime Prevention: A Review and Synthesis of the Literature." *Justice Quarterly*, 5:323-395.

Rosenbaum, D.P., A.J. Lurigio & P.J. Lavrakas (1989). "Enhancing Citizen Participation and Solving Serious Crime: A National Evaluation of Crime Stoppers Programs." *Crime and Delinquency*, 35:401-420.

Rosenberg, H. & P. Crane (1994). "Racine Community Policing: A Residential Perspective." Preliminary Report to the Racine Police Department. Racine, WI: Institute of Public Affairs.

Rothman, J. & J.E. Tropman (1987). "Models of Community Organization and Macro Practice." In F.M. Cox, J.L. Ehrlich, J. Rothman & J.E. Tropman (eds.) *Strategies of Community Organization*. Itasca, IL: F.E. Peacock.

Rumbaut, R.G. (1978). *The Politics of Reform in a Police Bureaucracy: A Case Study in Social Intervention and Organizational Change.* Ann Arbor, MI: University Microfilms International.

Sampson, R.J. (1986). "Crime in Cities: The Effects of Formal and Informal Social Control" In A.J. Reiss, Jr. & M. Tonry (eds.) *Communities and Crime.* Chicago, IL: University of Chicago Press.

———— (1987). "Communities and Crime." In M.R. Gottfredson & T. Hirschi (eds.) *Positive Criminology.* Chicago, IL: University of Chicago Press.

Savas, E.S. (1987). *Privatization: The Key to Better Government.* Chatham, NJ: Chatham House.

Saxe, S.J. & M. Reiser (1976). "A Comparison of Three Police Applicant Groups Using the MMPI." *Journal of Police Science & Administration,* 4:419-425.

Scaglion, R. & R. Condon (1980). "Determinants of Attitudes Toward City Police," *Criminology,* (17)4, 486-489.

Schumaker, P.D. (1975). "Policy Responsiveness to Protest-Group Demands." *Journal of Politics,* 372:488-521.

Schuman, H. & B. Gruenberg (1972). "Dissatisfaction with City Services: Is Race an Important Factor?" In H. Hahn (ed.) *People and Politics in Urban Society,* pp. 369-392. Beverly Hills, CA: Sage.

Senese, J.D. (1993). "Crime in High and Low Crime Neighborhoods: An Assessment of Social and Physical Dimensions." Unpublished paper. South Bend, IN: Indiana University at South Bend. (pp. 79-107).

Sheehan, R. & G.W. Cordner (1995). *Police Administration* (3rd ed.). Cincinnati, OH: Anderson Publishing Co.

Sherman, L.W. (1986). "Policing Communities: What Works." In A.J. Reiss, Jr. & M. Tonry (eds.) *Communities and Crime.* Chicago, IL: University of Chicago Press.

———— (1992). "Police and Crime Control." In M. Tonry & N. Morris (eds.) *Modern Policing.* Chicago, IL: The University of Chicago Press.

Sherman, L., C. Milton & T. Kelly (1973). *Team Policing: Seven Case Studies.* Washington, DC: The Police Foundation.

Sherman, L.W., J. Schmidt & D. Rogan (1992). *Policing Domestic Violence: Experiments and Dilemmas.* New York, NY: Basic Books.

Short, C. (1983). "Community Policing-Beyond the Slogans." In T. Bennett (ed.) *The Future of Policing,* pp. 67-81. Cambridge, UK: Institute of Technology.

Siegel, L.J. (1986). *Criminology* (2nd ed.). St. Paul, MN: West Publishing Company.

Simon, H. (1946). "The Proverbs of Administration." *Public Administration Review,* 6:53-67.

Skogan, W.G. (1978). "Citizen Satisfaction with Police Services: Individual and Contextual Effects." *Police Studies Journal,* 14:469-479.

_____ (1989). "Communities, Crime, and Neighborhood Organization." *Crime and Delinquency,* 35:437-457.

_____ (1990). *Disorder and Decline: Crime and the Spiral of Decay in American Neighborhoods.* New York, NY: The Free Press.

Skolnick, J.H. & D.H. Bayley (1986). *The New Blue Line: Police Innovation in Six American Cities.* New York, NY: The Free Press.

_____ (1988). *Community Policing: Issues and Practices around the World.* Washington, DC: National Institute of Justice.

_____ (1988). "Theme and Variation in Community Policing." In M. Tonry & N. Morris (eds.) *Crime and Justice: A Review of Research.* Chicago, IL: University of Chicago Press.

Slovak, J.S. (1986). *Styles of Urban Policing: Organization, Environment, and Police Styles in American Cities.* Washington, DC: Public Affairs Press.

Small, S.A., R.S. Zeldin & R.C. Savin-Williams (1983). "In Search of Personality Traits: A Multimethod Analysis of Naturally Occurring Prosocial and Dominance Behavior." *Journal of Personality,* 51:1-16.

Smith, D. (1987). "Research, the Community and the Police." In P. Willmott (ed.) *Policing and the Community.* London, UK: Policy Studies Institute.

Sniderman, P. (1981). *A Question of Loyalty.* Berkeley, CA: University of California Press.

Sparrow, M.K. (1988a). *Implementing Community Policing.* Washington, DC: National Institute of Justice, Perspectives on Policing.

_____ (1988b) "Implementing Community Policing." *Perspectives on Policing.* Washington, DC: National Institute of Justice.

Sparrow, M.K., M.H. Moore & D.H. Kennedy (1990). *Beyond 911: A New Era For Policing.* New York, NY: Basic Books.

Spelman, W. & J.E. Eck (1987a). *Newport News Tests Problem-Oriented Policing.* Washington, DC: National Institute of Justice.

_____ (1987b). "Problem-Oriented Policing." *Research in Brief.* Washington, DC: National Institute of Justice.

Spielberger, C.D., H.C. Spaulding, M.T. Jolley & J.C. Ward (1979). "Selection of Effective Law Enforcement Officers: The Florida Standards Project." In C.D. Spielberger (ed.) *Police Selection and Evaluation: Issues and Techniques*, pp. 231-251. New York, NY: Praeger.

Storms, L.H. (1990). "Policemen's Perception of Real and Ideal Policemen." *Journal of Police Science and Administration*, 17:40-43.

Swanson, C. (1978). "The Influence of Organization and Environment on Arrest Policies in Major U.S. Cities." *Policy Studies Journal*, 7:390-418.

Swanson, C.R., L. Territo & R.W. Taylor (1993). *Police Administration: Structures, Processes, and Behavior* (3rd ed.). New York, NY: Macmillan.

Sykes, G.W. (1986). "Street Justice: Amoral Defense of Order Maintenance Policing." *Justice Quarterly*, 3:497-512.

_____ (1990). "The Latest Advances in Making Excuses For The Way Things Are: Community Policing in the 1990s." Unpublished paper presented at the annual meeting of the Academy of Criminal Justice Sciences, Denver, CO.

Sylvia, R.D., K.J. Meier & E.M. Gunn (1991). *Program Planning and Evaluation for the Public Manager*. Washington, DC: Public Affairs Press.

Taft, P.B., Jr. (1986). *Fighting Fear: The Baltimore County COPE Project*. Washington DC: Police Executive Research Forum.

Taylor, R.B. & J. Covington (1988). "Neighborhood Changes in Ecology and Violence." *Criminology*, 26:553-589.

Teich, A.H. (1990). *Technology and the Future*. New York, NY: St. Martin's Press.

Thibault, E.A., L.M. Lynch & R.B. McBride (1985). *Proactive Police Management*. Englewood Cliffs, NJ: Prentice-Hall.

Toch, H. & J.D. Grant (1991). *Police as Problem Solvers*. New York, NY: Plenum Press.

Toffler, A. (1970). *Future Shock*. New York, NY: Random House.

Tonry, M. & N. Morris (eds.) (1992). *Modern Policing*. Chicago, IL: University of Chicago Press.

Topp, B.W. & C.A. Kardash (1986). "Personality, Achievement, and Attrition: Validation in a Multiple-Jurisdiction Police Academy." *Journal of Police Science and Administration*, 14:234-241.

Trojanowicz, R.C. (1980). *An Evaluation of the Neighborhood Foot Patrol Program in Flint, Michigan.* East Lansing, MI: National Neighborhood Foot Patrol Center, Michigan State University.

_____ (1982). *An Evaluation of the Neighborhood Foot Patrol Program in Flint, Michigan.* East Lansing, MI: National Center for Community Policing, Michigan State University.

_____ (1986). *An Evaluation of the Neighborhood Foot Patrol Program in Flint, Michigan.* East Lansing, MI: National Neighborhood Foot Patrol Center.

_____ (1988). *The Meaning of Community Policing.* East Lansing, MI: The Neighborhood Foot Patrol Center.

_____ (1990). "Community Policing is Not Police-Community Relations." *FBI Law Enforcement Bulletin,* Vol. 1 (October 1990), p.10.

Trojanowicz, R. & D.W. Banas (1985). *Job Satisfaction: A Comparison of Foot Patrol versus Motor Patrol Officers.* East Lansing, MI: National Center for Neighborhood Foot Patrol Center.

Trojanowicz, R.C. & B. Bucqueroux (1990). *Community Policing: A Contemporary Perspective.* Cincinnati, OH: Anderson Publishing Co.

_____ (1992). *Toward Development of Meaningful and Effective Performance Evaluations.* East Lansing, MI: National Center for Community Policing, Michigan State University.

_____ (1994). *Community Policing: How to Get Started.* Cincinnati, OH: Anderson Publishing Co.

Trojanowicz, R.C. & S.L. Dixon (1974). *Criminal Justice and the Community.* Englewood Cliffs, NJ: Prentice-Hall.

Trojanowicz, R.C. & F.M. Moss (1975). *Community-Based Crime Prevention.* Pacific Palisades, CA: Goodyear.

Trojanowicz, R., M. Steele & S. Trojanowicz (1986). *Community Policing: A Taxpayer's Perspective.* East Lansing, MI: National Neighborhood Foot Patrol Center, School of Criminal Justice, Michigan State University.

Turque, B. et al. (1990). "A New Line Against Crime." *Newsweek,* August 27, 1990:36-38.

U.S. Department of Justice (1991). *Crime in the United States.* Washington, DC: U.S. Government Printing Office.

U.S. Department of Justice (1993). *Crime in the United States.* Washington, DC: U.S. Government Printing Office.

Vera Institute of Justice (1988). *Community Patrol Officer Program Problem-Solving Guide.* New York, NY: Vera Institute of Justice.

Vernon, R.L. (1993). *L.A. Justice: Lessons from the Fire Storm.* Colorado Springs, CO: Focus on the Family Press.

Walker, J.L. (1969). "The Diffusion of Innovations Among the American States." *American Political Science Review,* 63:880-899.

Walker, J.P., A.P. Cardarelli & D.L. Billingsley (1976). *Delinquency Prevention in the USA: Synthesis and Assessment of Strategies.* Washington, DC: Office of Juvenile Justice and Delinquency Prevention.

Walker, S. (1977). *A Critical History of Police Reform: The Emergence of Professionalism.* Lexington, MA: Lexington Books.

———— (1980). *Popular Justice: A History of American Criminal Justice.* New York, NY: Oxford University Press.

———— (1984). "Broken Windows and Fractured History: The Use and Misuse of History in Recent Police Patrol Analysis." *Justice Quarterly,* 11:75-90.

———— (1992). *The Police in America: An Introduction.* New York, NY: McGraw-Hill.

———— (1994). *Sense and Nonsense About Crime: A Policy Guide.* Monterey, CA: Brooks/Cole.

Walsh, W.F. (1985). "Patrol Officer Arrest Rates: A Study of the Social Organization of Police Work." *Justice Quarterly,* 2:271-290.

Walsh, W.F. & E.J. Donovan (1990). *The Supervision of Police Personnel: A Performance Based Approach.* Dubuque, IA: Kendall Hunt.

Walton, M. (1986). *The Deming Management Method.* New York, NY: Perigee Books.

Ward, B. (1985). *The Community Police Officer Program.* New York, NY: New York City Police Department.

Wasserman, R. & M.H. Moore (1988). *Values in Policing.* Washington, DC: National Institute of Justice, Perspectives on Policing.

Weatheritt, M. (1983). "Community Policing: Does it Work and How Do We Know?" In T. Bennett (ed.) *The Future of Policing.* Cambridge, UK: Institute of Criminology (PPS. 127-143).

———— (1987). "Community Policing Now." In P. Willmott (ed.) *Policing and the Community.* London, UK: Policy Studies Institute.

———— (1988). "Community Policing: Rhetoric or Reality?" In J.R. Greene & S. Mastrofski (eds.) *Community Policing: Rhetoric or Reality?* New York, NY: Praeger.

Weber, M. (1947). *The Theory of Social and Economic Organizations.* Trans. A.M. Henderson & T. Parsons. New York, NY: Oxford University Press.

Weenig, M.W.H., T. Schmidt & C.J.H. Midden (1990). "Social Dimensions of Neighborhoods and The Effectiveness of Information Programs." *Environment and Behavior,* 22:27-54.

Weisburd, D., J. McElroy & P. Hardyman (1989). "Maintaining Control in Community-Oriented Policing." In D.J. Kenney (ed.) *Police and Policing: Contemporary Issues.* New York, NY: Praeger.

Wendel, F.C. & R.G. Joekel (1991). *Restructuring Personnel Selection: The Assessment Center Method.* Bloomington, IN: Phi Delta Kappa Educational Foundation.

Wiatrowski, M.D. & C. Campoverde (1993). *Community Consensus Building and Community Policing.* Unpublished manuscript. Florida Atlantic University, Boca Raton, FL.

Williams, H. & P.V. Murphy (1990). *The Evolving Strategy of Police: A Minority View.* Washington, DC: National Institute of Justice and Harvard University.

Wilson, J.Q. (1968). *Varieties of Police Behavior: The Management of Law and Order in Eight Communities.* Cambridge, MA: Harvard University Press.

_____ (1973). *Political Organizations.* New York, NY: Basic Books, Inc.

_____ (1975). *Thinking About Crime.* New York, NY: Basic Books, Inc.

_____ (1976). *Varieties of Police Behavior.* New York, NY: Atheneum.

_____ (1978). *The Investigators: Managing FBI and Narcotics Agents.* New York, NY: Basic Books, Inc.

Wilson, J.Q. & G.L. Kelling (1982). "Broken Windows: The Police and Neighborhood Safety." *Atlantic Monthly,* March:29-38.

_____ (1989). "Making Neighborhoods Safe: Sometimes 'Fixing Broken Windows' Does More to Reduce Crime than Conventional 'Incident Oriented' Policing: Community Policing." *Atlantic Monthly,* February:46.

Wilson, J.W. (1989). "Making Neighborhoods Safe: Sometimes 'Fixing Broken Windows' Does More to Reduce Crime than Conventional 'Incident-Oriented' Policing." *The Atlantic Monthly,* 263:46-53.

Wilson, O.W. (1950). *Police Administration.* New York, NY: McGraw-Hill.

Wilson, O.W. & R.C. McLaren (1977). *Police Administration* (4th ed.). New York, NY: McGraw-Hill.

Wilson, W.J. (1987). *The Truly Disadvantaged: The Inner City, The Underclass, and Public Policy.* Washington, DC: Urban Affairs Press.

Wright, J.C. & W. Mischel (1987). "A Conditional Approach to Dispositional Constructs: The Local Predictability of Social Behavior." *Journal of Personality and Social Psychology*, 53:1159-1177

————— (1988). "Conditional Hedges and the Intuitive Psychology of Traits." *Journal of Personality and Social Psychology*, 55:454-469.

Zhao, J., N.P. Lovrich & K. Gray (1994). "Moving Toward Community Policing: The Role of Postmaterialist Values in a Changing Police Profession." Unpublished paper presented at the annual meeting of the Academy of Criminal Justice Sciences, Chicago.

Zimbardo, P. (1992). *Psychology for Life*. New York, NY: Harper-Collins, Inc.

Zimmerman, A.M. (1990). "Taking Aim on Empowerment Research: The Distinction Between Individual and Psychological Conceptions." *American Journal of Community Psychology*, 18:169-177.

Author Index

Subject Index

About the Authors

James S. Albritton presently teaches in and is Associate Director of the Criminology and Law Studies Program at Marquette University. He has taught and done research in the field of criminal justice for the past 20 years and has devoted considerable attention to police matters over the last decade. A former police officer himself, Albritton attempts to bring that experience and perspective to bear on all aspects of his research and analysis of contemporary policing. His current interests include the comparative study of criminal justice and international systems of policing.

Robert B. Blair is a Professor of Sociology at the College of Wooster, Wooster, Ohio, since 1971. He received his Ph.D. in sociology from Northwestern University in 1974. Blair teaches in the areas of criminal justice, quantitative research methods, corrections, and introductory sociology courses. His current research interests include training of corrections staff, community policing, the prison officer role, and the adjustment of older inmates to prison.

Albert P. Cardarelli is currently a Senior Fellow at the John W. McCormack Institute of Public Affairs and Lecturer in Sociology at the University of Massachusetts Boston. He is a former professor and Co-Director of the Community Sociology Program at Boston University. He has published in the areas of juvenile delinquency, prisoner's legal rights, and child sexual abuse. Cardarelli is co-author (with J. Horowitz and B. Gomes-Schwartz) of *Child Sexual Abuse: The Initial Effects*. His research interests include legal theory, homicide, and community policing, and he is currently completing an edited volume on "Intimate Violence." Cardarelli has served as advisor to The Office of Juvenile Justice and Delinquency Prevention, the National Council of Crime and Delinquency, as well as various national, state, and local agencies involved in criminal and juvenile justice. He has a Ph.D. in Sociology from the University of Pennsylvania, and a J.D. degree from Suffolk University Law School.

Gary W. Cordner is a Professor in the Department of Police Studies at Eastern Kentucky University and a Visiting Fellow at the National Institute of Justice (NIJ). Previously he taught at Washington State University and at the University of

Baltimore. He has also worked as a police officer and police chief in Maryland. His Ph.D. is from Michigan State University. Cordner has co-authored texts on police administration and criminal justice planning, including *Police Administration*, 3d (Anderson, 1995), co-edited the volume *What Works in Policing? Operations and Administration Examined* (Anderson, 1992) in the ACJS/Anderson Monograph Series, edited the *American Journal of Police* from 1987-1992, and co-edits the *Police Computer Review*. He is continuing to evaluate police programs in public housing in Lexington, Kentucky and is engaged in a NIJ-funded study of the compatibility of community policing and police agency accreditation.

Rhonda K. DeLong earned her Bachelor of Science degree from Western Michigan University with a double major in Sociology and Criminal Justice, and is working toward completion of her doctoral studies at Western Michigan University in the field of Criminology. She holds a Specialty Degree in Alcohol and Drug Abuse and works full-time as a Substance Abuse/Violence Prevention Specialist for the Van Buren County Public Health Department. She has worked as a certified police officer since 1985. DeLong also teaches in the criminal justice program at Western Michigan University. She has served as Crime Prevention Organizer for the Vine Neighborhood in Kalamazoo, Michigan assisting in the implementation of prevention programs while working closely with the Department of Public Safety's Neighborhood Liaison Officers. Her research includes a variety of policing issues including use of force, community policing, and police training.

George M. Dery III is an Assistant Professor in the Division of Political Science and Criminal Justice at California State University, Fullerton. He is a former Deputy District Attorney for Los Angeles County and holds a J.D. degree from Loyola University in Los Angeles.

Michael E. Donahue graduated with a Ph.D. in Social Science from Michigan State University in 1983. He taught graduate and undergraduate courses in public administration, policing, and research methods at Appalachian State University in Boone, North Carolina and Armstrong State College in Savannah, Georgia. A former police officer and Director of Research and Planning with the Savannah Police Department, Donahue has written extensively on the police use of deadly force, police ethics, and criminal justice agency collaboration. Dr. Donahue currently serves as Associate Professor of Government and as Assistant Director of the Public Service Center for Armstrong State College. He is also an ongoing consultant for the National Institute of Justice in Washington, DC and Chair of the 1996 Olympic Criminal Justice Planning Committee for Chatham County.

Duane Dukes is an Associate Professor and Chairman of the Sociology Department of John Carroll University in Cleveland, Ohio. His areas of expertise include aggregate analysis of criminal violence, family violence dynamics, community policing, public perception of violence, program evaluation, and survey research methodology. Dukes is currently engaged in research on "Weed-and-Seed" needs in Euclid, Ohio, community police training in the city of Cleveland, and community police training for the Cleveland Metropolitan Housing Authority police. He is currently Vice-President Elect of the Society for Applied Sociology. He has regularly presented papers at the annual meetings of the Academy of Criminal Justice Sciences. He reviews for a number of journals in sociology and criminology, and contributes time to community anti-crime programs. Dukes is the recipient of the Cleveland Task Force on Violent Crime's 1986 award for Outstanding Service. In 1987 he received a Cleveland Faculty Fellowship for research on crime prevention programs within the Cleveland Safety Department. He is also the 1989 recipient of The William P. Dumont Community Service Award.

Sandra Gustavson earned the Master's Degree in Criminal Justice from Kent State University and has gained extensive experience in urban policing. Her first contact with the Cleveland Police Department came as a Consultant working with the Criminal Justice Institute in 1983. She joined the Department as a Project Director in 1988. She has worked closely with the Community Policing Unit, conducting analyses to establish baseline measures for efficiency and effectiveness in resource allocation. She conducted several surveys to measure citizen satisfaction with and response to community policing. She has also worked with the Cleveland Auxiliary Police, and was on-site consultant for Cleveland's most comprehensive Calls for Service Study. This led to the implementation of a Differential Police Response Program within the department for which she served as an advisor. She is currently involved in coordinating a citywide public safety and public service Radio Communications System for the city of Cleveland.

Michael A. Jones is a Project Manager for the Eastern Kentucky University (EKU) College of Law Enforcement's Training Resource Center. In this position, he is currently heading a national curriculum development team through a project with the National Juvenile Detention Association and the Office of Juvenile Justice and Delinquency Prevention. He is also the training coordinator for Kentucky's Family Resource and Youth Services Centers initiative. Jones received his undergraduate degree in psychology from Centre College in Danville, Kentucky and his master's degree in criminal justice/police administration from EKU. He has served as a consultant to the Lexington, Kentucky and Rapid City, South Dakota police departments, assisting them with citizen surveys required by the police agency accreditation program.

Peter C. Kratcoski is a Professor of Criminal Justice Studies and Sociology at Kent State University and serves as the Chairperson of the Department of Criminal Justice Studies. He received his Ph.D. at Pennsylvania State University and has taught at Pennsylvania State University and the College of St. Thomas. A co-author of several books, including *Criminal Justice: Process and Issues* and *Juvenile Delinquency,* he has also written numerous articles for journals specializing in criminal justice topics. His current research interests center on violent crime among the elderly, child abuse, community policing, and international comparisons of policing.

James R. Lasley is an Associate Professor in the Division of Political Science and Criminal Justice at California State University, Fullerton. He received his Ph.D. in Criminal Justice from the Center for Politics and Policy at the Claremont Graduate School in 1986. His research interests focus on ways to incorporate the ideas of CPTED (Crime Prevention Through Environmental Design) into community-based policing models.

Jack McDevitt is the Associate Director of The Center for Applied Social Research at Northeastern University and teaches in the College of Criminal Justice at Northeastern. His research interests include hate crimes, where he has recently co-authored *Hate Crime The Rising Tide of Bigotry and Bloodshed* (with Jack Levin) and the *1990 Hate Crime Resource Book* published by the FBI. In addition he has conducted substantial research on police and is the Editor of the *Police Discipline Newsletter.* He recently served as the Principal Investigator for a mayoral commission appointed to study management practices in the Boston Police Department. McDevitt has testified as an expert witness before the Senate Judiciary Committee and has served as a consultant to the Federal Bureau of Investigation, and The Bureau of Justice Statistics. He has a bachelor's degree from Stonehill College and a Master's degree in Public Administration from Northeastern University.

Vance McLaughlin earned his M.S. in Criminology from Florida State University and the Ph.D. from Penn State University. He taught both undergraduate and graduate courses in law enforcement at the University of North Carolina at Charlotte until 1987 when he accepted his current position as Director of Training with the Savannah Police Department. He was an original member of the Executive Board of the American Society of Law Enforcement Trainers. His most recent book is *Police and the Use of Force: The Savannah Study.* In 1994, McLaughlin was appointed Chairman of the 1996 Olympic Law Enforcement Training Committee for Chatham County.

Eric Metchik, Ph.D. is an Assistant Professor in the Criminal Justice Department of Salem State College, Salem, MA. He holds a Ph.D. in Psychology from Yale University and has previously worked as a Research Psychologist with the New York City Police Department, Psychological Services Section. His current research interests include alternative psychological selection criteria for police recruitment and the evaluation of juvenile aftercare programming.

Susan B. Noonan received a Masters of Science Degree in Criminal Justice from the University of Cincinnati and has continued post-graduate work in Sociology. During that time, Noonan worked as project coordinator on a National Institute of Corrections project and coauthored the "Impact of Technology in Corrections." Her current research interests are Community Policing and Police Community Relations. Since 1988, Noonan has worked with the Cincinnati Human Relations Commission as police community relations coordinator. Currently, she is actively involved with the Cincinnati Police Department in implementing community policing throughout the City. Noonan also teaches as an adjunct professor in the Criminal Justice Department at the University of Cincinnati, and is active in the Ohio Crime Prevention Association as well as the Academy of Criminal Justice Sciences.

Jeffrey Ian Ross was an Assistant Professor at the University of Lethbridge before assuming his current position as Assistant Professor of Criminal Justice Studies at Kent State University. He has conducted research, written, and lectured on political and criminal violence and policing for over a decade. His work has appeared in academic journals such as *Canadian Journal of Political Science, Comparative Politics Conflict Quarterly, Contemporary Sociology, International Journal of Group Tensions, Journal of Peace Research, Justice Quarterly, Low Intensity Conflict and Law Enforcement, Peace and Change, Police Studies, Terrorism, Terrorism and Political Violence,* and a variety of chapters in academic books, as well as articles in popular magazines in Canada and the United States. He is the editor of two forthcoming books, *Controlling State Crime* with Garland Publishing and *Violence in Canada: Sociopolitical Perspectives* with Oxford University Press. Ross teaches, among other courses, "Public Opinion and Propaganda," "Political Behavior," "Urban Politics and Government," and "The Politics of Policing." In 1986, Ross was the lead expert witness for the Senate of Canada's Special Committee on Terrorism and Public Safety.

Eli B. Silverman is Professor, Department of Law and Police Science, John Jay College of Criminal Justice, City University of New York. He has previously served as Special Assistant, Department of Justice, Washington, DC; Research Associate, National Academy of Public Administration, Washington, DC and Visiting Professor, Police Staff College, Bramshill, England. His research and publications focus on comparative community policing and the managerial aspects of policing in the United States and Great Britain. Silverman has served as a consultant and trainer to numerous state and local criminal justice including police departments, probation, and parole agencies.

Robyne Turner is Associate Professor of Political Science at Florida Atlantic University. She received her Ph.D. in Political Science from the University of Florida. Her publications have appeared in *Urban Affairs Quarterly, Journal of Urban*

Affairs, Publius: The Journal of Federalism, and *State and Local Government Review.* She is writing a book on the politics of downtown development in Sunbelt Cities, and her other areas of research include community development initiatives and sustainable community development for women. Turner is currently participating in an evaluation of a national demonstration project to develop community development corporations.

Robert L. Vernon recently retired from the Los Angeles Police Department (LAPD) as Assistant Chief of Police, where he served as Director of the Office of Operations. He received his B.A. from Northwestern University, his M.B.A. from Pepperdine University, and is a graduate of the FBI's National Executive Institute. During his 37 years with the LAPD, Vernon tested and refined several community-based policing programs, beginning with Team Policing and ending with Operation Cul-De-Sac. He now heads his own police management consulting firm in the Southern California area.

William F. Walsh is currently Director of the Southern Police Institute and Associate Professor in the School of Justice Administration at the University of Louisville. A former member of the New York City Police Department with 21 years of service, he holds undergraduate and masters degrees from John Jay College of Criminal Justice and a doctoral degree in Sociology from Fordham University, New York City. Walsh has written articles on issues related to both public and private police which have been published in the *American Journal of Police, Justice Quarterly, Journal of Police Science and Administration, Journal of Criminal Justice, Security Journal, The Justice Professional, Security Management* and *Police Chief.* He has co-authored *Police Supervision: A Performance Based Approach,* with Edwin J. Donovan and is currently re-writing and updating Wilson and McLaren's *Police Administration,* 5th Ed. with James Fyfe and Jack R. Greene.

Michael D. Wiatroswski is Associate Professor of Criminal Justice at Florida Atlantic University. He received his Ph.D. in Urban Studies from Portland State University in 1978. His publications have appeared in *Journal of Criminal Law and Criminology, American Sociological Review* and the *Journal of Quantitative Criminology.* Wiatrowski's current research interests include the theory and practice of community policing, community delinquency prevention, and community development.

Ann Winton is a clinical psychologist in private practice and an Adjunct Assistant Professor of Psychology at the John Jay College of Criminal Justice, City University of New York. She holds a Ph.D. in Psychology from Boston College and has served as a consultant psychologist with the New York City Police Department, Psychological Services Section. Her research interests include the rights of children in the legal system and the impact of AIDS and other chronic illnesses on family systems.